(UN)DOING
THE MISSIONARY
POSITION

Recent Titles in
Contributions in Women's Studies

(UN)DOING THE MISSIONARY POSITION

Gender Asymmetry in Contemporary
Asian American Women's Writing

PHILLIPA KAFKA

Contributions in Women's Studies, Number 158

GREENWOOD PRESS
Westport, Connecticut • London

Library of Congress Cataloging-in-Publication Data

Kafka, Phillipa, 1943–
     (Un)doing the missionary position : gender asymmetry in
contemporary Asian American women's writing / Phillipa Kafka.
          p.   cm. — (Contributions in women's studies, ISSN 0147–104X ;
no. 158)
     Includes bibliographical references and index.
     ISBN 0–313–30161–1 (alk. paper)
     1. American literature—Asian American authors—History and
criticism.   2. Feminism and literature—United States—History—20th
century.   3. Women and literature—United States—History—20th
century.   4. American literature—Women authors—History and
criticism.   5. American literature—20th century—History and
criticism.   6. Asian American women in literature.   7. Asian
Americans in literature.   8. Sex role in literature.   I. Title.
II. Series: Contributions in women's studies ; no. 158.
PS153.A84K34   1997
810.9′9287′08995073—DC20   96–27391

British Library Cataloguing in Publication Data is available.

Library of Congress Catalog Card Number: 96–27391
ISBN: 0–313–30161–1
ISSN: 0147–104X

First published in 1997

Greenwood Press, 88 Post Road West, Westport, CT 06881
An imprint of Greenwood Publishing Group, Inc.

Printed in the United States of America

The paper used in this book complies with the
Permanent Paper Standard issued by the National
Information Standards Organization (Z39.48–1984).

10 9 8 7 6 5 4 3 2

Copyright Acknowledgments

The author and publisher gratefully acknowledge permission for use of the following material:

From "Towards a Feminist Cultural Criticism: Hegemony and Modes of Social Division" by Donna Przybylowicz. In *Cultural Critique* 14 (Winter 1989/90), pp. 259–301. Reprinted by permission of Oxford University Press.

From "Domestic Violence among Pacific Asians" by Nilda Rimonte; and from "The Feminist Movement: Where Are All the Asian American Women?" by Esther Ngan-Ling Chow. In *Making Waves* by Asian Women United of California. Copyright © 1989 by Asian Women United of California. Reprinted by permission of Beacon Press, Boston.

From *Articulate Silences: Hisaye Yamamoto, Maxine Hong Kingston, Joy Kogawa* by King-Kok Cheung. Ithaca, NY: Cornell University Press, 1993.

From *Bone* by Fae Myenne Ng. Copyright © 1993 by Fae Myenne Ng. Reprinted by permission of Hyperion and Donadio & Ashworth, Inc.

From *The Loom and Other Stories* by R. A. Sasaki. Copyright © 1991 by R. A. Sasaki. Reprinted with the permission of Graywolf Press, Saint Paul, Minnesota.

From *Asian American Literature* by Elaine H. Kim. Philadelphia: Temple University Press, 1982.

From *Typical American* by Gish Jen. Copyright © 1991 by Gish Jen. Reprinted by permission of Houghton Mifflin Company. All rights reserved.

From *The Kitchen God's Wife* by Amy Tan. New York: The Putnam Berkley Group, Inc., 1991.

From *The Floating World* by Cynthia Kadohata. Copyright © 1989 by Cynthia Kadohata. Used by permission of Viking Penguin, a division of Penguin Books USA Inc.

For Olavi Koskinen, Jr.,
my heart's beloved husband and favorite in-house editor

Contents

Acknowledgments

To my acquisitions editor, Nina Pearlstein, for her support, and Gillian Beebe, my production editor, for her excellent editing skills; to Dr. Amy Ling, Director, Asian American Studies, University of Wisconsin, for her kind suggestions; to three brilliant and noble human beings, my children, Molly E. Holzschlag, Morris and Linus Kafka; and to my dear friend, Dr. Edward Weil, Dean of the School of Liberal Arts, Kean College of New Jersey.

Preface

The beginning is always difficult . . .
And I,
the beginning of an end, the end of a beginning,
sit here . . .
scrawl these paltry lines for you.

Marilyn Chin
"The End of a Beginning"

When Betty Friedan called attention to it in 1963, she called gender asymmetry "a problem with no name," it then seemed so natural an element of every aspect of our existence. But today it still flourishes, or two critics so disparate on the surface as the African V. Y. Mudimbe and Bette London would not have recently deplored "the thingification of women" and the "marginalization of the feminine." London views this marginalization as leaving "women readers no unappropriated space for gender-specific identification" (London 1993, 264). Not only can the "problem" now be named. There can also be a "rewriting" of it as a "(post)modern strategy" because it exposes what is "unsaid . . . suppressed." Such a rewriting "displaces the dominant logic—dislodging its hegemony and demystifying its 'naturalness'—and unleashes an alternative potential." It "disrupts patriarchal power" and intervenes in the operation of patriarchal ideology which works through "a double move." On the one hand, "patriarchal ideology" sets up "binary oppositions of gender differences," or gender asymmetry. On the other hand, it "naturalizes" these differences as "biological." In this text I will explore how selected contemporary Asian American women writers "inquire into the power relations requiring such suppression" (Ebert 1991, 889). Such writers as Maxine Hong Kingston, Amy Tan, and R. A. Sasaki do so from a feminist perspective. Some do so in allegorical terms, like Fae Myenne Ng. Some younger writers like Cynthia Kadohata do so from a postfeminist perspective, as if gender asymmetry had existed long ago in the distant past.

From approximately 1970 to 1985, Second Wave mainstream feminists— primarily white heterosexual middle and upper class privileged women—spoke as "women," for all women. They demanded the same rights as men and critiqued patriarchy without simultaneously demanding commensurate changes to the system. They thereby replicated phallocentric thinking by seeking change from within the culture's paradigms. About ten years ago, goaded on by ethnic and women of color feminists, mainstream feminists finally began including a "microlevel of differences" by pouring and stirring African American women writers into their discourse and theory. Nevertheless, mainstream feminists still focus on the works of white European and American women. Asian American women writers who confront gender asymmetry in their texts do not figure in mainstream feminist theory. It is time to give credit to their splendid contributions to feminist discourse and theory; time to begin a dialogue that speaks to our local as well as global affinities, our "collective identities in everyday life"; time to "conceptualize gender" so that it works "in the interests of women" rather than confining analyses to "the microlevel of differences [that] . . . inhibit . . . feminist intervention in the structures of the patriarchal totality" (Luttrell 1990, 638– 639; Ebert 1991, 902). It is time to talk to each other and to observe commonalities, which we have not yet done. We have emphasized the seemingly endless array of differences between women for far too long.

As Nancy Hartsock puts it, various groups' efforts were "fundamental to creating the preconditions for the current questioning of [patriarchal] claims to universality" (Hartsock 1990, 33). The contemporary Asian American women writers who are the subjects of my work, all born after 1950, have not only benefited from these various groups' efforts, primarily those of the feminist movement, but have also brought benefits to them in a variety of ways which my analysis of their work exposes. As a first generation American child of Polish Jewish parents who fled from the pogroms that preceded the Holocaust and therefore survived while all our relatives who remained behind perished, I am without prior knowledge of, complicity with, or connection to American culture and history. I am therefore inwardly unlike my mainstream sisters from whom I appear indistinguishable outwardly, while I am inwardly more like women of color from whom I appear different outwardly. What I learned I was taught in the public school system, originally as a struggling night school student and then on a graduate scholarship. I only began to read beyond the traditional canon after receiving a traditional Ph.D. It was not until 1976 during my first sabbatical as a young professor that I suddenly saw in the medium of ethnic American literature a public discourse that for the first time in my life mirrored my own life's realities: my own previously imagined individual, private sufferings as an outsider in this world by religion, class, ethnicity, and above all, gender. This literature was then called "minority literature" and defined as written by "Other Americans."

When I returned from sabbatical, I developed the first ethnic American literature course in higher education in the country. It crossed the multiethnic field, including African American, Asian American, Hispanic, and Native American, as well as other "hyphenated" American literature, and still does.

In addition to being a professor of ethnic American literature who has identified with, read, taught, and admired these authors for some time, I am also a "Second Wave" feminist, having joined the movement in 1971. My writing of this book originated as a desire to do more than express identification with and admiration for these authors to my students and colleagues with the hope of igniting their enthusiasm for them—to do more than just reading for classroom teaching and for presenting papers at conferences. I wanted to bring to a broader public's attention the work of these writers: to analyze where they are now and the directions in which they are going, as well as their attitudes in regard to that time in American literature and life when gender asymmetry was all-pervasive. I have attempted to determine all of this by analyzing what the authors I write about make of gender asymmetry in terms of the prior and current conditions for their female characters, how they depict these characters in response to their situations, and whether or not they give credit to the efforts of the mainstream feminist movement.

Furthermore, the fruits of my own personal experience and scholarly research across the ethnic field have recently led me to the same conclusions as Ebert's: that although the global system of rule outwardly assumes the form of "a differentiated, contradictory structure" it nevertheless produces "identical effects differently" from culture to culture. It may take the form of "late capitalist patriarchy in the United States" as distinct from "contemporary fundamentalist Iran," or as distinct from that "found in feudal Europe." Nevertheless, despite "all [these groups'] differences-in-relation to each other, they share the same dominant organization of differences" (Ebert 1991, 901). I passionately believe that once we realize this, we can reach out to each other—across to where we experience affinities. I disagree with all those who would separate Black and Asian American women from each other and from other ethnic women and women of color and mainstream women on the basis of ethnic, racial, class, and cultural differences.

Deconstructionist critics like Michel Foucault; Marxist critics like Fredric Jameson and Terry Eagleton; postcolonial critics like Edward Said and Abdul R. JanMohamed all critique Western imperialism's assumption of superiority to all cultures and races other than their own. Cornel West admires their analyses, and as an African American male he has good reason to do so, of course. He exults that "By questioning themes of degraded Otherness and subaltern marginality post-colonial discourses have come up with new theoretical . . . notions of exclusionary identity, dominating heterogeneity and universality or in more blunt language, White supremacy" (West 1989, 90). Henry A. Giroux, the distinguished advocate of "anti-racist teaching," joins West in problematizing "specific authorial positions" that emanate from and are supported by what he defines as "monolithic views of culture, nationalism, and difference" (Giroux

1992, 23)—what I have defined as "the missionary position" in my book's title. But like Foucault and other postmodern male critics, some of whom I have just cited, these critics suffer from a blind spot in relation to one glaring form of "supremacy." These male advocates of Marxist, deconstructionist, and postcolonialist theories all delight in taking to task the imperialist colonial and colonizing powers, as well as their mainstream colleagues for their ethnocentricity, racism, and class elitism—for what Said aptly terms "Orientalism." Meanwhile, they fail to extend their critique to include gender asymmetry. But their female counterparts—like Trin Minh-ha, Gayatri Chakravorty Spivak, and Chandra Talpade Mohanty—somehow have no difficulty whatsoever in seeing this as a global problem, as well.

Marxism especially has aroused the ire of many feminists "for its failure to describe the reality of women's lives, to acknowledge that our labor in the home was real, if 'unproductive' in classical terms, and to recognize the profoundly political nature of personal relations, especially those between women and men" (Gordon 1993, 11). Unfortunately, according to Gordon, "white feminists" were "prevented . . . by ethnocentrism, racism, class prejudice and pure ignorance about the rest of the world . . . from understanding how shaking off colonial rule or the redistribution of a nation's wealth might provide the women of that nation with varying shares of the benefits that result" (Gordon 1993, 11). However, even though they are the most visibly powerful because of their political, economic, and ideological control over other nations and cultures, imperialist and colonizing nations are not the only ones in "the missionary position." Postcolonial theorists and postmodern and deconstructionist philosophers are taken to task by Marxist materialist critics like Mas'ud Zavarzadeh for thinking so. As he puts it, the "discursive apparatuses" of postcolonialism remind Marxists of the "old modernist technologies of literacy" of the "traditional missionaries [because they] produce forms of liberalism, pluralism, and relativism that are amenable to Western-style bourgeois democracy, which is the name for new forms of postmodern totalitarianism of/as consumer society" (Zavarzadeh 1992, 27).

In turn, all these critics are also taken to task by ethnic feminist critics like R. Radhakrishnan (a male) and by feminist women of color critics like Barbara Christian for failing to participate in "political, economic, and ideological struggles" (Ebert 1993, 26). Ebert, who calls herself as "a resistance postmodern feminist critic" defines postmodernism as "a historical condition marked by a struggle over how to reconstruct the knowledges and social organizations of differences in the West" (Ebert 1993, 25). Christian defines postmodernism more concisely, as an "attempt to change the orientation of Western scholarship" (Christian 1987, 26). She sees the Lyotardian "poststructuralist discourses" as comprising only "one side" of postmodernism, and that side as "a neoconservative, apolitical anti-revolutionary side" (Christian 1988, 35). In addition, some feminist critics like Nancy Hartsock are also unhappy with the deconstructionist and postcolonial scholars for "remaining imprisoned in the terrain of Enlightenment thought and fail[ing] to provide the ground for alternative and more emancipatory accounts of subjectivity" (Hartsock 1990, 19). Instead, they operate as legitimate upholders of the "ruling bourgeois class."

Christian generously refrains from indicting white mainstream feminists who crusaded only for themselves, like their male postcolonial, deconstructionist, and Marxist colleagues. She faults the Marxists on the grounds that they "as usual, concentrated on themselves and were not in the slightest interested in the worlds they had ignored or controlled." Meanwhile she was expected, also as usual, "to know them, while they were not at all interested in knowing" her. "Instead they sought to 'deconstruct' the tradition to which they belonged even as they used the same forms, style, language of that tradition, forms which necessarily embody its values." The more she read the deconstructionists and the more she "saw their substitution of their philosophical writings for literary ones," the more uneasy she became. She saw that "they always harkened back to the masterpieces of the past, again reifying the very texts they said they were deconstructing" (Christian 1987, 56–57). Consequently, Black literary critics were "diverted into continually discussing the new literary theory" (Christian 1987, 57). She began to think that perhaps "the literature being produced is precisely one of the reasons why this new philosophical-literary-critical theory of relativity is so prominent. In other words, the literature of blacks, women of South America and Africa, etc., as overtly political literature was being preempted by a new Western concept which proclaimed that reality does not exist, that everything is relative, and that every text is silent about something—which indeed it must necessarily be" (Christian 1987, 57). Even faulting her for her omission of Asian American and other ethnic writers in her theory, Christian's profound insight into the elitism and the racism that "the language [of deconstructionist theory] creates" is "that it mystifies rather than clarifies our condition, making it possible for a few people who know that particular knowledge to control the critical scene." Moreover, since its publication, her next point—"that language surfaced, interestingly enough, just when the literature of peoples of color, of black women, of Latin Americans, of Africans began to move to 'the center' " (Christian 1987, 55) has influenced many readers, especially ethnic, women of color, and African American feminists.

In my Conclusion, after discussing what Chinese and Japanese American and other Asian American critics think about the (white) mainstream feminist movement, I call for dialogue. It is valuable for mainstream feminists to know how they are perceived. On the other hand, it is equally valuable for Chinese and Japanese and other Asian American and ethnic and women of color critics to avoid replicating the oppressors' mistakes. I consciously attempt in this Conclusion to adhere to "ground rules for communication across lines of difference and hierarchy that go beyond politeness but maintain mutual respect." I begin "a systematic approach to the all-important concept of cultural mediation" (Pratt 1991, 40) between mainstream feminist and Chinese and Japanese (and other Asian American) women writers. I call for "democratic action, not just a display of our identity labels." My aim in doing so is to end "the perpetuat[ion of] cultural constructs arising from specific, historic power structures" which in the form of "patriarchal status divisions have created immutable differences among women"(Ebert 1993, 25; Lapidus 1993, 25). In this work I envision an alliance that is not based on "hierarchies of oppression" cliques, or on "a politics of identity" based on shared ethnicity and/or race. I envision an alliance where "groups can constitute themselves as horizontal, homogeneous, sovereign communities with high degrees of trust, shared understandings, [and] temporary protection from legacies of oppression"; where groups can create space "for healing and mutual recognition, safe houses in which to construct shared understandings, knowledges, [and] claims on the world that they can then bring into the contact zone" (Pratt 1991, 40).

In my Conclusion I urge mainstream white feminists to do more than become aware of the existence of Asian American women writers. I suggest that they include and integrate their contributions in feminist theory: that they use Asian American women writers' artistic, aesthetic, and political representations of gender asymmetry as models to be taken fully into account as much as they now take those of mainstream and African American women writers and critics into account. It is painfully evident to me that too many of us are unaware of our affinities with other women. Although I by no means advocate an uncritical embrace, I argue that, instead of keeping the distance and even widening it, feminists can begin a cautious, wary dialogue with one another. Our distance is the result of doubts and suspicions, of ignorance about each other. Too many of us are convinced that our own group and our own agenda should come first. Such a position is based on the unexamined assumption that we cannot do it all at the same time—that we cannot talk to each other across the feminist fence, across ethnicities and races, across the globe. Accordingly, at the end of this text, I appeal for a more productive dialogue than has hitherto been possible between the feminist movement and Asian American women. In the face of ever-increasing divisions between us (which mirror contemporary global phenomena externally), I call for "border crossings" (Giroux 1992, 35) and for the creation of "a contact zone" (Pratt 1991, 39) where now there is no communication.

In the following chapters, I will discuss the authors' diversity of approach to gender asymmetry and the variety of potential solutions which they have suggested to this global problem. In spite of all this, a new system of possibilities will not necessarily emerge unless we are willing to enact actual ongoing confrontations with the ruling set of discourses about gender. To effect change there has to be dialogue between oppressed groups who form "a collective subject or group" that experiences itself as being "negated by other discourses and practices" (Lowe 1990, 143). Only when there is enough mass in a movement can a revolution comes about, or at the very least, effective demonstrations such as the highly controversial and publicized anti–Vietnam War rallies and the "Second Wave" feminist marches and "actions" during the late Sixties and early Seventies, in some of which I myself participated.

In the work that follows, it has also been my aim to create a transcultural or transglobal feminism where I once created a multiethnic vision of feminism. Even as I write these words, our dialogue is expanding. Through E-Mail and the

Internet, through the increased use of the "information superhighway," we will routinely enter "cyberspace" and expand our "contact zones" ever wider—from purely local affinities in the United States between ethnic and women of color and white mainstream feminists to routine linkages with women on a global basis.

Introduction

In 1982 Elaine H. Kim, in her ground-breaking introduction to Asian American literature, identified the "portrayal of ambiguity" (Kim 1982, xvii) as central to the Chinese American experience and defined the essential characteristics of Asian American women writers:

The links Asian American women cannot establish with their men they seek with one another. Motivated by the sense that there exist few adequate portrayals of Asian American women, writers have been attempting to depict the uniqueness and diversity of that experience as an integral part of the American and Asian American tradition. . . . [They] address themselves to themes that bring men and women together and that bring Asian American women together, always in an effort to shatter myths and stereotypes through self-expression so that Asian American women will emerge in positive self-affirmation. (Kim 1982, 253)

Eight years later, Amy Ling, the first scholar to write a truly comprehensive literary history of Chinese American women writers, theorized the source for their "ambiguity" as an "ambiguous consciousness, " as their being "between worlds." They therefore possess so acute a sense "of the gaze and judgment of others" that they devote their lives to having others "reconstitute or alter [their] views" of them (Ling 1990, 34). Ling's work, which covers approximately 100 years, beginning with the Eaton sisters and ending with Amy Tan's *The Joy Luck Club* (1989), concerns itself with this acutely self-reflexive duality. My work, dedicated to Dr. Ling, is a literary criticism written from an ethnic and global feminist perspective and begins with Amy Tan's *The Kitchen God's Wife* (1991)—precisely where Ling's work leaves off. Whereas Ling's work is a monumental and exhaustive literary history of Chinese American women writers, my work is limited to an analysis of selected works of contemporary Chinese and Japanese American women writers.

HONG KINGSTON'S INFLUENCE

In Chapter One, after a reprise of those elements in Maxine Hong Kingston's *The Woman Warrior* (1977) and Amy Tan's *The Joy Luck Club* which I consider most influential on younger Asian American women writers, I provide an extensive analysis of Amy Tan's later work, *The Kitchen God's Wife*. In Chapters Two and Three, I chart how Fae Myenne Ng in *Bone* (1993) and Gish Jen in *Typical American* (1992) continue the journey from ambiguity to "positive self-affirmation," and, even further, into advocating syncretism, or the blending of two cultures. In Chapters Four and Five I discuss the reverse trajectory of immigrant foremothers' hard prefeminist lives, compared to their daughters' and granddaughters' lives in R. A. Sasaki's *The Loom and Other Stories* (1991) and Cynthia Kadohata's *The Floating World* (1989).

Tan's and Myenne Ng's work extend Maxine Hong Kingston's feminist project of the late seventies and early eighties in *The Woman Warrior* and *China Men* (1980) into an incipient syncresis that Jen fully realizes. Unlike Hong Kingston, Tan, and Sasaki, these other writers, such as Jen and Kadohata, might better be defined as postfeminist rather than feminist. By postfeminist I mean that whether or not they accept "the feminist conviction of male domination and women's oppression," they perceive the feminist struggles as past and/or as being "insufficient in terms of the diversity of women's experiences" (Hite 1989, 193; Rosenfelt 1993, 270). In addition to Hong Kingston, these younger authors are influenced "consciously and unconsciously" in their representations of gender asymmetry by "the pioneers" (Hsaio 1992b, 131) who comprise the likes of Sui Sin Far (Edith Eaton), Jade Snow Wong, Merle Woo, Nellie Wong, Diana Chang, Louis Chu, and Frank Chin (if only in refutation of the latter). In the case of the younger Japanese American authors, such as Sasaki and Kadohata, their predecessors are Mitsuye Yamada, Toshio Mori, Monica Sone, Janice Mirikitani, and especially Wakako Yamauchi and Hisaye Yamamoto

Louis Chu's *Eat a Bowl of Tea* (1961) is widely considered as having an "ending which marks patriarchy's first serious fall into disrepute" in Chinese American fiction because Mei Oi, the wife of Ben Loy, commits adultery. In doing so, she violates Confucianism's "cardinal female virtue of chastity and marital fidelity." Also Ben Loy in accepting the child from that adultery "thus damages the Confucian image of patrilineal purity." Here Chu's influence clearly extends to contemporary Asian American women writers. Unfortunately, *Eat a Bowl of Tea* is syncretic only in that it reaffirms and perpetuates both the Western and the Chinese "patriarchal caricatures of Asian women" (Hsaio 1992a, 161). When Hsaio wonders whether "the patriarchal tradition" and "patriarchal views" can be purged in Chinese American literature, she is confronting gender asymmetry. She looks to later women writers, such as those whom I have selected for discussion in this work, to provide truer, "fuller portraits" of Asian American women than Chu and other Chinese American male writers have given us. I see these writers' representations of "the struggle and confusion that crossing cultural boundaries generates in the female psyche" as well as their cultures' "patriarchal views" as part of a cultural conspiracy in a global "subtext of gender erasure" (Hsaio 1992a, 153, 161; Stanford 1993, 17).

What Edward Said has perceived only in regard to "Orientalism," namely that it is "a flexible positional superiority which puts the Westerner in a whole series of possible relationships with the Orient without ever losing him the relative upper hand" (Said 1978, 7), is perceived by ethnic and mainstream feminists as characteristic of men in relation to women globally. Joyce Zonana critiques applications by "Western feminists" of Said's concept of Orientalism as a "literary strategy," not as a way "to restructure the West but as a conservative effort to make the West more like itself. Orientalism—the belief that the East is inferior to the West, and the representation of the Orient by means of unexamined, stereotypical images—thus becomes a major premise in the formulation of numerous Western feminist arguments" (Zonana 1993, 594). She accuses "global feminism" of being "a Western movement inapplicable to Eastern societies" (Zonana 1993, 595), as lost in "yet another thicket, the tangle of feminist Orientalist prejudice that continues to encumber Western feminist discourse" (Zonana 1993, 615). I fail to see how broadening postcolonial theories, such as the phallocentric Said's, to include gender issues globally diminishes Western feminists to the role of apologists for Western culture. In contrast to Zonana's "centric" thinking, Martha Chamallas points out about ethnic and transnational or global feminists that we are finding global patterns which arise "from relationships of affinity and social processes rather than from common essences." Citing Iris M. Young's *Justice and the Politics of Difference*, she lists five key patterns of "multiple oppression" against women—exploitation, marginalization, powerlessness, cultural imperialism, and violence and harassment (Chamallas 1993, 16). These oppressions are all global in scope, as well as local in origin.

SYNCRETISM

We will see the extended family model in all the works analyzed in this text because "traditionally, an individual's first loyalty was to his kinsmen [*sic*]. . . . [F]amily relationships dominated political and economic activities and served as a primary tool for social control. An individual's reputation was his [*sic*] family's reputation and one's personal affairs could not be strictly one's own" (Kim 1982, 102). For example, the "ancient" Confucian ideal of "family unity, economic interdependence, and mutual help" plays a large role in Jen's *Typical American.* This is a novel about the undermining of Confucianism when American success mythologies which valorize individualism over the family are followed. It is also about the eventual return to this philosophy in modified form through the utilization of syncresis (Goellnicht 1992, 193–194; Sledge 1980, 13–14).

All critics consider Hong Kingston's oppositional stance in *The Woman Warrior* and *China Men* to the Chinese cultural prescriptions for females as markedly feminist. Her feminist project continues on in Tan's emphasis on family control by males and in her representations of and solutions to gender asymmetry in *The Kitchen God's Wife*. Through Tan's work, Hong Kingston's groundbreaking work has been mediated into the works of other Chinese American authors such as Myenne Ng, who in *Bone* seems to actually make intertextual meditations on Tan's solutions.[1]

Like Hong Kingston, these authors represent individual characters as suffering from gender asymmetry in two cultures, in both private and public situations. In my Chapter One, on Tan's *The Kitchen God's Wife*, in Chapter Four, on Sasaki's *The Loom*, and in my Chapter Five, on Kadohata's *The Floating World*, we will see female characters coping with gender asymmetry primarily in their own cultures, as well as across cultures in their relationships with white fellow students at school, white husbands or lovers, and white employers.

The abstract, God-like omniscience in discourse and pose so characteristic of the Enlightenment is more of a pitfall than "identity politics," which at least serves as a corrective to the Enlightenment humanist model of a generic "man." Such a model of discourse has obliterated the existence of the female gender and of gender asymmetry (as well as other asymmetries) by defining "human being" as male, white, middle or upper class, and Christian. In the guise of the "rugged individual," this "generic man" has long flourished in the United States. He is represented as the homogenized All-American product resulting from immersion in a national "pot" where all his (temporarily) ethnic and racial differences are "melted" away. In Chapter Three, readers will see how Gish Jen in *Typical American* warns immigrants against being seduced by this ethnocentric and racist American model by having catastrophes befall them. Instead, her solution for immigrant Chinese and their first generation children lies in a pragmatic syncretism in which their original and new cultures are combined in ways that work best for them.

DOUBLE VISION, DOUBLE IRONY

When Kim observes that "women who rebel against the strictures of racism and sexism are frequent[ly portrayed]" (Kim 1982, 220–221) in the literature of Asian American women writers, it brings to mind another characteristic common to the writers covered in this text. They see double as a result of double suffering "as a racial minority and as women crossing between two patriarchal cultures, the traditional Chinese and the modern American" (Goellnicht 1992, 200). Characters like Maxine of Hong Kingston's *The Woman Warrior* and Winnie and Helen of Tan's *The Kitchen God's Wife* are situated in "a kind of guerrilla periphery" from which to employ "double irony," or "appropriative irony," or "a double movement" (Goellnicht 1992, 200: Chambers 1990, 21; Robinson 1991, 11). Robinson sees them as "double" because they are "simultaneously against normative constructions of Woman that are continually produced by hegemonic discourses and social practices, and toward new forms of representation that disrupt those normative constructions" (Robinson 1991, 11). No matter whether this technique is dubbed "double irony," or "double movement," or "appropriative irony," it works, because it not only utilizes the "marginal vantage point" of the writers to critique "the racist mainstream for its treatment of [their] forefathers, but [it is] also [used] to avenge themselves on those very forefathers, the malestream, for their sexist treatment of Chinese women" (Goellnicht 1992, 203). However, in my opinion, "triple irony" might be an even more accurate term than "double irony," since these women characters are represented as confronting three "malestream" or gender asymmetric cultures simultaneously— Chinese, Chinese American, and American.

This "tactic" also works because according to Chambers it creates a "crucial shift":

with all the play the [patriarchal] system allows, to produce different ends, that is, to change the products of the system. . . . [I]n particular, the disadvantaged of a system can use it against the advantaged. . . . [B]ecause a specific set of power relations is always mediated, it is possible to find a tactic (a "shift") that has the potential to move (to "shift") the positionality of the subjects with respect to the mediating system, or as Lyotard puts it, "Il y a toujours moyen de moyenner." (Chambers 1990, 21–22)

Chambers translates this last passage as " 'There's always a way to make [a] shift' " (Chambers 1990, 22), but it literally translates as "There's always a way of [making a] way[ing]." Ralph Chang, the presumptive protagonist of Gish Jen's *Typical American,* lives by this adage, but as a Chinese one. He periodically uses it when in trouble, as when he forgets to renew his visa, he reminds himself: *"Xiang banfa*: An essential Chinese idea . . . *to think of a way"* (27). An American expression that is analogous to this one and with which Ralph is still unfamiliar at this point in his life would have been: "In this challenging situation, let me try a bit of 'good old American ingenuity and know-how.' " In fact, all of the women writers discussed in this text represent their characters as living by this adage: first in relation to their struggle for survival as immigrants, and later as Asian Americans in a hostile, racist environment.

PARADOX

The writers depict "the part women play within relations of power" from diverse perspectives, not only from an "oppositional one." They convey not only frustration and impatience with, but also compassion for their female characters. Hong Kingston was the first to do so. As Kim points out: "One of the main points of *The Woman Warrior* is that a marginal person indeed derives power and vision from living with paradoxes. The narrator says: 'I learned to make my mind large, as the universe is large, so that there is room for paradoxes' " (Kim 1987, 93). Tan, Myenne Ng, and Jen follow Hong Kingston in consciously representing "tongue-tied" women who confront the system. The complexities of their perspectives and positions are represented in a nonjudgmental, nonbinary manner, again characteristics of postmodern writing. Simultaneously, they represent women characters "as victims, accepting the inevitability of domination"; as "consenting subordinates" who are "complying with those that affect their exclusion from history—that is, the ways in which hegemonic ideologies exact

compliance in marginalized subjects"; and as "resisting provided subjectivities."
At the same time, women can "accept, accommodate, ignore, resist, or protest"
power relations, that is, gender asymmetry (MacLeod, 1992, 534; Smith 1993,
396). In this text, we will see how Myenne Ng even abstracts diverse responses
through the use of allegory.

Hong Kingston's *The Woman Warrior* shows such diverse responses to the
culture as those of No-Name Woman, the suicide; Fa Mu Lan, the woman warrior; Brave Orchid, simultaneously a gatekeeper and a woman warrior; and the
conventional Moon Orchid, who goes mad. Readers of Tan, Myenne Ng, and
Jen will note that these younger writers also use paradox in representing their
characters' responses to gender asymmetry as simultaneously diverse and conflicting. They struggle continually to distinguish the real from the illusory, "to
sort fact from fantasy in order to come to terms with the paradoxes that shape
[their lives as members] of a racial minority group in America; their asking of
questions; their attempts to name the unnamed, to 'speak the unspeakable'; to
ask what is their . . . heritage; what it is that is externally imposed stereotype as
opposed to individual idiosyncrasy" (Goellnicht 1992, 199).

Also common to these writers and influenced by Hong Kingston, especially
in *The Woman Warrior*, is the feminist and postmodern emphasis on ambivalence and polyvocality. What Goellnicht says here of "feminist argument," that
it "critiques all systems that establish social relationships as hierarchies of power
and is perfectly capable of a both/and approach instead of an either/or one," can
be said of Hong Kingston and after her, Tan, Myenne Ng, and Jen. Certainly,
the "both/and" is implicit in Tan's endings in *The Joy Luck Club* and *The
Kitchen God's Wife*, as well as in Myenne Ng's *Bone* and Jen's *Typical American*.

UNRELIABLE NARRATORS AND INCONSISTENT
CHARACTERS

Hong Kingston's influence on Tan and the other younger writers also can be
seen in their use of postmodern techniques to further their feminist perspective—
techniques such as deconstruction, mimicry, and parody, especially the revising
of traditional myths in their attempts to end gender asymmetry. As Patricia Lin
(-Blinde) notes, Hong Kingston "chose to frame The Woman Warrior's story
very much in keeping with the vision and agenda of the post-modern writer" (Lin
1992, 333). Since Lin is a critic of Asian American women writers, her definition of the characteristics of postmodernism is useful here:

The disjunctured, decentralized perspective is an important characteristic of postmodernism. . . . Jameson in his critique of postmodernism . . . identifies pastiche as the only
interpretive mode that remains possible. As a mode, it capitalizes on the "already made"
by borrowing, even plagiarizing, and repeating bits and pieces of other works wholesale
with little or no commentary. Through this "metareferencing," that is, the placement side
by side of two fragments of a work, each work is flattened and emptied of its specific
contents, thus blurring the distinctions between past, present, and future. In the post-

modern era, what is finally left for the artist is the task of re-presenting representations. (Lin 1992, 337)

Cheung also includes "manifest and veiled plots," "unreliable points of view," and "unreliable narration" (Cheung 1993, 29) as characteristic techniques of postmodern writers. In this text, we will see how all the authors use unreliable narrators for the purpose of insisting "on their own voices, their [own] traditions, their [own] histories, and their [own] identities [to] turn the forms of personal narrative to their own purposes" and "to create a disruption of gendered binary opposition" in order to "force . . . readers to gain multicultural experiences" (Smith 1993, 407; Oh 1993, 14). Oh situates both Hong Kingston and Tan within the rubric of multiculturalism when he lauds Tan only as "another successful multicultural writer" like Hong Kingston, especially in her use of "strategic defamiliarization." In his opinion, such a technique "creates for her readers a somewhat confusing situation in which they feel as though they are overhearing the Chinese immigrant mothers, but not understanding everything they say. It also reinforces one of the novel's major themes: the troublesome exchange of ideas between immigrant mothers and their American-born daughters" (Oh 1993, 14). Hong Kingston and Tan are not only or primarily multicultural writers. They are ethnic and women of color feminists whose work aims to create "patriarchal hegemonic disruption" in both Oh's and Theresa Ebert's sense of it. Hong Kingston and Tan both use certain techniques to undo "the gender binary," not only in terms of "ideological constructions," but more importantly, to oppose "the systematic socioeconomic relations requiring and maintaining the specific forms of gender and sexual difference," that is, gender asymmetry (Ebert 1993, 39).

In their efforts "to elude cultural construction" (Friedman 1993, 245–246), the writers in question often represent female characters as inconsistent, contradictory, strange, or mad. Both Maxine and her mother in *The Woman Warrior* and Winnie and Helen of *The Kitchen God's Wife* are good examples, while Kadohata's Isura in *The Floating World* (influenced by Hisaye Yamamoto's "Seventeen Syllables" and "The Legend of Miss Sasagawara") provides perhaps the best example of all such characterizations.

SUBTERFUGE

After Hong Kingston's *The Woman Warrior*, the epic qualities of the magnificently delineated Brave Orchid give rise to another strategy common to the authors analyzed in this text. Arlene Elowe MacLeod, writing on Arab women, notes "subterfuge" as a dodge against gender asymmetry. Or as Sidonie Smith puts it more bluntly, "Lying is one kind of subversive ruse" (Smith 1993, 406). MacLeod describes "subterfuge" as "a useful technique in power struggles," not only because it is frequently employed by "subordinate groups" (MacLeod 1992, 550), but because it reflects "a more interesting and inseparable linkage of protest with accommodation" (MacLeod 1992, 552). We will see how Tan represents dodging as characteristic of Helen, as well as of Winnie in *The Kitchen God's Wife*. Tan's character Helen in this text and Myenne Ng's character Leon in *Bone* are embodiments of the rich quirkiness of character created when an author commits herself to such a nonbinary, paradoxical, ambiguous perspective, rather than a rigidly simplistic good-bad dichotomy. Suddenly at the end of *The Kitchen God's Wife*, although hitherto apparently consistent in her insensitivity, Helen reveals herself as a more sympathetic character when she clarifies the underlying causes of her seemingly "collaborationist" or "accommodationist" surface conduct. Similarly, Jen in *Typical American* represents her character Helen as being trained to have "enormous circumspection" in China.

Julia Kristeva sharply differentiates female thinking (which she defines as "semiotic") from male thinking (which she defines as "symbolic"). According to Kristeva, male "symbolism" is characterized by the abstract, the "thingified," with seeking to "make sense," to make "logical connections." On the other hand, female "semiotics" uses metaphor, metonymy, personal tone of voice, as well as many voices. Bifurcating these two modes of perception so sharply has brought down upon Kristeva the charge that she replicates the very binary thinking that she would undo in that "[t]he alternation between the semiotic and the symbolic that she postulates as a way beyond the rigid Lacanian [binary] categories" actually "replicates those categories" (Przybylowicz 1990, 266).

By glossing Kristeva's theories, as well as Mikhail Bakhtin's theory of "polyglossia" in relation to *The Woman Warrior*, Donald Goellnicht views Hong Kingston's narrative as a challenge and disruption of the "symbolic order with the semiotic" (Goellnicht 1992, 196), as is evident as well in the narratives of Tan, Myenne Ng, and Jen, as we will see. But this does not mean that these authors are essentialist feminists as is Kristeva. Tan, Myenne Ng, and Jen (as well as Sasaki and Kadohata) agree that it is their cultures, not human beings, that are designed asymmetrically. All the writers analyzed in this text oppose their cultures' constraining mythologies, religions, and prescriptions for women in a variety of ways that range from direct confrontation to subtle, muted representations of the waste of female lives caused by these oppressive forces.

Nevertheless, in postmodern feminist writing there are "[t]raits commonly identified as belonging to an intrinsically 'feminine' discourse—that is, the fragmented, circular, or otherwise antilinear (some would call it 'anti-phallocentric') narrative" (Edmondson 1991, 76). These include appropriation (adapting patriarchal forms to feminist purposes), juxtaposition (ironic arranging of materials), distraction (diverting attention away from the feminist message), indirection (using metaphor, impersonation, and hedging or equivocation to weaken a message), trivialization (using a form the dominant culture sees as irrelevant or unimportant), and deliberate incompetence (as in the domestic sphere). Pratt adds the following characteristics: "Exercises in storytelling and in identifying with the ideas, interest, histories, and attitudes of others, experiments in transculturation and collaborative work and in the arts of critique, parody, and comparison (including unseemly comparisons between elite and vernacular cultural forms); the redemption of the oral; ways for people to engage with suppressed aspects of history (including their own histories), ways to move into and out of rhetorics of authenticity" (Pratt 1991, 406).[2]

REVISIONING THE PAST

Hong Kingston's complex of writing techniques and perspectives has been characterized as "feminist subversive strategies" and " 'feminine' strategies of subversion." Among such strategies are "textual appropriation," sometimes "by cutting chunks out of all-ready written texts" and in other ways "defacing . . . patriarchal rhetoric and codes of behavior" which "threatens [sic] to bind rather than liberate" (Goellnicht 1992, 204; Henderson 1990, 243).

Nowhere is such controversial and influential "rewriting or rereading" more evident than in the work of Hong Kingston. King-Kok Cheung even suggests that contemporary African American women writers' representations of female characters, as illustrated by Celie in Alice Walker's *The Color Purple*, are indebted to Hong Kingston's female characters Fa Mu Lan, Brave Orchid, and the no-name aunt in *The Woman Warrior*. I would also add the narrator Maxine to Cheung's list of influential female characters. Maxine has been characterized as a female avenger "forged of words," or "a word warrior, a Fa Mu Lan of the pen instead of the sword" (Goellnicht 1992, 206). In becoming a woman warrior, Maxine is "subversively claiming her right to recycle myths and transpose gender, her right to authorship," just as the younger writers are doing, thereby shifting "the focus from physical prowess to verbal injuries and textural [sic] power" (Cheung 1992a, 176).

According to Cheung, through such female characterizations, Hong Kingston has provided contemporary African American women writers with "feminist models daring to assert autonomy, challenge patriarchy and shed feminine 'decorum' " (Cheung 1992a, 175). I would amend her claim to assert instead that contemporary African American women writers' characters are parallel in origin to Hong Kingston's, rather than influenced by her. Ethnic and women of color writers are all responding to the same problem: gender asymmetry. Thus they tend to create similar works of art and similar authorial strategies and techniques. These then define them in their time as "modern," "postmodern," "feminist," "postfeminist," and so on. In this light, what Cheung says of Walker and Hong Kingston is true, not only for Tan, but for Myenne Ng and Jen, as well. "They are feminist writers who seek to 're-vision' history (to borrow Adrienne Rich's word). If they are to be nurtured by their cultural inheritance rather than smothered by it, they must learn to reshape recalcitrant myths glorifying patriarchal values" (Cheung 1992a, 165).

In this text we will frequently see female characters represented by their authors as turning to their ancestral cultures in order "to reclaim beliefs that subvert the existing hierarchy" (Cheung 1992a, 184). In *The Joy Luck Club* far more than in *The Kitchen God's Wife*, Tan follows Hong Kingston's ironic tone of voice in a postmodern text that comes at readers like a random barrage of particles. Once we piece together these particles, we find a sequence of first person narrations comprised of mother-daughter sets. In an effort to transcend "disconnectedness and fragmentation" in *The Woman Warrior*, Hong Kingston employs the "thematic tune 'claiming America' " and "manages to join each seemingly isolated episode with different characters performing variations on the same theme against the background music produced by mini-tales and myths" (Wu 1992, 87). In Hong Kingston and in the other writers discussed in this text, this theme is also always interwoven with the issue of gender asymmetry. Theresa in *Typical American* even goes so far as to play variations on the Confucian family system to suit her own agenda. By revising and reconstituting it, she thereby subverts this system. Tan's character Winnie also does this by reshaping the myth of the Kitchen God by substituting the Kitchen God's wife for the Kitchen God. Such crucial "revis(ion)ing" shifts a strongly inscribed gender asymmetrical cultural discourse to the point where the noble wife actually emerges from invisible ink, from centuries of gender erasure. The Kitchen God's wife is the one who is canonized instead of her adulterous scoundrel of a husband. Where traditionalists like Frank Chin cry "heresy!" such a "revisioning" of old myths and customs and the creations of new ones strikes other critics as creative.

SILENCE/SILENCING

Cheung adds "the art of silence" to the list of techniques used by her own group as well as by women globally. This "art" includes various " 'strategies of reticence'—irony, hedging, coded language, muted plots—used by women writers to tell the forbidden and name the unspeakable" (Cheung 1993, 4). She also distinguishes between three kinds of female silences which are not always necessarily perceived by Asian American women writers as oppositional "in hierarchical terms"—as mainstream feminists tend to do—but as a complex means of communication. "[W]hether in the form of feminine and cultural decorum, external or self-censorship, or historical or political invisibility; at the same time they reveal, through their own manners of telling and through their characters, that silences—textual ellipses, nonverbal gestures, authorial hesitations (as against moral, historic, religious or political authority)—can also be articulate" (Cheung 1993, 3, 4–5).

In a humorous passage in *Typical American* the "hero's" wife Helen teaches their daughters Mona and Callie the strategic uses of "articulate silence" in conversation. The children's attempt to try out this technique on their "typical American" classmates fails when their strategy is ignored. Mona and Callie learn that typical Americans run roughshod over other cultures' subtleties not in their limited repertoire. What "typical Americans" do not hear or see they do not experience as reality. "[They] do not see what [they] do not see, and what [they] do not see does not [therefore] exist [so far as they are concerned]" (Maturana and Varela, 1992, 242). To use the term in a feminist sense, silence/silencing of women is one of the major issues in contemporary Asian American women's literature, as well as in women's literature globally.[3]

Traditionalists like Frank Chin and Benjamin Tong would perpetuate and reinforce this silencing by suppressing feminist projects such as the revision of myths or the creation of new ones. Kim has answered their outraged cries at great length. She devoted an entire chapter of *Asian American Literature: An Introduction to the Writings and Their Social Context*[4] to their attacks against feminist writers. Among others, she defended Hong Kingston for her "attempts to delineate her experience from the point of view of a Chinese American woman" (Kim 1982, 198). Not all male critics are negative, however. Donald Goellnicht, for one, is of especial interest because he courageously raised his voice in defense of the beleaguered writers to address Chin's complaints against them. And Qing-Yun Wu, another male reader of Hong Kingston's *China Men* was, like Chin, unsettled by Hong Kingston's creative revisioning—at first. He began by viewing her as "an unreliable author of autobiography or biography," but then she emerged for him "as a bold or even an audacious storyteller of history" (Wu 1992, 88).

Chin's attempt to "silence" the women writers has taken up so much space for more than twenty years in Asian American literary history that it might well be addressed at this point. He accuses revisionary feminist and gay Chinese American writers of colluding in a three-fold conspiracy against Chinese Americans. He argues that white Western stereotypes are reinforced culturally whenever revisionary writers create new myths and critique Chinese men. In this way they collaborate with and forward the Western project of emasculating or castrating (i.e., "Orientalizing") Chinese men. They also aid the U. S. government's anti-immigration legislation and the Western missionaries' imposition of Christianity on the Chinese. To the first accusation Goellnicht responded that Asian American men "do not usually experience the threat of sexual victimization, of bodily assault, faced in minority women" (Goellnicht 1992, 207). However, recent events such as the Los Angeles riots have vindicated Chin on this score.

In the second instance, Goellnicht reminded Chin of "the misogynous aspects of such legislation" historically, and linked his third charge with his repudiation of and dismissal of Chin for a "discourse [which] brims with misogynous rage" and for Chin's "sexist and homophobic tendencies" (Goellnicht 1992, 209). If Chin's wishes were to be fulfilled, the Chinese Confucian literature and culture he cherishes and valorizes unquestioningly and that minimalizes and objectifies women would permit " 'men's highly gendered views, arguments, and theories to pass as ungendered, generic' "(Stanley 1992, 14). From time immemorial the "ungendered, generic" masculine gender usage in discourse and hence in perspective has been naturalized as the normal state of affairs.[5] Chin wants to silence these writers in order to prevent them from representing women as "victimized and trapped in a hideous Chinese civilization" (F. Chin 1991, 3), as he puts it sarcastically. Their interpretations, revisions, and perspectives in relation to Chinese and Japanese culture and history are therefore "fake." Only his are "real" (F. Chin 1991, xi–xiii).

Chin's violent opposition to any revisions, any tampering with the "real" literature, myths, and folklore of "real" Chinese culture reveals that he sees himself as a "literary archaeologist," "a purist," "an agent of history" (Newman 1990, 104; Levi-Strauss 1966, 257), viewing what he "sever[s] and carve[s] up" from his cultural history as "real." Others who "sever and carve up" the same history so that it projects different views from his are "fake." Chin has no doubt that the way he interprets what has been written and passed on is an accurate representation of reality, of the way it was and is. This is why he feels always "under the threat of 'an infinite regress' " whenever he comes across interpellating variants such as the revisionary writers make.

Equally true of "the constitution of historical facts" is "their selection." Like many other self-selected upholders of pristine masculinist history, any revisionism, any change, seems to "confront" Chin "with chaos" (Levi-Strauss 1966, 257). To some extent, he is justified. As an upholder of tradition, he reviles destabilizations of Chinese ways imposed by Western colonialism and imperialism, particularly Christianity's depredations against the Chinese religion in the form of Christian missionaries (F. Chin 1991, 8–18). In doing so, he fails to notice the parallels between his perspective in relation to the ethnocentric racism of the West and its Christian missionaries and that of the Asian American feminist and gay writers toward gender asymmetry. Instead, he excoriates them as being guilty of "cashing in" and "selling out" (Kim 1982, 198). In doing so, he exposes "the frustration of [a revolutionary] who see[s] others awarded the victory, without ever being in the fight" (Newman 1990, 104) and a consuming jealousy of their successes with the mainstream public. He also assumes that their representations of gender asymmetry are (personal) insults to (his) "real" Chinese manhood.[6]

Because writers like Hong Kingston, Tan, and David Henry Hwang are against gender asymmetry, they are therefore denounced by Chin as "against men." In response, Hong Kingston has explained to the public that she cares "about men . . . as much as I care about women" (Pfaff 1980, 27). This defensive posture signals a feminist perspective as opposed to a postfeminist one. From the latter perspective, Hong Kingston's generalization is reductive. Feminist critique of males signifies a hatred of male characters as little or as much as criticism of one's government signifies that the critic is a traitor or anti-American. As a matter of fact, all of the writers whom I discuss in this text depict male characters in a "by and large . . . positive" way characterized by "compassion" mixed with "a kind of subversive triumph" (Goellnicht 1992, 203). Some of these writers create unforgettable male characters, as illustrated in Hong Kingston's penetrating portrait of Maxine's father in *China Men*; in Tan's complex characterization of Winnie's father in *The Kitchen God's Wife* (strongly influenced by Hong Kingston); in Myenne Ng's creation of Leon, who seems to come alive off the page in *Bone*; and Sasaki's moving delineation in *The Loom and Other Stories* of Jo's father in Hiroshima and his response to his imminent death.

When Kim states that Chin considers "the masculinity of Asian American men . . . as threatened by the comparatively large number of Asian American women writers" (Kim 1982, 180, 198), I would modify this statement to read that Chin's own threatened masculinity is projected onto other Asian American men's. The acclaim given to certain Chinese American writers, especially Jade Snow Wong, Maxine Hong Kingston, and Amy Tan seems to him to come at the price of his comparative obscurity while gifted with considerable talent, equal or superior to theirs. Therefore, he concludes, there must be a conspiracy against him, that is, against all Chinese men. According to him, the conspiracy is orchestrated by Hollywood, mainstream white feminists, and "American publishers [who] went crazy for Chinese women's dumping on Chinese men" (F. Chin 1991, 27). Only conspiracy could account for the success of such "fakes," he argued. Even though she had contained herself for so long and hitherto put up with "a one sided argument because the women don't answer. We let them say those things because we don't want to be divisive" (M. Chin 1990, 66), Hong Kingston finally exploded at this point:

Attacks by the men on the women. Saying that somehow, we have achieved our success by collaborating with the white racist establishment. We are in bed with the white literary establishment; that's how we get published. Or they say, we pander to the white taste for feminist writing. We're just panderers if we write this kind of stuff. We write, we put out exotic visions, images, because whites find it romantic. All these issues that David Hwang did in *M. Butterfly* are very feminist. . . . It's a very crazy plot they have in their heads. Their assessment of the publishing industry is so wrong. (M. Chin 1990, 66–67)

What also enrages Chin is that these women writers do not restrict themselves to representing specific situations in their individual characters' lives. Instead, they critique the deep level structure of traditional Chinese culture in terms of gender asymmetry. This then becomes a political issue to him—of women refusing privatization, of contending instead that the situations they expose are not individual cases of abuse, but the results of an unjust system in relation to all women. Chin sees this move as a Western imposition of and disruption to the Confucian system of order and hierarchy of positions, "the Confucian ideal of marriage" and "the Confucian ethic"—which is military (F. Chin 1991, 28–52). "The soldier is the universal individual. . . . Life is war. . . . All behavior is strategy and tactics. All relationships are martial. Marriages are military alliances" (F. Chin 1991, 6).

Even in the face of such a hierarchical conflictual model, Chin denies gender asymmetry in Confucianism. He insists that in Confucianism, and in the poetry and myths and tales that comprise Confucian Chinese literature, "[t]here is no sexual dominance . . . [no] male dominance and the inferiority of women as a moral universal" (F. Chin 1991, 7). Thus Chin denies the fact that Chinese literature and culture is in Bakhtin's language "ideologically saturated." But language has never been just a simple vehicle of transcendent universal abstract truth and reality. There is in fact always a tension between those "purists" who would stabilize language into a unitary, officially recognized system and those "revisionists" who would destabilize and diversify it (Bakhtin 1986, 271–272). Ultimately, those perspectives, insights, and judgments in the literature and culture that Chin considers objective can only reflect his own opinions and those who agree with him. He uses the same arguments and takes the same tone and stance as Black Power and Afrocentric spokesmen in relation to African American women (Goellnicht 1992, 293) and other women of color and ethnic women writers. "Among the minority writers," Hong Kingston stated in an interview, "It looks like there is an argument going on, between black men and black women writers, between the Chicano men and the Chicanas, between the Asian-American writers, the men and women, the same argument is being carried out. And it's not even an argument; it's so one-sided" (M. Chin 1990, 66).

One of Chin's and other ethnic and men of color's most influential arguments with their women is that "You are conspiring against us if you allow the mainstream feminists who are racist and hate men, any kind of men, to use you to advance their agenda. You are naive to allow these white women to use you when you should stand by (and behind) your men of your own kind." Undeniably, this argument, designed to distance and estrange, to erect barriers of suspicion between white mainstream feminists and ethnic and women of color feminists, has been successful on ethnic women and women of color. However, ethnic and men of color have failed to take sufficient notice of the fact that this argument also perpetuates gender asymmetry and the status quo in order for them to continue to remain in control over their women. By denying the validity of women's perspectives in relation to the culture and in labeling any expression of revisionism the tools of white Western religion, white male publishers, and white mainstream feminists, Chin is using tactics of intimidation, harassment and abuse. He would prevent the women of his group from free self-expression, their First Amendment rights, and their rights as authors—equal to Chin's—to express their own viewpoints and their own creativity.

Initially, Chin's outrage came as a shock to Hong Kingston and caused her much undue suffering, more than others, because as the first and most successful Asian American feminist writer "to step out of line" it was she who bore the brunt of the attacks:

I was really shocked when I came out with my first book. At that time there were some Asian-American men who were all we had of our literary community. And I expected, when my book came out, for them to say, welcome. Welcome to the community of artists. Because there are so few of us. So here's another one to add strength to our numbers. And, instead, the men just right away went into this big thing. (M. Chin 1990, 67)

To illustrate with only a few of many examples, if thinking like Chin's had prevailed, Shakespeare's plays might never have been performed or published, since most of them were derivative and revisionary; Elizabeth Cady Stanton's woman's version of the Bible; Eugene O'Neill's plays, which were powerful Freudian revisions of Greek tragedies; and a multitude of composers and artists who produce variations on any themes would all be consigned to oblivion. To gag the Chinese American women writers is to sacrifice them at the altar of perceived heresy without regard to their rights to self-define and express their issues and needs. Further, to play one group of women against the other in order to forward his position is unconscionable, although Chin's distrust of white mainstream feminists is well-founded. However, Chin conveniently ignores the fact that other ethnic and women of color feminist critics have also paid scant, if any, attention to Asian American women writers. Since this is the case, why do Chin, as well as Asian American women critics, express reservations only about white mainstream feminists and not about other ethnic and women of color critics who also neglect them? I will take up this issue in the Conclusion, after devoting Chapter Two to Fae Myenne Ng, Chapter Three to Gish Jen, Chapter Four to R. A. Sasaki, and Chapter Five to Cynthia Kadohata, authors who are even more undeservedly ignored than Hong Kingston and Tan by all these groups of critics—by ethnic, women of color, and mainstream feminists alike. So far as I am aware, my Conclusion is the first call for a dialogue between Asian American women writers and critics and mainstream feminist movement critics. I seek to offset all such hitherto fairly successful efforts as Chin's to divide and conquer women by silencing them. These efforts are all designed to prevent dialogue between mainstream feminists and Asian American and other ethnic and women of color feminists by nipping in the bud our nascent attempts to express our affinities across race, class, and ethnic lines, as well as across cultures and around the world.

Following the lead of Hong Kingston, we will see the younger Chinese American women writers grappling with the global problem of gender asymmetry. Tan will confront it directly in *The Kitchen God's Wife*. Myenne Ng in *Bone* will create a historic allegory of women in relation to it. And Jen in *Typical American* will both satirize and celebrate Chinese and American success mythologies. We will see Sasaki in *The Loom and Other Stories* illustrate the tragic results of gender and racial constraints on women, while Kadohata in *The Floating World* rejects them entirely and writes as if they do not exist.

NOTES

1. See end of Chapter Two.

2. Christopher Wise adds the use of "originless voices, the exploration of dreams and the unconscious, the fragmentation of the ego, and a self-reflexive awareness of fiction *as* fiction" (1992, 121). [Emphasis in original]

3. The ethnic Latina feminist critic Linda Alcoff and her colleague Laura Gray add children to the list. "The violations and silencing of women and children [are characteristic of modes of] dominance and ancient structures of asymmetrical discursive relationships" (Alcoff and Gray 1993, 265).

4. See her Chapter Six, "Chinatown Cowboys and Warrior Women: Searching for a New Self-Image" (Kim, 1982, 173–213).

5. On "gender erasure," Paula Bennett argues that women are "not necessarily 'invisible' within our system of representation." Nevertheless, "like members of other

minoritized and colonized groups," [that] they "experience themselves as invisible or 'lacking' seems beyond dispute. The causes of this lack are political, however, they can be changed" (Bennett 1993, 256).

6. Hong Kingston's *The Woman Warrior* became a bestseller with the public and in academia, and Hong Kingston even became a media figure. Equally infuriating to Chin was the enormous success of David Henry Hwang's *M Butterfly*. Tan's *The Joy Luck Club* not only became a bestseller, but was adapted into a movie. Ironically, although Chin deems himself a conservator and Hong Kingston a desecrator of traditional literature, Hong Kingston, not Chin, was recently chosen to host and introduce a series of traditional Chinese folktales on mainstream television. Indeed, Chin might have been the better choice, given the medium, since he is gifted with a charismatic personality and a flair for showmanship.

Chapter 1

Amy Tan, *The Kitchen God's Wife:*
"Chasing Away a Big Stink"

TAN'S SUBSTITUTION OF THE MOTHER-DAUGHTER PLOT FOR THE YIN/YANG PRINCIPLE

In Amy Tan's *The Joy Luck Club*, Lindo Jong of "The Red Candle" is Waverly's mother. A rebel like An Mei's mother in *The Joy Luck Club* and Wei Wei's (Winnie's) mother in *The Kitchen God's Wife*, Lindo is, unlike them, a brilliant manipulator and subverter, as well. She ingeniously sabotages Chinese marriage customs and superstitions in order to achieve her own ends: to break out of an arranged marriage. Again, unlike the other rebels, Lindo succeeds without repercussions to herself. On her wedding day to a lout, after four years of slaving for his obnoxious mother, Lindo uses their superstitious belief that if the wedding candle goes out during the night, bad luck will befall the groom. She arranges it so that the candle goes out. Lindo's comment after she has achieved her covert goal foreshadows the equilibrium that Tan depicts between mothers and daughters at the end of *The Joy Luck Club*: "I would always remember my parents' wishes, but never forget myself" (*Joy* 53). Technically Lindo was obeying her parents in marrying the man they had chosen for her, but not in fact. She thus plays both ends against the middle. Again, in the chapter "Four Directions," featuring Lindo and Waverly, the moral is that mothers are eerily correct about everything. It is up to the daughter to come to terms with and accommodate the mother.

Also enduring horrifying experiences with her first husband (as do An Mei of *The Joy Luck Club* and Winnie of *The Kitchen God's Wife*) is Ying-Ying St. Clair of *The Joy Luck Club*. A tormented woman who suffers periodic bouts of madness as a result of her first marriage to a brutal husband, she is convinced that she cannot disclose her past suffering in China to anyone. In order to escape her "domestic" situation she subverted it illegally. Re-creating herself in the artificially (en)gendered image of a "China Doll" Oriental woman that fits her future white American husband's fantasy desire, she allows him to woo and win her as if she were single. She then elopes with him to the United States, deserting her legal Chinese husband. As a by-product of this "metaperformance," in Judith Butler's sense of the word, Ying-Ying's denied selfhood is submerged. She grows ever more silent and deaf, estranged from others, incapable of being understood and therefore heard by her American husband if she should speak. This is the price she pays herself for her deception. She has traded in the harshest forms of gender asymmetry in China for inauthenticity—for a more benign gender asymmetry in the United States, but gender asymmetry, nevertheless.

Ying-Ying is furious with her daughter's inertia, her passivity in not acting on her own behalf in decision making during her marriage and subsequent separation, especially when she recollects the extremes she herself went through in order to escape her marital predicament in China. Nevertheless, by continuing to keep silent about her past, Ying-Ying prevents her daughter from finding out that her mother has paid her dues and therefore from moving on past her current state of resignation to gender asymmetry. She has endured a relationship in China with an even meaner husband than Lena's cheap, philandering white American husband, whose name ironically is "Rich." Ying-Ying identifies herself with a tiger, a far cry indeed from acquiescence, obedience, and passivity, the three Confucian obediences for women.

To briefly summarize, by the end of *The Joy Luck Club*, the daughters have learned to accept their mothers as they are. They have also learned to be at peace about the gap caused by generational variations in environment, cultural internalizations, belief systems, and practices between their Chinese mothers and themselves. Tan here illustrates ethnicity in terms of Sollors's (1986) concept of "consent and descent." Between the generations from immigrant to American-born there occurs a romanticizing process of reconnection to the country of origin. In coming to terms with the past and with the originating culture, there is a reinvention of that past that links the post immigrant generation to the former culture. In both *The Joy Luck Club* and *The Kitchen God's Wife*, daughters are empowered to continue the syncresis of their mothers' linking of the past with the present for them—that is, if and when the mothers tell their stories to their daughters. In *The Joy Luck Club* the mothers remain fixed, of the past. They do not seem to bend in their turn—to reach outward to the new ways represented by their daughters, to modify, and to accept them. The daughters seem to have to do all the work of interpreting their mothers' innermost thoughts.

Following Hong Kingston's feminist model, Tan ends with her daughters at peace about their mothers' ambivalence, paradox and uncertainty. It does not even matter at the end that the mothers have different values from their daughters and live by them. The daughters adapt to their mothers. They do not judge their mothers' differences any longer as superstitions imposed upon them to harass them and make their lives miserable. The failure of their conflicting ideologies to mesh is no longer a source of suffering. The mothers are loved and accepted on their own terms. But the reverse does not hold, thereby creating an asymmetry between women on an intergenerational level. A like tolerance and/or acceptance is not demanded of mothers as it is of daughters. The onus of understanding, of modifying any positions, is placed all upon the daughters.

Tan would then seem to be perpetuating the traditional Confucian hierarchical systems that require worship of ancestors and obligations of filial respect and duty to "the ancient notion of family accord" (Sledge 1980, 14). However, in most traditional Chinese literature females and female issues and relationships are of little consequence, peripheral to the heroics of heroes, to their manifold masculine activities. What is revolutionary about Tan's mother-daughter relationships is that she is transferring the Confucian model of yin/yang from men and women to mother/daughter relations. Of the younger generation of Asian American women authors, Tan most closely follows Hong Kingston's feminist lead in *The Woman Warrior* in reversing the traditional perspective. Her immigrant "mother" characters confront brutal gender asymmetries both in China and the United States. Their daughters, despite their American birth, are by no means immune to gender asymmetry, either. Tan shows much of the daughters' suffering, in fact, as due to men individually, even though the gender asymmetry they experience in the United States under masculine systems of control and dominance is nowhere near as brutal as what their mothers experienced in China. In both cases, however, the men whom both generations encounter have made the rules for their own advantage and for women's oppression. Derrida (1976) has explained "difference" as that which is within but which is projected externally and then seen as the Other. By male-centered logic, its (male) discourse is primary, of course—seamless, transparent, rational: the way things should be—while the female Other is deviant and dangerous. In terms of crucial destabilizations of this masculinist construct of "difference" in gender relations, Tan's female characters make changes that are not superficial. A major question I will address in this chapter is that of the response of Tan's female characters to gender asymmetry.

When she was a child, the gatekeepers subjected Ying-Ying to such acculturation. The woman is "Yin—darkness within, where untempered passions lie. And man is Yang, bright truth lighting our minds" (*Joy* 92). However, in a revolutionary move, the traditional yin/yang paradigm is reversed by Ying-Ying and integrated into one seamless whole, just as in the male-centered cultural regime. The only difference is that the entire paradigm relates only to women. In "Walking Between Trees" she likens herself to a tiger "gold [female] with its heart, black [male] with cunning, hiding gold between trees, seeing, not being seen, waiting patiently for things to come" (*Joy* 282). Tan substitutes the traditional concept of yin/female and yang/male by making mothers yin, instead, and daughters yang. She thereby undoes one of the key tenets of the Chinese world view; that the yin/yang relationship between male and female is the fundamental basis for all relationships. Despite Ruth Y. Hsiao's argument that this is nothing new, that since Louis Chu's *Eat a Bowl of Tea* "overtly or subversively, the literature has repeatedly attacked the Confucian fathers" (Hsiao 1992a, 154), Tan's move is more than an attack. It is a daring discursive ideological displacement. Mothers and daughters are represented as in the relationship that the Chinese (as well as all patriarchal cultures globally) have traditionally prescribed as fundamental: the relationship of man/woman.

Instead of working with a male/female yin/yang model as fundamental, Tan substitutes the never-ending, circular flow of continuity from mother to daughter: This conceptualization also includes the destabilization of gender asymmetry. The male/female model sounds good, as if balance between the two is cultural bedrock, an assumption that Tan challenges. In her view the traditional yin/yang binary also diverts the mother/daughter flow into a conduit or feeder for the perpetuation of gender asymmetry. In so doing, it irretrievably disrupts the mother/daughter relationship in various ways—from the creation of artificial barriers between mother/daughter to the most tragic of all—the loss of the mother. We will see how this notion of Tan's becomes one of the major elements of *The Kitchen God's Wife*. It is similar to Western feminist psychoanalytic modifications of Freud's Oedipus complex paradigm for "object relations," as when Nancy Chodorow maintains that both sexes are products of bonding with the mother. The son separates and distances himself from the mother in a necessary move to establish his own identity, whereas the daughter need never split off, or returns at the onset of maturity. As I have previously shown, the trajectory of *The Joy Luck Club* follows this latter revisionary path of reconciliation, as does *The Kitchen God's Wife*, as we will see.

MALE CHARACTERS

Wen Fu

In another reversal of gender asymmetry, Tan sets up her male characters as foils to her heroines. Male characters are given more importance in *The Kitchen God's Wife* than in *The Joy Luck Club*, but are minimally delineated in both works. They are either abrasive and unappealing, or remote and benign. Although referring to the male characters of Hisaye Yamamoto, Elaine Kim's words could well describe the male characters of both *The Joy Luck Club* and *The Kitchen God's Wife*: "[T]hey [the men] remain in the shadows as guardians of the prison doors, for the most part conventional and colorless in comparison to the women who are the central figures" (Kim 1987, 99). Wen Fu of *The Kitchen God's Wife* is the one exception. The excruciating details of Winnie's long struggles over years of marriage to him do not occur in a vacuum. They are set within the context of the culture of the time and place and of historic events from 1938 to 1945, after Japan's invasion of China, followed by limited American assistance to the Chinese.

Tan's purpose in the sometimes over-minutely detailed situations given over to Wen Fu is twofold. First, she exposes in perhaps too many ways the excesses that she believes men are permitted to indulge in when only men are in control. In this light, Wen Fu can be viewed as embodying Chinese patriarchal laws and customs that take gender asymmetry too far. On one occasion Winnie even becomes the object of public censure in the media. After being chastised in court, she is sentenced to a prison term for being a bad wife and mother. Wen Fu's lies are believed by all. Secondly, Tan's strategy is to overload readers with domestic and public situations that provide so many trials and tribulations to Winnie as to garner all the sympathy she can for her before she violates two of the strongest cultural commandments for women ever constructed. Tan's difficult task is to create a female character who retains readers' respect as a "heroine," even though we are not trained to accept a woman who will abandon her husband, and even more shocking, her small children. Only after having suffered *ad nauseam* every conceivable form of abuse does Winnie finally rear up and strike back (like Samuel Richardson's Clarissa and Alice Walker's Celie of *The Color Purple*. Unlike Clarissa, but like Celie, she does so with the help of a community of female friends).

In order to make her case against him and his culture as strong as possible, Tan has constructed Wen Fu with the greatest of care as an extreme by-product of his cultural regime. He masquerades as his older, smarter, deceased brother in order to be chosen one of the band of famed pilots, the fabled "flying tigers." This elite group flew under the American General Claire Chenault, "that famous American general with a lady's name" (Tan 1991, 165). All of them share the same class values and privileges, as well as Winnie's dowry, which Wen Fu depletes by entertaining them. He is their "top man," "the most" of what they are trained to be. They all seem to be intimidated by him. Unlike the rest of his group, who all die, Wen Fu survives the war. He survives everything—Tan's commentary on the incredible staying power of the extremes of the system he embodies. Tan has Wen Fu live and die triumphant, surrounded to the end by admiring, loving friends. Her aim, once again, is to outrage her readers' sense of justice, although her strategy backfires to some extent, because she also outrages our sense of credibility, at times. Wen Fu's treatment of his wife and all other women forms a large part of an incremental pattern designed and repeated painstakingly by Tan through Winnie's narrating voice. Each anecdote redounds to the credit of his wife to such an extent that eventually readers are moved to so great a distaste for Wen Fu that the very sight of his name becomes unbearable. However, so many repetitions on the same theme create "overkill" and could have used some editorial pruning.

Wen Fu is a womanizer.[1] First he charms and plays with women and then seduces and/or rapes them. Like most of his sort, he has contempt for women. He even sleeps with one in his wife's bed while she is at the hospital bearing their child.[2] After Winnie becomes disenchanted with him, he performs sadistic, perverse, and painful sex acts on her, as well as on other women. His brutality and selfishness extend even to beating his own baby violently and allowing it to die. While Winnie is away in the hospital giving birth, Wen Fu repeatedly rapes the fourteen year old servant girl who becomes pregnant and dies while trying to abort the fetus.

When Winnie confronts Wen Fu, his response is to hit the baby who was "crying hard." He hit her again and again until the baby "rolled up into a little ball . . . making small animal sounds" (262). Blackmailed in this manner, Winnie caves in and agrees to beg her husband to forgive her, although it is he who needs forgiveness. Not surprisingly, the baby then turns strange. It loses its mind from fear and stress. When the baby grows very ill, Wen Fu is in the midst of a mah jong game with his buddies, one of them a doctor. On the grounds that his wife " 'is exaggerating, ' " he does not permit the doctor to stop playing: " 'The baby sneezed once, she thinks it's pneumonia' " (265), he claims. Furious that Winnie contradicts him, Wen Fu shouts that he wouldn't care if the baby died, that actually his wife is trying to chase him home before he loses all his winnings. The other men respond with nervous laughter while the doctor sits back down to the game. Later that night when Winnie brings the dying child to Wen Fu and shows her to the group, Wen Fu calls her a " 'stupid woman' " for not telling him that the child was so ill and expresses outrage at her lack of maternal feeling: " 'What kind of mother are you!' " he demands (266).

After Wen Fu slaps Winnie publicly, she distances herself for the first time, to the point where she actually begins to theorize the situation from a feminist perspective. Winnie's response is to resent both her husband for criticizing her in private and in public and the kind of cultural training where no one present in the room had defended her, had had the courage to tell Wen Fu that they had heard her inform them all that the baby was dying. She begins to view her suffering not only in personal and private terms, but in relation to the group. In this light, she judges the group as not so much "wrong" as "dangerous" because "[i]t fed Wen Fu's power, made him feel stronger." When he forces her to kneel down in public and beg forgiveness while their neighbor Helen assists him, she begins to wonder why no one defends her, why they stood there acting as if she were the one in the wrong. She is aggrieved that "[t]hey did not protest and tell Wen Fu, 'This is enough,' when he told me to beg forgiveness, again and again" (253).

Soon after their marriage, Wen Fu begins to abuse her physically and emotionally. He forces her "to say dirty words . . . for a woman's body parts." He undresses her naked, and because she will not say what he wants her to say, drags her "toward the door like a bag of rice . . . then pushed me outside into the corridor . . . where anyone passing by could have seen me, naked like that" (169). He also made her strip naked, go on her hands and knees, then pretend to be "desperate" for sex, while "he would pretend to refuse," giving as reasons that she "was not pretty enough," or that she "had been a bad wife that day" (170). Wen Fu also forced her to "stand in the room naked, shivering in the night chill" (170). She "had to beg and beg, my teeth chattering, until I truly was begging so I could get off the cold floor" (170). He would name body parts, and then she had "to say the same coarse word, then put my fingers there, touch myself—here, there, everywhere—while he watched and laughed." In the mornings he would often complain that she "was not a good wife," that she "had no passion, not like other women he knew" (170).

Interestingly, she "was not angry. I did not know I was supposed to be angry. This was China. A woman had no right to be angry" (170). When Betty Friedan published *The Feminine Mystique* (1963), which started the "second wave" of feminism, she called sexism the problem with "no name." Gender asymmetry then (and still today in many parts of the world) was such that the language discourse contained no female gender referentiality. Gender was erased, and few women were in evidence in the male world in any of its public institutions. Friedan pointed out that women had difficulty in complaining about that for which no language existed, what was nowhere but everywhere historically and in our world and time. First we had to become aware—and this was against the grain of our cultural training—that our suffering was not due to something wrong with us individually. Rather, something was amiss with our world about how gender was constructed, Friedan claimed. But few people in any given generation question their training. A critical mass of enough men and women first have to perceive things similarly and then have to come together in sufficient numbers. There have to be safe structures set up for women to express their grievances, to create a discourse such as "sexual harassment," "wife [or child] abuse," "battering," and even "gender asymmetry," which becomes acceptable over time in common usage. Only then can the nature of our grievances be expressed and solutions put forward. Anger is only the first step in the long process. However, anger is forbidden to women.

In the early days of their marriage, the knowledge that Wen Fu was still dissatisfied with her is the only supposed source of Winnie's unhappiness. She had been taught that she "would have to go through more suffering to show him I was a good wife" (170). She observes that her husband is sadistic, not only with her, but with his friends, as well. "I saw that my husband did this laughing-scaring game not just with me, but with his friends. And I also began to see that what he did was wrong, cruel, but no one else seemed to see this. . . . He accused and tormented, shouted and threatened. And just at that point when you did not know which way to move, he took the danger away, became kind and forgiving, laughing and happy. Back and forth, this way and that" (180). Winnie then drops the use of the first person singular in order to prove that everyone in the group agreed with her—that her observations are based on reality and not biased due to her hatred of Wen Fu: "Of course, we were confused, fooled into thinking we always wanted to please him. And when we did not, we tried hard to win back his good nature, afraid we would be lost without it" (180).

With Winnie's dowry money Wen Fu buys a car for himself, which he promptly destroys in a joy ride. Later, he gets into an accident with a jeep he had commandeered without permission. While speeding, he almost runs into a truck going his way. Wen Fu is then forced to swerve, and the jeep flips over. A girl he had taken with him is killed, "crushed underneath" the vehicle (248), as is the case with any woman around Wen Fu. Later we will see Gish Jen using the same situation in *Typical American*—a man out of control driving his vehicle over a woman—again to signify gender asymmetry. In representing Wen Fu as "off the deep end," Tan may be referencing the Monkey King, but with a twist. The playful, but amusingly destructive sexual trickster of Chinese myth and folklore, has here gone amok, been turned into a monster. This technique is intertextual with Hong Kingston's in *The Woman Warrior* when she shaped and adapted Chinese myths and folklore to suit her perspective in her work.

Because Winnie meets another man at an officers' dance and dances with him, when they return home Wen Fu pulls her by the hair and throws her to the floor.[3] Pointing a gun at her head, he makes her fill out divorce papers (which she eagerly does): "You see, you are divorced. . . . Worth nothing. You have no husband. You have no home. You have no son" (308), he pontificates. Then he demands that she go down on her knees and beg him not to divorce her, to tear up the papers. With the gun still at her head, he next proceeds to rape her, "telling me I had lost the privileges of a wife and now had only the duties of a whore." He forces her to "do one terrible thing after another. He made me murmur thanks to him. He made me beg for more of his punishment. I did all these things until I was senseless, laughing and crying, all feeling in my body gone" (309). The next morning she leaves Wen Fu, but he finds her. "He was not kind. . . . And if you think that was the worst part of my life, you are wrong. The worst was always what happened next, and then after that, and then after that. The worst was never knowing when it would stop" (311).

Occasionally Tan provides readers with comparative relief from these brutal scenes by describing Winnie's suffering through metaphors, instead. At one point Winnie describes herself as "like a chicken in a cage, mindless, never dreaming of freedom, but never worrying when your neck might be chopped off. . . . But of course, even the stupidest chicken will fly away when the cage breaks open" (313). And when Winnie undergoes three abortions in the space of five months, she puts it as: "That bad man was using my body. Every night he used it, as if I were—what?—a machine!" (312). After Wen Fu chases his mistress away, he returns to Winnie's bed, while continuing to sleep with many other women. He can do this, Winnie concludes, because "we were all the same to him, like a piece of furniture to sit on, or a pair of chopsticks for everyday use" (282). Indeed, she often ponders the nature of Wen Fu's character, so much so that she seems to verge on an obsession about him. By this means, Tan gives to Wen Fu a three-dimensionality usually lacking in traditionally conceived and created "villains."

Cowardly as he is, Wen Fu became a successful flyer through lying his way into the air corps. During air battles he would beat a quick retreat. He teases and bullies his friends, and they interpret this as personality. He lords it over everyone and gets away with it. In the guise of a war hero, he shamelessly uses his uniform and war record to bluster about his sacrifices wherever he goes. Actually his grotesque appearance, injuries, and disabilities were caused by himself during his adulterous junket with the jeep. After the war ends, Wen Fu, Winnie, and their son Danru return to Shanghai to her father's house. Here Wen Fu literally and metaphorically proceeds to undermine and destroy the old man's house, that is, Winnie's patrimony. With his army record as a hero, he takes over his father-in-law's decaying mansion and enters into an orgy of "selling and spending" everything in sight for his own benefit. As one example, he sells a "magistrate's table" that "had been in [Winnie's] father's family for many generations, at least two hundred years" (329). When it can't get through the door, and the purchaser wishes his money back, Wen Fu takes a chair and cracks the carved table legs in half. If anyone attempts to say one word against him, he blackmails them with being thrown in jail " 'along with this traitor' " [Winnie's father] (330). Many years later, when Wen Fu finally dies, Tan puns on the cause of his death—"heart failure"—an affliction he suffered from all his life, since he was the most heartless of men. Ironically, Tan also causes Winnie's second husband, Jimmy Louie, who is a good man, to die young and suddenly of the same disease. [4]

Old Jiang

Winnie's father serves as another example of a man's "inappropriate" behavior in terms of the manner of his suffering and death. Initially he denounced the Japanese and threw tea at one of his precious paintings to prevent the conquerors from benefiting in any way from their booty. Later, however, under intense, incessant pressure, he caved in and collaborated with them. As a result, he is condemned by his neighbors and suffers a stroke. Winnie generously defends as a "mistake" her father's having thrown away his "honor" in order to protect his life by "becoming a traitor. . . . How can you blame a person for his fears and weaknesses unless you have felt the same and done differently? How can you think everyone can be a hero, choosing death, when it is part of our nature to let go of brave thoughts at the last moment and cling to hope and life?" (327). These complex questions bring Winnie to peace and understanding about her mother as well as her father. "[F]orgiving him with [her] heart," she realizes that if she blames her father she would also have to blame her mother for running away, for leaving her "so she could find her own life" (327). She would also have to blame herself for all the wrong choices she herself had made. This catharsis about one's parents is precisely where Tan had left off at the end of her first work, *The Joy Luck Club*.

Winnie's mother in *The Kitchen God's Wife*, (as well as An Mei's mother in *The Joy Luck Club*) may not have anticipated the intensity of her husband's vengeful reaction when she ran away. On one level, his conduct is literal. At a deeper level, it reflects the patriarchal system. Shame and "loss of his manhood" are reinforced whenever he is reminded of his wife abandoning him. She had outsmarted and outmaneuvered him and the culture by escaping from the marital coils in which she felt trapped. Her flight from both husband and child in order to fight with the Communists under Mao Tse tung against the traditional Chinese system fills her husband with rage and her abandoned child with endless sorrow. Under these circumstances, it is not difficult to understand why the sight of Winnie also sets Old Jiang off, so that for years he cannot stand the sight of her.

This is the case, especially because immediately prior to his wife's flight he had been bullying her in the mistaken certainty that there was nothing she (or any woman) could do to improve her situation. This was the way things were and had always been in their culture, he had insisted. She, as well as all other women, had to put up with it. He (literally the father and symbolically the male ruler) had consciously chosen to take advantage of the privileges he enjoyed as a male to tyrannize over his wives and children. When he had the opportunity to work with Winnie's mother to transform the system, he had lorded it over her and perpetuated it, instead. However, he had failed to take account of the possibility that he could not intimidate this exceptionally spirited young woman. He was caught by surprise by her response. Nothing in his training or his own experience had prepared him for such conduct, even his first "second" wife's suicide. Tan represents the response of suicide as the same and yet the opposite of Winnie's mother's response of flight.[5] Both choices represent a refusal to live any longer under the traditional system. In Tan's view, neither choice is acceptable. Nevertheless, Winnie takes pains to do her father justice; to represent him as ultimately paying as high a personal price for his loyalty to his cruel culture as these two out of his many wives had paid for their rebellion against it. The Japanese invaders bring this autocratic male great personal humiliation and suffering for the second time in his life. This time he yields, a course of conduct that directly reflects on himself as less than a man in terms of his culture's masculine codes of honor. He may not have chosen the stroke he suffered as a result of his enforced collaboration with the Japanese, but certainly his decision never again to use his voice for the rest of his life is chosen as self-punishment. Since only male voices matter and female voices are silent and silenced, his silence is a sign of self-imposed male gender castration.

Tan creates a fascinating stress between Old Jiang's personality (the result of his rigid masculine acculturation) and the extreme challenges to that acculturation with which he is confronted and that ultimately defeat him. Beneath the mask of the rigid code of honor within which his life as a mandarin is played out, readers experience a heart-wrenching glimpse at the end of his life of his individual qualities. At any given time Old Jiang only wanted to do what he had been trained by his culture was the appropriate thing for a man to do. The trouble is that cultural prescriptions by gender do not always accord with what is humanly nurturing. His "feminization" at the hands of the Japanese humanizes him to the point where he is finally able to set eyes on Winnie again and even live with her again. That he finally reveals parental feeling and concern for her welfare, if only in secret, is enough to redeem him in Winnie's eyes, because after learning that his daughter hates Wen Fu, her father gives her the last remnants of his secret hoard of wealth. He then dies, and in the course of doing so pulls a brilliant practical joke on Wen Fu reminiscent of Edgar Allen Poe's "The Cask of Amontillado." He tricks his son-in-law into believing that a fortune lies concealed somewhere in the foundations of his mansion. In his quest for it, Wen Fu destroys the house around himself as he digs. By this means, Old Jiang dooms his own house by depriving his own progeny of their rightful inheritance.

At the same time he has arranged it so that all the spoils of Wen Fu's usurpation will evaporate and he will be left only with dust and decay.

Around this time, Winnie, like her father, grows consciously subversive, quietly finding "ways to fight back" with wit and graceful ferocity. For example, she once "stole a mah jong tile from the set," effectively sabotaging her mother-in-law. Again, when Wen Fu's mother chooses Winnie's old room, Winnie informs her that a woman had died in that room under mysterious circumstances. Her mother-in-law then forces Winnie to switch rooms with her. When Wen Fu ignores the threat of "[i]nsects and disease" entering the house by refusing to spend the money to fix the broken windows, Winnie "sprinkled little bugs in his dresser and under the padding of his bed" (330) in the room he had taken over from her father.

All during this time, Wen Fu treats Winnie as if she "were a folding chair" (330), rolling her over, unbending her arms and legs with no words exchanged. When it was over, he would go to his room, and she would immediately wash herself where he touched her and throw the water out the window. Nilda Rimonte indicts the Asian community when it explains "domestic violence" by "blaming the circumstances" such as joblessness and poverty. Such excuses serve only to deny the problem, as well as to deny "the victims the right to look for alternatives," while ignoring "their need to seek help." Even more damning, the community "does not question the man's assumed right to beat women during times of stress, or the woman's assumed obligation to respect that right" (Rimonte 1989, 329). In this final indictment lies another distinction between Asian, African, and European cultures as compared to American culture. In contemporary American culture, a man will experience public censure and indictment if he physically beats a woman. However, the American failure to regard verbal insults and harassment as forms of spousal abuse does parallel the other cultures. For this reason, Rimonte's conclusion about spousal abuse still holds for all women in all cultures globally, that after the woman is "brutalized," she is then forced to collude in her own "victimization" through community "pressure." Thus it is the community that fosters and perpetuates gender asymmetry by nurturing "the ancient patriarchal family structure" (Rimonte 1989, 329).

Rimonte goes on to draw a sharp contrast between the Western family structure and that of the Pacific Asian one, but regardless of family structure, only by getting clear about the system and how it works for their disadvantage will women break the chain of victimization. They will then be empowered to substitute alternative values while reversing the system's abuses. Tan has Winnie reach a point by the end of the text where, contrary to the tenets of the prevailing patriarchal system, she is capable of making these distinctions. She questions her culture's valorized concept of "family" and "family values" which is designed to reproduce its own form, that is, to perpetuate male workers and female servants to those workers. Tan suggests that women should look to alternate forms, such as Winnie's disruption of the "Kitchen God's wife" myth.

A question emerges here as to whether or not Tan's notion of community is influenced by Carol Gilligan's observations (*In a Different Voice* 1982) concerning gender relational differences. According to Lawrence Kohlberg (*The Philosophy of Moral Development* 1981) men go by abstract principles of justice as the highest form of social contract. Women go by specific relationships, by webs of affiliation. Certainly the latter way is characteristic of all the females in this work, from Winnie to the fourteen year old victimized servant girl who kills herself after Wen Fu's rape impregnates her. Winnie's acts of subversion and heroism, her clever perceptions and wit, her functioning with and in a community of women, her nurturing of children and others, her practicality and involvement in everyday matters are not mere survival mechanisms of an intrinsic female essence, however. Unlike Julia Kristeva and Hélène Cixous, Tan does not claim these qualities as inherently female before acculturation. Instead, she is suggesting that these qualities might be cultivated for use as solutions to gender asymmetry that impact on males on the other side of the binary split.

Dr. Phil, Doctor to the Dead

As seemingly unlike as two men can possibly be on the surface, Winnie's and Pearl's husbands are not as different as they appear. Tan uses Winnie's caustic humor against Pearl's white husband to forward her own message against the Western white phallocentric system of rule. She depicts Dr. Phil, not as a healing doctor, but as a pathologist, a doctor to the dead. His irreverent wisecracks thinly disguise his impatience and skepticism with the past and with different, hence "inferior" cultures. He takes arrogant pride in his "rational," "scientific," objective mind. He feels superior to his "ignorant" Chinese immigrant mother-in-law, whom he perceives as silly because she is superstitious. He includes his wife in his sneers whenever Pearl inclines so much as a minute fraction of an inch in her mother's direction. He manipulates his wife into feeling embarrassed by and then distancing herself from her mother by defining Winnie's rituals as irrational, mind-controlling games devised to keep Pearl in line through guilt. They are inferior because they are different from his rational, "objective" ways which, of course, are the only correct and enlightened ones. By his attitude and in his discourse he also manipulates Pearl by withholding his approval of her as his equal unless she accepts his world view. Tan thus represents the underside of the contemporary Western white male's supposedly "kinder, gentler" perspective. Dr. Phil (like Charlotte E. Perkins Gilman's Dr. John in "The Yellow Wallpaper") is the epitome of the Western man of reason and science who believes in and relies on machine technology and the superiority of his and the machine's "abstract" and "objective" perspective. Early in the text, we find him playing with his beloved new computer.

On the other hand, Tan shows males like Jimmy Louie who are just as involved in caring and other female forms of "immanence" as opposed to "power" in Simone de Beauvoir's distinction between female and male forms of power in *The Second Sex*. Jimmy Louie is a human being who does right to all alike, who does not act in conformity with a gender symmetrical system. To balanced characters like Winnie and Jimmy Louie, gender asymmetry is irrelevant. Such characters are feminist because they perceive "the old binary oppositions" as having "outlived their usefulness in codifying and interpreting the American experience, and the Chinese immigrants who have been living by them." They also practice syncresis because they are now "ready to settle down into integrated life" (Sau-ling C. Wong 1993, 120). Winnie can be defined as feminist by the end of her life, so much so that she opposes the constraints of her cultural indoctrination. She becomes yin and yang in her own being.

Although ultimately her female characters do not have unique claims to an essence opposite to that which is "evil" or "bad" in men, Tan does focus primarily on women's problems and women's solutions. No characters in her texts, no matter how "bad" were not made "bad" by their culture. If they had such tendencies to begin with, they were further entrenched in them by their culture's teachings. Winnie's mother-in-law, as well as her cousin Peanut's mother-in-law, as well as the mothers-in-law of other women characters in this text, obediently followed their culture's prescription for mothering men. According to Tan, they thereby created monsters while they self-righteously imagined themselves good and proper wives and mothers for abiding by the legitimate and sensible rules of their culture. They back their sons totally, even in the sons' tantrums and egomania, and they regard the property of their daughters-in-law as now belonging to them by right of their motherhood to their sons who own their wives and their wives' property. These women perceive themselves as finally entitled to receive all the benefits the culture at long last gives them as mothers and mothers-in-law, for which they have had to wait so long and patiently, enduring so much along the way. They do not perceive that these hard-won benefits perpetuate exploitative and abusive relationships between mothers-in-law and daughters-in-law, nor that they are functioning as tools of the patriarchal system.

In Tan's work, a "bad" man puts into practice what the gender asymmetrical system decrees about the privileges and duties of masculinity. In exposing the culture's workings in relation to gender, Tan exposes that which is "bad" in man as due to the system of gender asymmetry. None of their qualities is inherently gender specific to the male characters. The gender asymmetric system under which Tan represents her characters as living gives any men who wish to indulge themselves in such conduct the opportunity to act in tyrannical, adulterous, bullying, cruel, and sadistic ways without retribution. She describes the men who choose to conduct themselves in these ways as still fitting within the parameters of what is considered legitimate and acceptable behavior for males in Chinese culture. As I have already pointed out in my Introduction, Tan's perspective is disputed, even excoriated in some quarters as being erroneous and anti male.[6] Tan does concede that in her view "bad" men who adhere to their culture's prescriptions in letter and spirit are rewarded, as are their women collaborators. Some women, like Helen, Winnie's long-time friend, are imperceptive, crude, and insensitive—or rather, they are permitted or encouraged to be that way when they so choose. They can also be sensitive and caring, as Winnie eventually finds out. According to Tan, how and/or in what ways characters are "bad" depends to a large extent on the culture's construction of gender.

COLLABORATORS/GATEKEEPERS

Old Aunt, New Aunt, Winnie's Mother-in-Law, Peanut's Mother-in-Law

Tan presents a scale of female characters in terms of their responses to the system. First there are those women who adhere with servile fidelity to their culture's asymmetrical prescriptions for females. Whether self-serving or unthinking, they act as "consenting subordinates" (MacLeod 1992) by perpetuating it against their own kind. They impose whatever their culture's "regime of truth" (Foucault 1980, 131) dictates upon those females who are within their sphere of influence, who are junior and subordinate to themselves in the hierarchy. They suppress themselves and other females, collude in gender erasure, and, at the very least, assist in depriving other females of the nurturing and positive image making that humans need for a healthy and productive sense of self. Like Hong Kingston before her, Tan represents these gatekeepers as using "brainwashing" techniques, primarily in the form of adages.[7] One of Tan's favorite techniques for conveying her antagonism to the system is to have the adage givers expose the evil of the system by means of the very adages they cite to reinforce it. Ying-Ying in *The Joy Luck Club* is treated to these adages in her childhood: "It is wrong to think of your needs. A girl can never ask, only listen" (68), or "The girl stands still and the dragon fly comes to her" (70). And as Maxine of *The Woman Warrior* was raised by her mother, so Winnie of *The Kitchen God's Wife* is raised by Old Aunt, with dire threats and frightening stories. This is the Chinese way of ensuring obedience, according to Winnie:

"Do you want to be sent away forever and become a beggar, just like your mother? . . . Do you want to get a terrible disease that eats away your face, same as your mother? . . . Look at that poor girl. . . . The girl was wearing ragged pants too short for her thin legs. Her eyes had no feeling left behind them. And then Old Aunt said the girl was a slave, sold by her father because she would not behave after her mother died. . . . So willful, that rebellious! What kind of family would want you for their son's wife? Maybe I should marry you off to Old Shoe Stink! . . . " I think all the mothers in our village threatened to marry their daughters to Old Shoe Stink. And those daughters must have obeyed. Otherwise, Old Shoe Stink would have had twenty wives!

I do not think Old Aunt said these things to be mean to me or to lie for no reason. I am not being generous in saying this. Giving threats to children was the custom in old families like ours. Old Aunt's mother probably did this to her when she was a child, handing out warnings about another kind of life, too terrible to imagine—also giving examples of obedient children too good to be true. This is how you made children behave. This was how you drove selfish thoughts out of their foolish heads. This was how you showed you were concerned for their future, teaching them how they too could keep order in the family. (132–134)

Old Aunt, who represents the traditional Chinese matron, relentlessly stuffs cultural prescriptions into her younger female charges. " 'The girls' eyes should never be used for reading, only for sewing. The girl's ears should never be used for listening to ideas, only to orders. The girl's lips should be small, rarely used, except to express appreciation or ask for approval' " (102). She seizes upon Winnie's first menstruation as an opportunity to further indoctrinate her into perpetuating gender asymmetry: " 'The bleeding is a sign. When a girl starts having unclean thoughts, her body must purge itself. That is why so much blood is coming out. Later . . . if she becomes a good wife and loves her husband, this will stop' " (183). There were always sad endings reserved for girls who married only for love "with scary morals given at the end: 'Lose control, lose your life!' 'Fall in love, fall into disgrace!' 'Throw away family values, throw your face [honor, reputation] away!' " (340). These used to make Winnie cry the most because they reminded her of her mother's own life, "as sad as a story" (340). Old Aunt blamed Winnie's mother's Christian education for her tragic fate: " 'The foreign teachers want to overturn all order in the world. Confucius is bad, Jesus is good! Girls can be teachers, girls do not have to marry. . . . Upside-down thinking!—that's what got her into trouble' " (103).

Before Winnie's wedding, her father socializes her in the same manner as has Old Aunt. After asking her opinion of a painting, he orders her " '[f]rom now on . . . [to] consider what your husband's opinions are. Yours do not matter so much any more. Do you understand?' " (145). Winnie adds that as a future bride, she had been grateful to her father for having "taught me this useful lesson in such a subtle way" (145). She is here recreating for her daughter the way she once was in her loving innocence. "Now you see how I once was. I was not always negative-thinking, the way you and Helen say. When I was young, I wanted to believe in something good. And when that good thing started to go away, I still wanted to grab it, make it stay" (152). After Winnie marries, she finds herself involved in a traditional Chinese marriage custom. As a bride, she undergoes a kind of graduate school of obedience training under her mother-in-law's tutelage. Some of this woman's choicest sayings were: "To protect my husband so he would protect me. To fear him and think this was respect. To make him a proper hot soup, which was ready to serve only when I had scalded my little finger testing it. . . . 'Doesn't hurt!' my mother- in-law would exclaim if I shouted in pain. 'That kind of sacrifice for a husband never hurts' " (168). In a remarkable exhibition of acuity, Winnie blames her mother-in-law, not Wen Fu "for having given birth to him, for tending to all his desires as if she were his servant, for always feeding husband and son first, for allowing me to eat only after I had picked off bits of food stuck to my father-in-law's beard, for letting the meanness in her son grow like a strange appetite, so that he would always feel hungry to feed his own power" (257).

At this point in Winnie's life, 1990, these statements are being made anachronistically. But in her youth, Winnie was taught to believe that all this suffering added up to "true love, the kind that grew between husband and wife." She did not perceive any of the outrages that are assigned blame by the mature Winnie who has long since fled from the oppressive Chinese culture to the United States. Note that she adds: "I had also learned this in the movies, both Chinese and American. A woman always had to feel pain, suffer and cry before she could feel love" (168), which exposes the awesome global extent of gender asymmetry.[8]

This passage is followed by an even more remarkable one. Winnie realizes that in blaming her gatekeeper mother-in-law, she may have been "wrong . . . to blame another woman for my own miseries." Such is usually the case when one is not self-reflexive, continually on guard against internalizing cultural shibboleths unthinkingly, for "that was how I was raised—never to criticize men or the society they ruled, or Confucius, that awful man who made that society. I could blame only other women who were more afraid than I" (257). Here Winnie clearly realizes the collaborator role of the older women like Old Aunt and her mother-in-law who are the gatekeepers for the traditional culture and perpetuate it out of fear. It takes a combination of intelligence and compassion to see beyond one's oppressor(s) to the system that sets the hierarchies of oppression in place, as Winnie finally does in the scene where she realizes that her husband's male network supports him completely. She reasons that women's obedient passivity rather than active opportunism reinforces the system. She explains that fear is trained into women by the culture. Still Winnie blames women gatekeepers, despite her conviction that their fear kept them in place. She even distances her present self from her youthful self, as when she tells us that whenever her baby girl would begin to cry in response to Wen Fu's noisy shouting, the infant "would not stop until I told her more lies" such as, "if she were good, her 'life will be good too.' How could I know that this is how a mother teaches her daughter to be afraid?" (258).

REBELS

Winnie's Mother, Winnie, Peanut

At the other end of the scale from the gatekeepers are women who pay a steep price for open rebellion against the system. They are made to experience loss, abandonment, suicide, death, or death in life, that is, social ostracism. Nevertheless, these heroic women continue to attempt to improve intolerable conditions and are forced to flee, like Winnie and her mother, in order to fight again elsewhere. Midway in Tan's scale, between the collaborators and rebels, she places the saboteurs, the covert revisionists who attempt by a variety of means to shape the cultural order to improve their situations. These women's problem solving provides temporary, personal relief for themselves and their friends and relatives.

In the final story of *The Joy Luck Club,* "A Pair of Tickets," Jing Mei returns to China with her father after her mother has died in order to be reunited with her two older Chinese sisters whom their mother had been forced to abandon in her flight from the Japanese. This is a call from Tan for American -born Chinese women to syncretize both Chinese and American ways in order to combine the best of both cultures: one's Chinese-constructed self (as in the Chinese mothers)and one's American training (as in the Chinese American daughters). In *The Joy Luck Club,* Tan unifies the two in order to achieve harmony. In *The Kitchen God's Wife,* she goes further. Unless the older generation's stories are transmitted to the next generation of women, all these struggles will go for naught. Only when this is done, as when Winnie tells her story to her daughter, can a productive syncresis become possible. Communication is necessary between the Asian immigrant mother generation(s)—Mother Courage (Winnie, "a winner")—and the Asian American daughter ("Pearl," the postcolonial pearl of great price).Pearl is "married" to or is in syncresis with Western ways, as represented by Dr. Phil, the rational, scientific, and technological American man. Otherwise there is a gap between each woman in endless continuity of generations. Each generation will believe that the other will judge her and that she will be found wanting, as is so painfully the case throughout *The Joy Luck Club* and *The Kitchen God's Wife.* The mother suffers from guilt over maternal abandonment; the daughter from guilt over being abandoned. As the result of the loss of her mother, An Mei in *The Joy Luck Club* concludes that life has taught her to desire nothing, "to swallow other people's misery, to eat my own bitterness" (241).[9]

Tan subverts the original context of the traditional Chinese cautionary tale of the run-away wife by representing An Mei's mother's flight (and later in *The Kitchen God's Wife,* Winnie's mother's flight) from an intolerable domestic situation. Tan also uses the mother's flight to illustrate one of the results of open rebellion: the by-product of choosing an alternative life is the suffering over the loss of her mother of the child left behind. Still, if the mother had not been forced into taking such an extreme position—to have to flee as a form of rebellion—the daughter would never have been deprived of the mother. Winnie in her turn, in keeping with the tradition begun by her mother, also flees her marital prison. Tan sees rebellion as forbidden by the culture, to be prevented from happening at any cost. One of the most effective ways of stopping it is through social ostracism, to deny that the rebel even exists. The runaway mother is turned into an object of pity and victimization by the family's public face-saving claim that she has committed suicide. Whatever story is made up about the fighter, she is excised from the rolls of the family, the community, the body politic, the culture.

Winnie's mother, miserable under the Confucian Chinese system of gender asymmetry in the form of polygamy, as well as with class inequities, cuts her hair and runs away to become a Communist revolutionary. Her grandmother, the widow of a Manchu official of the Ching dynasty, had temporarily circumvented her daughter's rebelliousness by going to an old friend of her husband's, Jiang Soo-Yen. Jian, in turn, had then "bought" Winnie's mother as a "second second" wife to substitute for his first second wife who had just committed suicide. But before her enforced marriage to Old Jiang, Winnie's mother had chosen for her male companion a brilliant young Marxist student from the country, from a family of fishermen. And although she had been trained in a Christian Missionary school, her choice of a peasant Communist male reveals that she had rejected both the Confucian philosophy and the Christian religion. From the beginning, Winnie's mother was known as a girl with "a fighting temper." In this regard, Winnie points out that "[m]aybe that's why I was the same way" (102). Much later in the text and in her life, Winnie gradually comes to understand and interpret the meaning of her mother's actions and life trajectory in terms of gender and class asymmetry and of feminist rejections of them.

So far as her mother's birth family, her husband, and his other wives are concerned, Winnie's mother no longer exists. Under the patriarchal system, the female rebel and the abandoned child suffer doubly. Winnie's eternal sense of loss goes forever unmitigated. Reinforcing this harsh reality of suffering (perhaps the most tragic loss of all in her life) is the child's perspective on the loss of her mother: that the hounded woman, passionately devoted to an ideal, chose exile/ death/ freedom over her own personal love for her child. More likely, however, Winnie's mother felt that to leave the child with her wealthy father, co wives, and numerous siblings would lessen the little girl's suffering and sense of loss. At the very least, Winnie could continue her comfortable existence. Either way, the mother did not factor in her young child's sense of irrevocable loss and abandonment. And if she did, she did not permit it to dissuade her from joining the Communist Revolution. She sacrificed her private pleasures, small as they were, for what she considered a higher cause. Never will the void left by her mother's abandonment be filled, even to the child's last days on earth. Now past seventy, Winnie still remains inconsolable:

In my heart, there is a little room. And in that room is a little girl, still six years old. She is always waiting, an achy hoping, hoping beyond reason. She is sure the door will fly open, any minute now. And sure enough, it does, and her mother runs in. And the pain in the little girl's heart is instantly gone, forgotten. Because now her mother is lifting her up, high up in the air, laughing and crying, crying and laughing, "*Syin ke, syin ke!* There you are!" (109)

Later on, when she creates Lady Sorrowfree and describes for Pearl the benefits the goddess will bring future generations of women, she uses identical language.[10] Historically, many such "runaway wives" stories (as the Chinese folktales define these rebels) are similar in every culture and generation globally. Winnie's gradual and arduous transition from acceptance of her culture, to questioning, to disbelief, to revision and subversion is rare. For the most part, "cautionary tales" prevent continuity, forcing each new generation of rebellious women to reinvent the oppositional wheel anew.

SABOTEURS

Helen, Auntie Du

Another woman provides solace for Winnie during the bleak period of her marriage to Wen Fu. Married to a fellow army officer of Wen Fu's, Helen is a crude, earthy country girl just Winnie's age. When Winnie confides in Helen that her husband is forcing her to have sex with him even while she is pregnant, Helen berates her, instead of giving her much-needed sympathy and support, as expected. She demands of Winnie why she shouldn't do this for her husband, because when he loses interest in her he will go elsewhere. " 'And then you'll know what it means to be unhappy with a husband.' " She tops off her "scolding" with a folk saying, a habit also characteristic of her: " 'Eh, if you think a dish won't be cooked right, then of course, when you taste it, it won't be right' " (188). Winnie, from the mandarin class, finds Helen coarse and vulgar, especially about her body functions. As a result, she feels superior to her. She is convinced that she has nothing in common with her but accidental propinquity, an elitist attitude she retains to some degree all her life, although she always sympathizes with the lower classes philosophically.

In this unusual manner, Tan begins to weave another major thread into a complex pattern consisting of diverse female characters who all confront gender asymmetry in different ways. In 1990, it appears to Pearl that her mother has an elderly sister-in-law, one with whom she battles and for whom she frequently expresses contempt. Nevertheless, the two women have forged an enduring relationship:

No one would believe me now if I said Helen is not my sister-in-law. She is not related by blood, not even by marriage. She is not someone I chose as my friend. Sometimes I do not even enjoy her company. I do not agree with her opinions. I do not admire her character. And yet we are closer perhaps than sisters, related by fate, joined by debts. I have kept her secrets. She has kept mine. And we have a kind of loyalty that has no word in this country. (72–73)

The Kitchen God's Wife contains two major contrapuntal voices. The daughter's begins the book, but the mother's voice abruptly begins in Chapter Three and continues to the last chapter. Winnie's voice is first heard complaining about Helen—that she has "foolish thinking" which "turns into good fortune" (61); that even though Helen is neither smart, nor pretty, and "was born poor, she has always had luck pour onto her plate," whereas Winnie, who was pretty and had good luck to begin with, "dried out, then [her luck] carved [suffering] lines on my face so I would not forget" (62). Such a use of "double-voiced discourse," as I have previously pointed out in the preface, is considered to be a characteristic of postmodern writers. There are other fundamental differences between the two women, as well. Whereas Helen wants to forget the past— " Useless to regret. You cannot change the past," Winnie thinks about "old things " (62). She has a different kind of luck. She looks "at everything in my life two ways, the way it happened, the way it did not" (68). But for a long time Winnie "didn't know" she "had a choice" (69).

One of the major themes of this text is that Winnie discovers the existence of choice in the face of all contrary cultural prescriptions for women. In contrast, Pearl sees no choice. She and her husband used to quarrel about what Pearl defined as her duty to her family and what Dr. Phil, a witty man, defined as her being "driven by blind devotion to fear and guilt . . . manipulated into thinking" that she "had no choice," and that she "was doing the same thing to him" (15). Lately, however, after Pearl was been diagnosed with multiple sclerosis, she and her husband "no longer fought self-righteously over philosophical differences concerning individual choice" (15).

Winnie and Helen begin their relationship only because they are neighbors. As such, it is impossible for Helen not to know what Wen Fu was like. Yet she and her aunt Du who lives with her appear not to notice. Because Helen is childless, Winnie assumes that Helen's lack of sympathy is due to jealousy. However, by the end of the book, Winnie suddenly discovers that Helen (as well as Auntie Du) did know and did care all along. Helen handled the situation in her own way—shrewdly, indirectly, covertly. She is not the collaborationist she appears to be, but a saboteur. She fights guerrilla warfare, with maximum safety for herself and her allies. Helen's primary concern all along was that Winnie's husband never realize that she did know about all his evil doings. If so, she brilliantly reasoned, he would have deprived Winnie of her proximity, of whatever small comfort she could be to her. This revelation is amazing in its profundity. It is profound that a woman who seems so insensitive and so self-absorbed as Helen should all the time have known and cared and have had her friend's best interests at heart! Here what Rimonte points out about the difference between Pacific Asians' and white women's acculturation is relevant: "Traditionally" [as does Helen] they "conceal and deny problems [such as domestic violence] that threaten group pride and may bring on shame" (Rimonte 1989, 328). Rimonte attributes this to heavily inscribed training to avoid disgracing or dishonoring one's family at almost any cost, including one's own well-being. As Winnie tells Pearl: "In China back then, you were always responsible to somebody else. It's not like here in the United States—freedom, independence, individual thinking, do what you want, disobey your mother. No such thing. Nobody ever said to me, 'Be good, little girl, and I will give you a piece of candy.' You did not get a reward for being good, that was expected. But if you were bad—your family could do anything to you, no reason needed" (132).

Rimonte rightfully critiques the community that stresses "economic and social adjustment pressures" and ignores the problem of gender asymmetry. However, she also maintains that the cause of the problem is oppression of Asian American men, and that if this were "removed from the environment," they would stop abusing their womenfolk (Rimonte 1989, 328). However, since even under conditions when economic, political, and social stress are absent, such abuse has not ceased, Rimonte is letting abusive men off the hook by arguing that the problem is due to changes that threaten the man. In actuality, gender asymmetry itself leads to abusive tendencies. Without checks and balances, all situations involving one individual's or one group's domination over others lead to abuse of the dominated by the dominant. Rimonte claims that because the man's culture has acculturated him to "privileges and esteemed place" the Asian Pacific man feels that his woman should adhere to their traditional culture, which benefits only himself. If she rejects her culture, she is therefore rejecting her man (Rimonte 1989, 329). This is Wen Fu's point of view, as well.

In musing about why Helen and she are still friends, Winnie concludes not so much that they are alike in any way, but that "[m]aybe it's because we fought so much in those early days. Maybe it's because we had no one else to turn to. So we always had to find reason to be friends. Maybe those reasons are still there" (194). Readers can guess "those reasons": unity under fire. Here King-Kok Cheung's acknowledgment of authors Alice Walker and Maxine Hong Kingston in terms of their "protagonists' resilience and the authors' determination" can well be said of Amy Tan's delineation of Winnie and Helen in *The Kitchen God's Wife*: that they "dare to be themselves—to listen to their own pains, to report the ravages, and finally, to persist in finding strengths from sources that have caused inestimable anguish. Their way of breaking out of enforced silence is not by dissolving into the mainstream but by rendering their distinctive voices" (Cheung 1992a, 184–185).

Another saboteur on the level of Helen is the woman Pearl calls Grand Auntie Du, actually Helen's Aunt, aged ninety-three. At the beginning of the book, she has just died and been given a Buddhist funeral by Helen and Winnie. How they do it enables readers to see an example of these women's syncretism of Western and Eastern spirituality. They "stopped going [to Church]" after Winnie's husband, a Baptist minister, suddenly died. At the same time, Du and Winnie never gave up their "other beliefs, which weren't exactly Buddhist, just all the superstitious rituals concerning attracting good luck and avoiding bad" (19). Unobtrusive as it may seem, such syncretic "rituals" nevertheless side-step the gender asymmetry of both Buddhism and Christianity. Much like Brave Orchid (Maxine's mother in Hong Kingston's *The Woman Warrior*), Winnie believes in ghosts (not only the white human kind) and merges "religion, medicine, and superstition . . . with her own beliefs" (29). To her, "*nothing* is an accident. . . . Everything has a reason. Everything could have been prevented" (29) [Emphasis in original].

Yet another form of subversion on a lower scale is revealed by Winnie's Old and New Aunts (her paternal uncle's first and second wives). Publicly, New Aunt loudly objects to her daughter's leaving her husband and joining the Communists. She says terrible things about Peanut to Winnie when the latter expresses her wish to see her cousin. Suddenly, in the midst of her vituperation, New Aunt throws "a piece of paper down on the bed" and leaves. A few minutes later, Old Aunt enters Winnie's room and "[s]et[s] a small wrapped package on the bed" (339), claiming that she had borrowed something from a friend and wanted it delivered. The addresses on both the package and the piece of paper are identical. By this means Tan conveys that these collaborators do not practice what they preach. Their concern for Peanut causes them to send her assistance while publicly vilifying and disowning the female rebel.

COMMUNITY OF WOMEN

Despite the fact that in China the community formed by fathers' and uncles' wives was an enforced one occasioned by polygamy, nevertheless much as in *The Color Purple*, *The Woman Warrior*, and *The Joy Luck Club*, women forge a community of friendship and assistance in order to "gather strength through a female network" (Cheung 1992a, 172). Tan would add that they did this, not only to ease the force of the blows against them from a harsh and hostile world, but to subvert, transform, and even rebel against it.

Instead of hating her husband's mistress as she is trained to do, Winnie identifies strongly with Min. She feels compassion for her "pretty skin, foolish heart, strong will, scared bones." The war had made many people "full of fear, desperate to live without knowing why" (272). "What kind of woman would be so desperate she would want to be a mistress to my husband?" (272) she demands of the reader with her characteristically blunt wit. And she perceives their sisterhood in oppression, when she asserts that "I was no better than she was" (272), despite their differences in class and background and therefore in treatment. Min would tell Winnie risqué stories (which seemed glamorous to the sheltered, upper class young woman) about "old boyfriends, dance parties . . . Shanghai nightclubs" where she had worked as a singer and dancer. She had also worked in an act that emphasized sadism against women in "an amusement arcade in the French concession catering to foreign customers, a very wicked and dangerous place for women" (273) and had also sung to "entertain crowds in the open restaurants" (275) at Sincere, the department store on Nanking Road, until the store was bombed. For these reasons, not despite them, Winnie found Min to be "good company." She was also a good soul, was "sincere," appreciated Winnie's cooking, admired her jewelry and clothes, and "never complained, never ordered the servants around," "thanking them for the smallest favor," and "she would hold Winnie's baby Danru when he was crying " (273).[11] Although it is contrary to what she has been taught to feel for such a young woman, Winnie feels pity for her and also admires the girl's resiliency, despite the ever-downward trajectory of her life. The many good times they have together before Min is thrown out by Wen Fu provide the only rays of sunshine in both women's otherwise drab lives. They take endless pleasure in one another and in one another's company, especially while dancing. Some years later when Winnie learns that Min ended up by committing suicide, she genuinely grieves for her.

Now in 1990, Winnie and Helen are living out their long lives as squabbling partners in a jointly owned florist shop. Still, an undying sense of connectedness due to shared past sufferings underlies their essential class differences. Helen has come from such great poverty that at one time she had to dole out beans by number to her sister. She has all along been witness to Wen Fu's abusive treatment of Winnie, as has her Auntie Du. Winnie loves Auntie Du for many reasons, primarily for her courage, honesty, and loyalty. But both Auntie Du and Helen, trained to internalize gender asymmetry, served at Wen Fu's side over-long. Eventually they both were caring enough to apologize to Winnie for the error of their ways and to forge the closest of life-long ties with her. More than that, both women assisted Winnie in her quest for freedom from Wen Fu and in whatever else she needed. At the end of the book, Helen is even returning to China with her friend, for her friend, for no other reasons.

Winnie does not entirely blame the female gatekeepers, the collaborationists like her maternal grandmother, or her Old and New Aunts. She does not even entirely blame her mother-in-law and the co wives who had made her mother and herself so miserable with their endless intrigues against one another to secure Old Jiang's favor. Such women are unthinking participants in their own oppression for a long time before or if ever they take a stand, as Helen and her aunt finally do. In having these former collaborators rise up against the system, Tan reveals yet another way for women to relate to it. They repudiate the system and befriend Winnie, although extremely late in the game. It is only on page 411 of a 415-page book that Helen finally admits "something": not that she lied—so she euphemizes—but that she " 'said many wrong things' " (411).

Wen Fu is not only an awful husband as an individual, but every one of his problematic features of personality, conduct, and attitude are meant by Tan to signify representations of the Chinese codes for male gender behavior carried to extreme limits, as I have previously pointed out. It is therefore highly significant when Helen admits that " 'I always told you Wen Fu was not a bad man, not as bad as you said. But all along I knew. He was bad. He was awful!' She waved her hand under her nose, chasing away a big stink. . . . 'I tried to make you think he was a nice man' " (411). Also by making such an admission, Helen, who has always justified Wen Fu's evil behavior on the flimsy grounds of his disfiguring accident, now reveals to Winnie that she lied to protect Pearl, to prevent Winnie from blaming Pearl [as his daughter]: " 'He was mean, a very bad man' " (412), she concludes, together with the story.

Through a process of revisionary self-reflexivity in relation to gender asymmetry, Tan creates a ranking of women characters in a community of women. There are those women—collaborationists and gatekeepers—who are entirely the product of their "cultural regime of truth." They actively obey and work hard to further and perpetuate the system of gender asymmetry. Many of them, unthinking, "vindicate the code" by which they live "but whose desirability and justice" they never bother "to examine" (S. Wong 1993, 16). Conversely, there are those women who rebel against it early. There are many stories scattered through the text to illustrate what the culture defines as and intends for future generations to learn about the "bad endings" to which these women come. These are used as cautionary tales by the gatekeeper women as part of the cultural training to indoctrinate little girls into the right paths: to toe the customary line and never "to seek fulfillment beyond what creature comforts and a rather unreflecting kind of social approval can give" (S. Wong 1993, 17). The example of Winnie's mother is successfully used by the gatekeeper women as a cautionary

tale until Winnie questions whether her mother's fate as a result of her disobedience was necessarily sealed. In fact, one day she suddenly realizes that her
mother's life might just as well have been one of fulfillment and happiness. This
gives Winnie hope for the first time of possibility in her life.

Then there are women who separate themselves from the system even while
living within it. They use it to manipulate it, to serve their agenda; to expand it
to include their desires, their perspectives. For example, Auntie Du uses the
system any way she can to get Winnie out of jail. When her lies in court prove
fruitless and Winnie is jailed anyhow, she takes it upon herself to go to the
authorities who have arrested Winnie. She boldly lies again, informing them that
Winnie is related to two high-ranking Communists, an exaggeration of Cousin
Peanut's and her lover's status. Peanut had only become Communist in order to
serve her own ends, having resorted to a women's shelter set up by the Communists after fleeing from her marriage and there linking up with a young Communist student. Auntie Du warns the police that they will be punished severely
when the Communists take over for arresting so importantly connected a woman
as Winnie. Duped by Auntie Du's brazen lie and evidently frightened for their
skins, the police release Winnie from prison.[12]

CLASS ASYMMETRY

The Kitchen God's wife is compassionate to those less fortunate than herself,
as well as to the homeless. She does not take advantage of gender asymmetry
when it is in her favor, nor class asymmetry, for that matter. However, she does
not question her status, whereas Winnie and her mother do. Winnie's mother
repudiates her life as "second second" wife to a wealthy industrialist in Shanghai. Before she leaves, she shows her little girl that her dissatisfaction with her
lot is not only due to her personal, private misery with her co wives under polygamy. She also refuses to continue to lead a life of class privilege any longer. As
for Winnie herself, she will be raised and live as upper class, but she will never
forget her mother's perspective and will always be sensitive to it. This is evident
in the sardonic way in which Winnie informs the reader of class asymmetry, as
when she says of her accommodations in Kunming during World War II, that she
had enjoyed the luxury of "a sink with a drain, but no running water, only running servants. That was the Chinese way. The cook and the servant had to go to
the pump in the backyard and carry in the big, heavy buckets. Maybe they had
to carry these upstairs as well. I don't remember now. When you have never
had to do these things yourself, you do not think about what someone else has to
do instead" (238).

Once when a pig did not get out of his way, Wen Fu shot it in the stomach,
even after the pig's owner came to take it away He then threatened the owner,
which also reveals his class snobbery and elitism (224–225). On another occasion, he went into a hospital kitchen and "chopped up the table, the walls, the
chairs . . . knocked over jars and dishes . . . dumped out all the food," then
"threatened all the cooks and their helpers, who were watching from the door"

that if they reported this he would " 'come back and chop your bones in half ' "(257). There are two reasons why Wen Fu gets away with this. Because he was in uniform and swathed in bandages, people jumped to the conclusion that he was a "war hero." Actually he had been injured in an accident while carelessly driving a jeep, as previously mentioned. Also as a pilot, he is not only to be respected because he is serving his country, but also as a member of the upper classes. In intimidating the hospital kitchen staff who were peasants, Wen Fu arrogantly assumed these privileges and cultural assumptions and played them up for all they were worth.

THE CINDERELLA MYTH

According to Bruno Betelheim (1976), the Cinderella story began in China in the ninth century A.D. In *The Kitchen God's Wife* as in the Cinderella myth, the heroine has lost her own mother and is raised by a stepmother who has three wicked daughters. Similarly, Winnie's father's house in Shanghai contains five wives and their children, her step siblings, who are all preferred over her. Winnie is raised by New and Old Aunts who have a selfish daughter Peanut who is also preferred over her, although Winnie, not Peanut, should have been her father's "rightful heiress." Cinderella is also neglected by her father. Peanut becomes more like Winnie's stepsister than her cousin. At one point, Peanut is supposed to marry Wen Fu, her Prince Charming, but something goes wrong, and he woos Winnie instead. When Winnie, infatuated with his oily charm, marries her Prince Charming, she feels as triumphant in love as Cinderella. But Cinderella's story ends where Winnie's revision of the story of the Kitchen God (aka Wen Fu) and the Kitchen God's wife (aka Winnie) begins. Jimmie Louie, Winnie's true Prince Charming, does come, but only after she is unhappily married. They do meet at a ball. They do dance just once. The heel of her shoe does break off (in a variant of Cinderella's loss of her slipper). Winnie does eventually marry him, and they do live happily ever after until his premature death. However, in Tan's variant, Winnie is not carried away by Prince Charming. He is unable to free her from Wen Fu's clutches and to keep her from prison, but Tan represents Winnie's supportive community of women friends as doing so. They enable her to follow Jimmy Louie to the United States where she marries him and lives from then on forever free from Wen Fu and all he represents.

WINNIE, THE TRANSFORMER

Originally, the reader leans toward ascribing the role of heroine solely to the narrator, Winnie's daughter, Pearl, only to have that role taken over by her mother. Again, this is another of Tan's unexpected reversals of stereotypical characterizations and plot set-ups. Gradually, the mother's voice emerges. It is only toward the end that we discover the tale with which to read the mother's life: the key to the reader's dawning realization that Winnie is an epic heroine in her monumental struggles against gender asymmetry. Only when actively involved in the process of moving forward in an effort to free herself from her intolerable situation can Winnie, like her mother, eventually begin to think for herself, to realize "that all these stories [about her mother] were false—only stories" (340). She does not feel what happened to her mother was the result of "a bad education [as she has been taught] but bad fate." As Winnie observes: "[H]er [mother's] education only made her unhappy thinking about it—[and as for her mother] that no matter how much she changed her life, she could not change the world that surrounded her" (103). In terms of women's response to gender asymmetry, this is one of Tan's major points about open rebellion. It must combine personal solutions with those designed to change the system. Or as the feminist philosopher Donna Przybylowicz puts it, we must always

look at the specific historical situations that produce the category of the feminine and not see it as the product of one mechanism. . . . Although it is necessary to relate sexual differences to the practices that construct them, it is also important to realize that overdetermination among disparate subject positions produces a system of sexual division that, no matter how heterogeneous the various structures of sexual differences may be, situates the female in the inferior position. (1990, 283)

Even more daring, in recollecting that her grandmother was "in no big hurry to marry off her daughter" because she "could take care of her into her old age" (103), Winnie remarks heretically that "[t]hat's what Confucius would have said. I don't know why everyone always thought Confucius was so good, so wise. He made everyone look down on someone else, women were the lowest" (103). Further, the possibility occurs to her that her mother was not so much concerned with her own life as with changing "the world." This realization provides yet another unlinking of the chains of cultural prescriptions that have hitherto bound Winnie and frees her to enter the "forbidden territory in one's mind" (S. Wong 1988, 8). Only after arriving at this point can it occur to Winnie to reverse the cultural message entirely about what the culture naturalizes as a given and what everyone around her had believed inevitable (including herself). For example, her mother's life, like any other rebellious woman's life, did not have to come to "an unhappy ending." In fact, it begins to dawn on her that the exact reverse can occur. Heeding all the admonitions may not in any way prevent "disaster from coming into my life." Instead, her mother's life might now be "filled with joy" and she too "could find the same thing." Winnie aptly defines the crucial process she has undergone in order to reach her feminist perspective as having "finally come to a true thought of my own" (434). Here Winnie's illumination is much like that of Maxine's at the beginning of *The Woman Warrior* when she meditates on her No-Name aunt's fate. Sifting among the possibilities enables her to come up with alternative versions to what the culture decrees. Of crucial significance is the fact that creating alternative versions to Confucianism will support both characters' negotiations with the oppressive system:

If she [Hong Kingston] seems to highlight the savagery and cruelty of Chinese morés . . . it is because her protagonist perceives, in what glimpses she can catch of this (to her) alien culture, some "objective correlative" of her feelings toward the role played by Necessity in her own Chinese-American life. The fate of a woman such as her aunt may have been better in real life, or it may have been worse. Historical correspondence does not matter. . . . The process of wrestling "ancestral help" entails a laborious and active penetration of what hitherto has only been forbidden territory in one's mind. (S. Wong 1988, 7–8)

As Donald Goellnicht in his penetrating analysis of Hong Kingston's *China Men* points out: "[R]eligion reveals itself as one of the powerful institutions of the masculine symbolic order that entrenches male privilege" (1992, 196). In the process of separating herself from the gender (and class) asymmetry of her culture, Winnie also separates herself from and critiques perhaps the most impregnable bastion of patriarchy, her religion, presumably Christianity. "When Jesus was born, he was already the son of God. I was the daughter of someone who ran away, big disgrace. And when Jesus suffered, everyone worshipped him. Nobody worshipped me for living with Wen Fu. I was like that wife of Kitchen God. Nobody worshipped her either. He got all the excuses. He got all the credit. She was forgotten" (255).

Tan represents the result of Winnie's having to confront a powerful enemy every day of her life in the person of her own hostile spouse as molding her into a far stronger woman than she would otherwise have been had she obediently followed her training without question. Nevertheless, the reformative act for which Winnie will live in literary history only becomes real when Winnie bridges the gap with Pearl by sharing her past with her daughter. Tan has shaped and organized the novel to prepare readers for the message at the end of the text through Winnie's present to her daughter. This is as far as she goes. The rest, syncresis, is up to the new generation. At first, Pearl is flippant about the strange gift her mother forces on her: "Cheaper than the lottery" (55) she quips, doubtless to Dr. Phil's delight. But then Winnie "startles" them by exclaiming " 'No! . . . Sometimes he is in a bad mood. Sometimes he says, I don't like this family, give them bad luck. Then you're in trouble, nothing you can do about it. Why should I want that kind of person to judge me, a man who cheated on his wife? His wife was the good one, not him' " (55).

In brief, this is the story of the Kitchen God as Winnie tells it, according to Pearl. A rich farmer blessed with a hardworking wife " 'had everything he could ask for—from the water, the earth, and the heavens above' " (54). But " '[h]e wanted to play with a pretty, carefree woman named Lady Li.' " He brought her home and " 'made his wife cook for her.' " He then allowed Lady Li to chase " 'his wife out of the house.' " The two lovers despoiled his land and emptied his pockets. Once everything was all gone, Lady Li ran off with another man. Zhang became a beggar and began to starve. One day he fainted and awoke to find himself being cared for in his wife's house. He " 'jumped into the kitchen fire just as his wife walked in the room' "—and ended up " 'burning with shame and, of course, because of the hot roaring fire below' " (54–55). When the Jade

Emperor in heaven heard everything, he made Zhang a Kitchen God " '[f]or having the courage to admit you were wrong. . . . Every year, you let me know who deserves good luck, who deserves bad' " (55).

Winnie despises the Kitchen God, much as she did Wen Fu, who shares many of the god's qualities when he was a man on earth. " 'He is not Santa Claus. More like a spy—FBI agent, CIA, Mafia, worse than IRS, that kind of person! And he does not give you gifts, you give *him* things [Emphasis in the original]. All year long you have to show him respect—give him tea and oranges' " (55). During Chinese New Year, the gifts have to be even better, because " 'You are hoping all the time his tongue will be sweet, his head a little drunk, so when he has his meeting with the big boss, maybe he reports good things about you' " (55)

In fact, if Wen Fu epitomizes the Kitchen God, Winnie is the Kitchen God's wife. As far as Winnie is concerned, this long-suffering female nonentity has for too long been on the receiving end, a background foil to Kitchen God. Let him be her foil for a change, Winnie decrees, and proceeds to make a fateful decision, her solution to gender symmetry: " 'I'm thinking about it this way,' she finally announced, her mouth set in an expression of thoughtfulness. 'You take this altar. I can find you another kind of lucky god to put inside, not this one.' She removes the picture of the Kitchen God. 'This one, I take it. Grand Auntie will understand. This kind of luck, you don't want. Then you don't have to worry' " (56). Winnie sets out to replace the unpleasant Kitchen God with a more inspiring goddess, at least to women. First she buys " 'a goddess that nobody knows' " that might " 'not yet exist' " (413). She paints it gold and puts her name on the bottom, while Helen joins in her project by purchasing good incense. The goddess is going to live " 'in her new house, the red temple altar with two candlesticks lighting up her face from both sides. She would live there, but no one would call her Mrs. Kitchen God. Why would she want to be called that, now that she and her husband are divorced?' " (414) Winnie demands rhetorically. After reading this passage, readers are now aware that Winnie and her mother are both united in the one deity, Lady Sorrowfree.

Winnie takes Pearl up to her bedroom, advising her on the proper medicine to take for her multiple sclerosis and there relates to her the magical, mystical properties of the statue. Both her connection to the goddess and her sardonic humor are once again in delightful evidence: " 'See how nicely she sits in her chair, so comfortable-looking in her manner. Look at her hair, how black it is, no worries. Although maybe she used to worry. I heard she once had many hardships in her life. So maybe her hair is dyed' " (414). She tells Pearl that the goddess wants her to speak, that she understands English, that she bought the goddess for her. Finally melting at these scarcely veiled allusions to herself and her mother, Pearl breaks down and cries. Winnie believes that Pearl is upset because she has paid " 'too much' " for the goddess, an erroneous assumption on her part, which is ironically correct on a deeper level. The price she has paid to come to this point is indeed inordinately high. Pearl is crying for what she now finally realizes is the beauty, the tragedy, the greatness of her mother, aka the Kitchen God's wife, now Lady Sorrowfree.

Winnie proceeds to explain to Pearl what the " 'goddess will do' " for her; that is, the nature of the goddess's properties and attributes. When she is afraid, Pearl can talk to her and " '[s]he will listen. She will wash away everything sad with her tears. She will use her stick to chase away everything bad.' " Most importantly, Winnie has deified and named the anonymous wife of a minor god. " 'Lady Sorrowfree, happiness winning over bitterness, no regrets in this world. . . . But see how fast the smoke rises—oh even faster when we laugh, lifting our hopes, higher and higher' " (414–415).

Winnie tells the story from the perspective of the abused wife of the Kitchen God. As the Kitchen God's wife, Winnie speaks to women globally who are abused by their men folk. What she is attempting to do is factor into the story validation of the Kitchen God's wife and her character. She also addresses the culture that worships him while it forgets her. She has subverted the Kitchen God and retold his narrative, but in private. For at the present time there is no public forum worldwide to support and validate Winnie's revisionism.

It is Winnie who by taking on the existing order and shaping it to her needs goes even further than any of the other women characters represented by Tan as challenging gender asymmetry. This includes Winnie's mother who rebels against her culture, but within the confines of Communism, which, when all is said and done, is a rival male-run system to an already-existing male-run system. Left with the Kitchen God seated on his altar by Auntie Du who is in effect passing on the torch, Winnie first boldly removes, then tears up and throws away the Kitchen God's picture. And this is the action of a woman who saves everything! Instead, she substitutes a female goddess, a projection of her mother and herself on the altar. Then she refuses to invoke the source of power and healing as from a deity's wife, because in actuality the deity, not his wife, still remains the real source of power. She solves this problem by giving the wife the title of Lady Sorrowfree, decreeing her to be a new goddess in her own right, as well.[13]

Winnie thereby uses the system as referent from which to substitute her own system. It is not enough, Tan suggests, to distance oneself from gender asymmetry (although this is a necessary first step) and to complain about it. Making a lateral move by running away to another patriarchal structure, as Winnie's mother did, still keeps it in place. Women must consciously remain a part of the culture. Then they must devise creative strategies from within so that the structure expands to be more open to the possibility of gender equity. Tan represents Winnie as syncretizing two systems: Confucianism and Christianity. Both of these are global hierarchical institutions that have historically imposed gender asymmetry on women under the guise of training them about how life should be lived. Both systems uphold and reflect gender, as well as race and class asymmetry.

Tan here reveals an essentialist feminism, right down to having her own goddess, just as men have created their own gods in their image. Derrida in his discussion of "difference" informs us that it emanates from within. Thus, men have first created their own male gods in their image and goddesses to suit their specifications. Then they have separated themselves from the male deities to worship them as different and higher entities, while the female deities are subordinated to the male deities. Next, they demand of everyone else that they all join in worshipping these deities in hierarchical ranks that were their own projections in the first place. In like manner, Winnie creates a goddess, Lady Sorrowfree, out of her own needs, her own vision, her own interests. By so doing, Winnie is making a statement: if men can allocate to themselves the right to create their own male and female deities and their own myths, then women can also. Winnie questions why women must go along with men's projections. From her point of view a masculinist perspective places the focus on the Kitchen God. His wife (Everywoman) is peripheral. She fades off and is forgotten by the tale's end, except as an instrument in his death and transfiguration into the Kitchen God. Her nameless name is put in lower case—"the Kitchen God's wife"—whereas the god's name is in upper case. Yet she alone is the one who has shown mercy, even in this male version. Thus, from Winnie's feminist perspective, it is the Kitchen God's wife who has been wronged. In this way, through Winnie's character Tan suggests that women must take the initiative to point out the asymmetric discourse of the existing models and to reshape existing gods, myths, and customs in order to project and reflect themselves.

Winnie in her final epiphany and transfiguration into Lady Sorrowfree becomes her own mother in her enduring fantasy of her mother's return when she will be lifted up and held once again in her mother's arms. Lady Sorrowfree also reflects her feelings as a mother in relation to Pearl, especially in regard to Pearl's illness. The healing solutions Winnie calls for are laughter and women's "jouissance" (Cixous). She promises that "when we laugh" Lady Sorrowfree will lift "our hopes, higher and higher" (415). She also calls for the creation of a female discourse, community, goddesses, self-definitions, and self-autonomy within the existing structures and systems, and possibility where once there was only gender asymmetry. This is reflected in Winnie's setting up the new goddess on the old altar. She is not advocating all this through a political process. Rather she performs a linguistic and semiotic subversion that reverses the situation by creating in Lady Sorrowfree a revision of the Kitchen God's myth: "a talk story [that] allows a shift into pure fantasy . . . to project an alternative world untrammeled by the oppressive rules of society," as a way of redeploying, like Hong Kingston, "fable, dream, and fantasy to evoke a world independent of time-worn rules, monocultural imperatives, and binary oppositions" (Cheung 1993, 123, 125). Unfortunately, the problem with such a solution to gender asymmetry is that "subversive or resistant perspectives" in Tan's text "cannot undo the power of what is socially 'dominant' " (McCormick 1993, 662). Patriarchal "binaries" will not go away "simply through the discursive deconstruction of 'opposition.' " This can only happen "when the socioeconomic conditions producing the contradictions in society are eradicated through the construction of nonexploitative social relations" (Ebert 1993, 45).

Hong Kingston wishes "to be welcomed back to the fold of the community via her art: 'The swordswoman and I are not so dissimilar. May my people understand the resemblance soon so that I can return to them. What we have in common are the words at our backs.' " And Hong Kingston's writing, according to Cheung, "constitutes the symbolic return" (1993, 100). In contrast, Tan through her art has Winnie recuperate a sense of community, but newly formed by herself as a means of transcending or fulfilling the longing or need for the original constraining community.

PEARL, THE SYNCRETIZER

In terms of Tan's women characters' responses to gender asymmetry, the question still remains at this point as to where Pearl fits in the continuum, especially in terms of two such formidable foremothers. The first two chapters are in Pearl's voice. Tellingly, Pearl's first words are about her mother and their discord. As we have seen, this is the basis of Tan's first work, *The Joy Luck Club*: "Whenever my mother talks to me, she begins the conversation as if we were already in the middle of an argument," Pearl complains. Then Winnie's voice begins, giving an order to her daughter and son-in-law in which the major components of her authoritative treatment of her daughter are expressed: " 'Pearl— ah, have to go, no choice,' my mother said"(11). From the very beginning of this work, then, Pearl is "not really sure why I still give in to my family obligations," as well as being on the defensive about them to her husband. As far as she is concerned, whenever she is with her mother "I feel as though I have to spend the whole time avoiding land mines" (16). She is emotionally paralyzed. Her multiple sclerosis is a physical manifestation of her psychic dilemma: the inability to choose between the two conflicting pulls on her heart (mother) and mind (Dr. Phil). Pearl has never been able to bring herself to confide to Winnie about her illness because "I think of the enormous distance that separates us and makes us unable to share the most important matters of our life. How did this happen?" (34). Thus at the beginning of *The Kitchen God's Wife*, as in *The Joy Luck Club*, there exists a chasm between mothers and daughters.

In replacing the Kitchen God's wife with Lady Sorrowfree, Winnie is supposedly imposing changes of community structure only on her daughter, but is in a way imposing them on the men around her, as well. This is the case because Pearl is married to Dr. Phil. Thus he is Pearl's Kitchen God in the home where Winnie wants her daughter to set up an altar presided over by a goddess named Lady Sorrowfree. Under his caustic scrutiny, readers cannot imagine Pearl actually lighting the incense and praying to Lady Sorrowfree for her health. Still, the mere presence of the goddess in their home would be subversive. Also subversive is Pearl's intention to return to China with her mother and Helen to select appropriate Chinese herbalists to treat her multiple sclerosis. Again, this is a repudiation of her husband's Western scientific notion of "doctoring." Also subversive is that while there the three women all intend to drink from the wondrous spring of happiness that Winnie and Helen drank from so many years ago in the early days of their relationship. Significantly, Winnie still remembers the location of this spring. Pearl is on the road to syncresis with her hyphenated American mentality's "consent" to Western rational humanism (Dr. Phil) and her ancestral Chinese female ways of being, knowing, and spirituality (Winnie, the mother). Unlike Winnie's, Pearl's will be the double way, such as *The Joy Luck Club* presages: a way in which Pearl feels comfortable. She will neither repudiate that which is Chinese in her life (the "silly" superstitions of her mother), nor obey what the Western system (Phil, the doctor of and to the dead) prescribes. She will combine both, and in doing so carve out her own way. It is at this tentative point of imminent syncresis at which *The Kitchen God's Wife* ends.

CONCLUSION

When the feminist critic Marianne Hirsch (1989) concludes that "only in the work of black writers such as Toni Morrison and Alice Walker [is] matrophobia and the endemic cultural exclusion of the mother's subjecthood . . . challenged effectively" (461), she is unaware of or remiss in omitting the work of Asian American women writers such as Maxine Hong Kingston and Amy Tan, as well as the others who will be discussed in the following pages. In fact, where Tan ends, both in *The Joy Luck Club* and *The Kitchen God's Wife*, she carries Derrida's concept of "binarism" and Foucault's notion of "discourse" one step further. "The theoretical problem facing us in cultural criticism at this moment is not how to fit anomalous positions into a fixed dualistic conception of dominant ideology and counterideology of discourse and counterdiscourse. Rather, it may be the reverse: heterogeneities, pluralities, and contradictions are givens in culture" (Lowe 1990, 143). "Anomalous positions" or "non-equivalences and non-correspondences" between mothers and daughters are facets of "a multivalent approach to Asian American literature which steers away from the 'East-West' or the 'dual personality' model and stresses instead a synergistic vision" (Lowe 1990, 143; Cheung 1993, 23). "Synergistic vision," or what critics of Asian American literature prefer to call "syncresis," is used not only to combine "East-West," the two halves of the hyphenation in Asian American. It is also used by Asian American women to confront gender asymmetry, not only in Asia, but also in the United States. In this chapter, I have shown how Amy Tan looks to solutions that will syncretize East and West: the East as embodied in Winnie, the past generation of Chinese immigrant women, and Pearl, the future hyphenated Chinese-American "daughter" who will serve as a bridge, a syncresis between Winnie and Dr. Phil, Winnie's Western son-in-law and Pearl's husband. This syncretic feminist approach and vision are also characteristic of the work of other contemporary Chinese American women writers. Fae Myenne Ng in *Bone* allegorizes and historicizes gender asymmetry and Gish Jen in *Typical American* has an ironist's field day playing with the clash of philosophical and economic values in Chinese and American culture and tradition. Like Tan and Myenne Ng, Jen suggests that this clash be resolved by syncresis.

NOTES

1. Wen Fu's behavior was not considered reprehensible at that time, as Francis L. K. Hsu points out. Hsu recounts attending a wedding feast in 1929 where the bridegroom "called in some prostitutes whom he had known previously to pour the wine and sing for the guests." Some of those present thought "he had gone too far," but "nobody thought him crazy. And the bride did not even raise her eyebrows" (Hsu 1981, 146).

2. This is a connubial detail not uncommon in ethnic American women's literature. See Alice Walker, *The Color Purple* and Sandra Cisneros, "Woman Hollering Creek" in *Woman Hollering Creek and Other Stories.*

3. Jimmy Louie (who later becomes her second husband) is the man she meets at the dance. Wen Fu's seemingly extreme response is explained by the fact that "[t]hroughout Chinese history, there has never been social dancing as Westerners understand the term. . . . Western-type social dancing can seldom occur between persons other than lovers or married couples at home, or prostitutes and their customers in a brothel. Under these latter circumstances, dancing either assumes a greater sexual intimacy than in the West or serves as a preliminary to intercourse, but is not an end in itself as in America" (Hsu 1981, 60).

4. Elaine Kim reports that Wen Fu and his kind still bloom and thrive in the Asian American community. One of her interviewees, a social worker at an Asian Community Center, was beaten up by a male client because she did not show him the respect he deserved as a man several years older . . . and for not giving him enough assistance. When she refused to apologize, he beat her with his fists. Her eye was swollen shut for days with an ugly purple bruise. But when she wanted to press charges against him for assault, some people in the community thought she should just "forgive" him. "No one has the right to harm another person just because he's facing personal problems. How could I be blamed for losing his job? Because I'm young and female, many people feel that I should be nothing but a servant obedient to everyone else. Some people think it's all right for men to beat women anyway. There were those who asked me what I had done to provoke the attack and others who said that I shouldn't make a big deal out of it. He only hit me a few times, and no bones were broken, they said. None of them realized how terrified I was to be alone with a man who acted like a maniac. I thought I might be killed" (Kim and Otani 1983, 16).

5. Such a response is not uncommon historically in most cultures. Indeed, Hong Kingston opens her work *The Woman Warrior* at this point, and we will see in *The Kitchen God's Wife* that Tan is intertextual with Hong Kingston when she ends Winnie's musings on her lost mother much as Hong Kinton ends Maxine's musing over the suicide of her No-Name Aunt.

6. See Frank Chin's "Come All Ye Asian American Writers of the Real and Fake" (1991) for Chin's attack on Hong Kingston and other Asian American writers, among them Jade Snow Wong and Amy Tan on these grounds. Also see Calvin Hernton, *The Sexual Mountain and Afro-American Women Writers* (1987), for a detailed examination of this subject in relation to African American men and women that opposes Chin's position.

7. Adages are used in Chinese American literature to convey information indirectly. In *The Kitchen God's Wife*, Winnie points this out to Pearl about Helen that "she does this when something else is bothering her and she can't say" (188). It is common to Chinese, including Winnie herself, and not at all unique to Helen.

8. On this issue, see Chapter Four of this text, which reveals the similarity between Winnie's response and that of the mother in Sasaki's *The Loom and Other Stories.*

9. Here one wonders whether An Mei's and Wei Wei's stories in both texts may not be based on the lives of Tan's own foremothers—much as Alice Walker inserted the story of her paternal grandmother who was slain by a jealous husband into *The Third Life of Grange Copeland*, *In Search of our Mothers' Gardens*, and *The Color Purple*.

10. See the end of this chapter.

11. This is much like the source of Celie's attraction for Shug in *The Color Purple*: the attraction of opposites, who are opposites only in experience and not actually in perspective. Interestingly, both Celie and Winnie become extremely attached to their husband's mistress rather than becoming distanced and inimical, as their respective cultures would decree. Also possibly intimated is an attraction that Winnie feels for Min. It is she who suggests that Min call herself "Miss Golden Throat," which Min does in her future career.

12. This is reminiscent of the tragi-comic efforts of Sophia's community to free her from jail in *The Color Purple*.

13. In many Latina and Chicana texts, the Virgin Mary is used more conservatively. Mary, forwarded by the patriarchal church, serves as mediator between humanity and her son. See, for example, Cherríe Moraga, *Loving in the War Years* and Judith Ortiz Cofer, *Silent Dancing: A Partial Remembrance of a Puerto Rican Childhood.* But Sandra Cisneros in "Woman Hollering Creek," *Woman Hollering Creek and Other Stories*, is the exception. Like Tan, she represents a goddess (created by a woman character) who erases a preexistent male deity. Thus no male authority figure can assume "the missionary position" above these female characters and their female deities. Interestingly, feminist archaeologists have long contended that dominant male deities arose with patriarchy and erased preexisting dominant female deities.

Chapter 2

Fae Myenne Ng, *Bone:*
"Nina, Ona, and I,
We're the Lucky Generation"

THE MEANINGS OF "BONE"

Technically, Myenne Ng's *Bone* resembles Tan's *The Joy Luck Club*, but is even more "chaotic" and fragmented in order to create a sense of "perceptual defamiliarization" (Haddad 1992, 149) so that believable characters and realistic situations can also be abstracted into allegorical meanings. In the process, Myenne Ng moves from the past to the present, from the present to the past, and in between, in abrupt, confusing changes characteristic of much feminist and postmodern writing. The plot line, which revolves around the death of "the obedient daughter" Ona and its after-effects on the Leong family, is an allegory of gender asymmetry.

Myenne Ng offers two possible solutions to this problem as embodied in Ona's two surviving sisters, Nina and Lei. Through the allegory, Myenne Ng links personal and family problems to historical and political ones, primarily gender and race asymmetry. What Cheung (citing Jameson) maintains of Joy Kogawa and Hisaye Yamamoto can also be said of Myenne Ng: "National allegory does provide a valuable angle for a view of emergent literature" in that "Third World" texts, no matter how private they seem, "necessarily project a political dimension in the form of a national allegory: the story of the private individual destiny is always an allegory of the embattled situation of the public third-world culture and society" (Cheung 1993, 14).

Although *Bone* is such an allegory—simultaneously public and private—and although I am not challenging the validity of Cheung's argument, nevertheless, her argument can just as well be maintained in relation to mainstream texts also, because all cultures and all humans are constructed in a given space and time. So-called "Third world" texts have no monopoly on the "personal is political" argument and aesthetic, although traditionalists like to imagine that their chosen canon is neither personal nor political. They argue that they do not take positions; that they are not specifically situated; that they are objective and omniscient and therefore produce and/or study and teach truly aesthetic and universal works of art. They deem ethnic and "Third World" texts parochial and narrow because they are personal and therefore of little aesthetic value or universal appeal, unless a political motivation can be said to be aesthetic. In order to circumvent such mainstream "authoritarian narration" and to "signify the instability of [its self-serving definitions of] 'truth' and 'history' " (Cheung 1993, 15), Hong Kingston and Tan utilize "modes of 'double-voiced' discourse," or syncresis. From their perspective, as well as Myenne Ng's, syncresis solves the problem. It is a combination that is "neither schizophrenic nor bisectable into East and West, neither merely preserving the ancestral culture nor dissolving into the mainstream" (Cheung 1993, 19). Among other things, according to Cheung, the characteristics of such discourse are the uses of "the juvenile" as well as mature narrators and perspectives; the "journalistic and the poetic, and of 'memory' and 'counter-memory' " (Cheung 1993, 15).

Although Myenne Ng uses only one voice, the narrator Lei's, readers hear other voices through her sensibility. Lei's is a young voice, and she has a perspective that readers discover is unreliable. By this means, Myenne Ng adds a ludic touch: an ironic, broader perspective beneath and beyond the narrator's troubled perspective. DuPlessis (1985) terms this kind of writing (which is characteristic of the works covered in this text) "a feminine aesthetic." To her, this "fragmented narrative style" reflects the "doubleness" or "dualism" of women; their "insider-outsider social status"; their "gender position . . . by . . . relation to power." DuPlessis and other essentialist feminists call for women writers to "invent" a written form to match this experience of "doubleness." In addition, they demand "a female aesthetic" theory that "will produce art works that incorporate contradiction and nonlinear movement into the heart of the text." Hong Kingston, Amy Tan, and Myenne Ng already employ both the form and theory that these feminists advocate, although the feminists seem to be unaware of it. These writers already "attack the heart of the unified master discourse" because it has no room for female discourse, except situated on the bottom or out on the edge (DuPlessis 1985, 278). In *Bone* this bottom edge is precisely the site from which Ona falls, as the daughter who believes most in and is most obedient to the "Father" ("the unified master discourse").

"[F]our cultural dilemmas" have been identified for traditionally oriented Asian American women: binaries of "obedience vs. independence"; "collective (or familial) vs. individual interest"; "fatalism vs. change"; and "self-control vs. self-expression or spontaneity" (E. Chow 1989, 368). That these four dilemmas are also experienced by women on a global basis indicates similar cultural inscriptions for all women, not only for Asian American women. These are precisely the four dilemmas of Myenne Ng's four female characters in *Bone*, which provides yet another reason why the text works so well on an allegorical level. Women of all cultures can relate to its dilemmas. By "encoding volatile political material in allegory" Myenne Ng criticizes both "the ethnic community and the larger society for their intolerance of difference and for their mechanisms of exclusion" (Cheung 1993, 72). Furthermore, characteristic of all the writers analyzed in this text and of Asian American literature in general, as well as ethnic and "Third World" writers, is the advocacy of syncresis, "the need for balance between . . . two emphases" on one hand, and "the subordination of the individual to the family and community" on the other, "while the individual is supreme in modern Western societies" (Kim 1982, 172). This "need for balance" or syncresis is a second major element in Myenne Ng's allegorical presentation of the characters in *Bone*.

Before discussing either of the allegorical meanings behind Ona's suicide and the family's responses to that suicide, or Myenne Ng's effort to syncretize East and West in order to achieve balance through allegory, it is useful to explore some of the meanings of the term Bone, which is itself allegorical. Lei informs us that it means the "sucking out the sweetness of the lesser parts. . . . 'Bones are sweeter than you know,' . . . [Mah] always said . . . 'Clean bones' . . . 'No waste' " (2–3). The bones of Grandpa Leong, the embodiment of the family's Chinese traditions and ancestry, are "restless bones" because they have not been buried properly. That is, the cultural prescription has not yet been properly fulfilled by the inheritor of Grandpa Leong's tradition, his "paper son" Leon Leong. Because "overcrowding had become a problem at the cemetery and most old timers had only leased their burial plots for three, five, or nine years, hoping to be sent back to China by relatives," the Chinese Association places an ad in *The Chinese Times*. Nowadays, in contrast, "the dead are forgotten. People get busy. Times change, even feelings. It happens" (76). As a result, "the unclaimed graves were disinterred and the bones grouped by family surnames and then reburied" (77). That Grandpa Leong has no direct heirs and that Leon does not fulfill his will and provide continuity is telling. It is Myenne Ng's observation from a historical perspective, as well as from a contemporary Chinese American perspective, that Chinese traditional culture is moribund.

Lei, whose full name is Lei-lah Fu Leong Louie, is called Lei Leong before her marriage. This name closely resembles her creator's—Lei/Fae and Leong/Myenne Ng. Lei embodies both the problem which begins the text, as well as the syncretic solution which ends it. This is done in terms of her desire to syncretize—to know "[h]ow to get the bones back"—how to re-graft one's roots, one's ancestry onto alien cultural soil. She is informed that it is too late to do so, that she should "[b]ow to the family headstone" because "the right gesture will find your grandfather" (79). By the very act of titling this book *Bone*, then, the author is reconnecting with her ancestry. She is paying her respects through historic referentiality to her cultural traditions, at the same time that she is undertaking to show how the old and the new can be syncretized.

DIVERSE RESPONSES TO THE ALLEGORY OF GENDER ASYMMETRY

Myenne Ng nowhere gives feminism the credit, but instead uses the term "history" to convey her conviction that somehow times have evolved so that when Lei and her sisters are born, the world has possibilities for women that it never had before. The examples that Lei cites when she uses the term "history" are all from traditional patriarchal China and its laws and customs, specifically in relation to women:

We're lucky, not like the bond maids growing up in service, or the newborn daughters whose mouths were stuffed with ashes. The beardless, soft-shouldered eunuchs, the courtesans with the three-inch feet and the frightened child brides—they're all stories to us. Nina, Ona, and I, we're the lucky generation. Mah and Leon forced themselves to live through the humiliation in this country so that we could have it better. We know so little of the old country. We repeat the names of grandfathers and uncles, but they have always been strangers to us. Family exists only because somebody has a story, and knowing the story connects us to a history. To us, the deformed man is oddly compelling, the forgotten man is a good story, and a beautiful woman suffers. (36)

Lei believes that the previous generation's struggle, "the humiliation" they experienced "in this country" is what made "it better" for "Nina, Ona and I." The struggle that she seems unaware of, the feminist struggle, has also made it possible for Nina to have her abortion, to tell about it and live, and continue living without being "a tragedy queen." It is also a struggle that makes it possible for her to say in a restaurant so casually about a waiter: "Cute." "Nice ass." "The best" (26). Trivial as this last example may appear on the surface, Mah's and Leon's struggles did not include the rights the sisters now have: to perceive "bond maids" as in the past, to marry or not marry as they will, to be casual about men sexually. Mah's and Leon's struggles were for survival and improvement in their lot. They were private and personal and would have ended with themselves had there not been several powerful mass movements supplementing their efforts.

One of them, the Second Wave feminist movement specifically, made it possible for their daughters to pursue an education and careers, to be "liberated" psychically from their "bond maid" status. Because of this movement, beautiful women like Nina no longer have to suffer, as, for example, Maxine's "No-Name" Aunt did in Hong Kingston's *The Woman Warrior*. As Hong Kingston herself (perhaps the major influence for Myenne Ng's notion of history) puts it: "Our roots go way back. We're old souls. We need to speak for all those people who didn't have a chance to speak, all those women who were illiterate, all those court women who were embodied in the architecture and couldn't get out—their feet bound, so they would not wander away from the courtyard. We're almost like mediums for those ancient voices. I feel close ties to my Chinese roots" (M. Chin 1990, 65).

Like Pearl of *The Kitchen God's Wife*, Lei is raised by a beloved stepfather. Lei's mother had married her first husband, Lei's biological father Lyman Fu, "for a thrill," but her second husband Leon "for convenience" (2). Lei believes that this marriage "was a marriage of toil—of toiling together. The idea was that the next generation would marry for love" (33). For the most part, this is why Lei feels such guilt about her own love match. At the same time as she feels she is fulfilling her mother's and Leon's wishes for her, she feels sorry for them because they do not know what love is, what marrying for love is, a typical attitude on the part of American-born children in relation to their immigrant parents' ways: "The old way. Matches were made, strangers were wedded, and that was fate. Marriage was for survival. Men were scarce: dead from the wars, or working abroad as sojourners. As such, my father, Lyman Fu, was considered a prince. Mah married my father to escape the war-torn villages, and when he ran off on her, she married Leon to be saved from disgrace" (34).

Lately a family tragedy has created heartbreak and division. Mah and Leon have split up, and the remaining sisters are traumatized as a result of the middle daughter Ona's suicide, a jump off the thirteenth floor of the "last of the four housing projects built in Chinatown [San Francisco]" (4). It takes the entire work for Myenne Ng to give readers sufficient data about this death to determine its cause literally and allegorically. The significance of Ona's suicide resonates historically in traditional Confucian culture where shamed children or relatives do away with themselves when cursed.[1]

Literally, the fall is represented as due to the unbearable stress of Ona's finding herself in a triangle between two men she loved equally, as well as her inability to express her opinion to them, because they will not listen: "There is no healing in silence" (Gamble 1993, 12), or, as Myenne Ng shows in *Bone*, silence is death. The first part of Ona's triangle was her lover Osvaldo Ong. The second was her father who had threatened the withdrawal of his love and relationship with her if she continued seeing Osvaldo. Ona had always been very attached to Leon, even more than her sisters. Unable to bear the stress of two equal but opposing demands on her—one of paternal prescription, the other of her lover's claims—she did away with herself.

Allegorically, the loss of Ona as daughter and sister reflects the price of the traditional system's abuses, not only in her sacrifice of herself, but in the varying responses of each of her sisters and of her father and mother. Had there been no gender asymmetry, had there been no cultural constructs about the nature of gender roles—what is appropriate or inappropriate—Ona would not have died. Furthermore, the members of her family and community members who also loved her would not have suffered.

Myenne Ng circles around the suicide from all angles until she zeroes in on Ona's reasons. Once we get clear about those reasons and the responses of her sisters, and her parents, we realize that Myenne Ng is projecting the diverse responses of contemporary Chinese Americans to gender asymmetry, specifically in relation to Chinese cultural traditions. These responses cover a broad range. The parents do not celebrate the feminist solutions as do the younger generation. When Nina, for example, tells them of her abortion, Ma responds with the assumption that her daughter is a "disgrace" for being "mistreated by men." In Mah's view, as well as that of traditional Chinese culture, Leon has saved her from disgrace by marrying her when her first husband abandoned her.

The response of obedience is represented allegorically by Ona. Separation (which comes at a steep price) is represented by Nina who is in flight from the culture's constraints. Finally, there is mediation (which also has its price) as represented by the narrator Lei—she who bridges—the syncretizer who links and spans both disparate "sisters" or sides. Just as the narrator Maxine of *The Woman Warrior* is "at every turn blind to the ideological forces that shape her perceptions," so is Ona. And as "the full-fledged author [Hong Kingston] knows better" (Cheung 1993, 79), so does the narrator Lei by the end of the book. First, in order to grow wiser, women have to repudiate becoming trapped in the roles that the patriarchy assigns them (symbolized by the skimpy Playboy-type uniform Ona wears on her last job). On the other hand, women should reject Nina's detached, entirely self-centered approach. Such a strategy paradoxically replicates the abuses of gender asymmetry in reverse: another dead-end chauvinism. The third element is Lei, the bridge between past and present, because more than anything else, she wants her mother not to suffer any longer. "I'd seen her break. Now more than anything, I wanted to see her happy" (9).

THE PARENTS' RESPONSES TO ONA'S DEATH

After Ona's death, Lei's parents "acted as if all they heard were their own hearts howling." Caught "between [Leon's] noisy loneliness and [Mah's] endless lament" (24), Lei chooses to stay with her mother "on Salmon Alley," her former home, and to visit her husband on weekends. Nina, the youngest daughter is a flight attendant (an appropriate postmodern pun for a woman in flight from the "Bone," the responsibility or burden of her past). As is to be expected, she arranges for her mother's flight back to Hong Kong. From Lei's perspective, this return is not a triumphal march, "of offering banquets and stories of the good life . . . in the land of gold and good fortune" (24). Rather it is for Mah "to go back for solace and comfort . . . to tell her story: the years spent in sweatshops, the prince of the Golden Mountain turned into a toad, and three daughters: one unmarried, another who-cares-where, one dead" (24). Mah and Leon "hit on" Lei after Ona's death because of the Confucian Chinese rule that the older sibling is held "responsible" for all younger ones. "Mah said something about how everything started with me, since I was the first one, the eldest, the one with the daring to live with Mason when I wasn't married. She said it in that irrational way she has. " 'That's why Ona went bad. That's why Nina left' " (41).

Then the parents started on Nina:

[They] joined forces and ganged up on her, said awful things, made her feel like she was a disgrace. Nina was rotten, doomed, no-good. Good as dead. She'd die in a gutter without rice in her belly, and her spirit—if she had one—wouldn't be fed. They forecast bad days in this life and the next. They used a word that sounded like dyeen. I still can't find an exact translation, but in my mind it's come to mean something lowly, despised.
"I have no eyes for you," Mah said.
"Don't call us," Leon said. (25)[2]

It isn't as if either parent is so traditional:

They made up rules as they needed them, and changed them all on a whim. Mah had her ways when Leon was out at sea, but when he came home all her rules relaxed. Nina called their parenting chop suey, a little bit of everything. There were nights we had to speak Chinese at the dinner table and there were other nights we could laugh and talk English all we wanted and even take our bowls out to the front room and eat while watching *I Love Lucy*. One day we could run wild in the alley until way after dark and stay up all night eating candy and watching television. The next day we had to sew culottes until our eyes crossed. (117)

Lei describes how hard and enterprising a worker Leon was, that on the ships Leon had worked at every job possible. After his wife's infidelity, he stayed ashore, working days at a grocery and nights as a welder at Bethlehem Steel. He continually percolated with ideas for getting the family out of their rut of poverty. But all this activity of Leon's meant that he never saw his family. Without Mah's ceaselessly reminding the children of him, they would not even have known that he was employed on ships. What made the children remember him was Mah's "excitement" and the "majestic welcomes home" (34) she arranged for him.

The narrator also describes negative aspects about Leon, as well as the positive—"how ugly his words could become"—that she attributes to the hard life both Leon and Mah led. On this basis she queries the reader as to whether "their discontent" was irrational. She then records the couple's essential grievances against one another. For Mah, he was not there for her when the children were born. It didn't even occur to him to go to see her at the hospital. And always "the need for 'Money! Money!! Money to eat with, to buy clothes with, to pass this life with!' " Leon's grievances against Mah are also recorded: " 'What about living or dying? Which did you want for me that time you pushed me back to work before my back brace was off?' " (35). He also maintains that he hands over all his earnings from " 'that dead place' " to his wife (35). When they get into these arguments, they get violent. It is unclear which one of them takes up weapons, or whether it is both of them. Sadly, they count on the children's' interference to mediate between them, to prevent them from going over the edge. Lei can't count the times she and her sisters have "held them apart." With dread she recollects "[t]he flat ting! sound as the blade slapped onto the linoleum floor, the wooden handle of the knife slamming into the corner. Which one of us screamed, repeating all their ugliest words? Who shook them? Who made them stop?" (35).

Clearly by mainstream American standards, Leon, Mah, and their children are a "dysfunctional" family. But traditional Asian American standards "permit some violence" toward women and children and other social inferiors in order to mold their "behavior" and to express "frustrations," according to Nilda Rimonte. One can't help but wonder why Rimonte deems any of these situations permissible for the expression of violence. On the other hand, unlike much current thinking in terms of wife abuse, Rimonte argues that just because "violence as a form of power and control is rooted in and sanctioned by a culture does not mean . . . that the culture is itself the problem." As far as she is concerned, the violent batterer is to blame, not the culture.

Although Rimonte is addressing only Asian American family situations, I would again extend the problem of battering to what happens to women, if not physically, then verbally, in every culture around the globe. Rimonte feels that if we hold the individual culture responsible, then the individual would get off the hook and that there would therefore be "no victimizer" and no victim. "[T]hen no law has been broken, and therefore there is no crime." Those who wish to improve conditions could well become "paralyzed by the enormity of" such an undertaking where the effort to change is addressed to the culture, its systems and all its beliefs, values, and norms (Rimonte 1989, 335).

Moreover, after having internalized a patriarchal model, women become "codependent" because of their "desire for recognition by powerful others," which "creates a vulnerability to 'addictive' relationships and institutions" (Haaken 1993, 326). All too frequently, studies of the "nontraditional family" tend to be studies assuming solipsistically that any other mode of the family than the patriarchal, nuclear model is deviant and dysfunctional. Inherent in these studies is the culturally naturalized assumption that difference in structure and gender such as is characteristic of single parent families, female headed households, and gay and lesbian parent families is synonymous with the deterioration of the family. From a feminist perspective, such a definition of dysfunctional is both sexist, racist, and homophobic in its "imposition of middle-class definitions of normative family values." Consequently, for many this has meant that "these concepts have been less than liberatory":

Lines between functional and dysfunctional are not so clearly drawn in a world where poverty and racism undermine parental capacities. Under such conditions, women of color have developed protective traditions based on extrafamilial sources of support, while the middle-class family has been defined historically as the primary and ideal social unit, one of the consequences of which has been weakened ties to community life. The deterioration of family life, then, creates a greater sense of cultural crisis within the middle class because it represents a negation of its own mythic autonomy. (Haaken 1993, 340)

The feminist ending of *Bone*, especially in relation to Mah's and Leon's behavior modifications, is foreshadowed by Haaken's solution to this "dysfunction": "In a humane society, the vicissitudes of early development perhaps would be less crucial; both men and women would have ongoing possibilities for rebuilding a wounded sense of self. Codependence might refer, in that better society, to an ideal based on working for cooperative, shared concerns rather than to a disease that requires a formulaic program of individual spiritual recovery" (Haaken 1993, 342).

DIFFERENCES BETWEEN MAH'S AND LEON'S AND NINA'S AND LEI'S RESPONSES TO ONA'S DEATH, AND THEIR ALLEGORICAL MEANINGS

Leon covers over his sense of guilt about Ona's death by maintaining that it was due to "bad luck" caused by his not having kept his promise to return his sponsor's bones to China when the old man passed away. Such intensity covers over his torment about having abused his daughter's love for him by giving her an impossible ultimatum that he didn't mean in his heart, but which his position as father/male authority figure traditionally demands. At first, instead of facing this fact—what his adherence to tradition has cost him—he sublimates his guilt about Ona into a concern about the "bones." Not burying them properly has brought him "bad luck." By this subterfuge, he can "let it all hang out." "He didn't care what other people asked; all he wanted to talk about was how much he loved Ona. . . . Leon was looking for someone to blame" (103).

Here the question arises as to the allegorical meaning of Myenne Ng's representation of Leon after Ona's death as having "become dreamy, lost" (49). His ability to concentrate has left him and he is experiencing "something" that "disconnected between his mind and his heart" (49). Like Winnie's father Old Jiang in *The Kitchen God's Wife*, Leon has consciously chosen his gender role acculturation over his personal feelings. But unlike Winnie's father, Leon's suffering is caused by the surfacing in his consciousness (which he is battling) of the chasm between what he has been taught and what he feels. He is beginning the uncomfortable process of questioning his training. At first, Leon tries to revert to tradition in his grief. "He wanted a Chinese wake. Something fancy. He wanted to invite all his friends . . . He talked about hiring an El Dorado, having Ona's poster-sized picture riding high above the cab for everyone to see. He wanted to take Ona for her last walk. He wanted to hire a professional wailer. He wanted to fill all of Chinatown with his grief " (123). In contrast, his youngest daughter Nina, the postfeminist, rolls her eyes and declares that

[S]he didn't want any of that hocus-pocus, which sent Leon onto a rant about Confucian rites. When he warned about ancestral retribution and Nina muttered, "What ancestor?" Leon was so pissed off he blamed everything on Mah and said, "Just like you, no manners, bad home education." Mah called Leon a do-nothing bum. He called her a bad mother, the world's worst wife. I tried to stay out of it, but when Nina shouted at them to shut up, I yelled at Nina to show more respect. (124–125)

The difference between the feminist and postfeminist position is here brilliantly encapsulated in the daughters' contrasting responses to the past, to tradition. The only difference between Mah's and Leon's response is that Leon desperately points the finger at everything and everyone else except his tradition and himself for being obedient to it—with disastrous results. Meanwhile, he is internally struggling with his suppressed awareness that both have been responsible for Ona's suicide. Mah, on the other hand, openly points to herself and her shortcomings in terms of her training, without questioning her training. Guilt ridden, she "blamed herself for what happened" and believes that "the bad luck started with her" (102) for her having married the charming, irresponsible Lyman Fu who had ultimately deserted her and her baby. She also blames herself for having had an affair with her boss Tommie Hom.

Lei's reaction is to churn up her shortcomings in her relationship with Ona. She is also guilt-ridden for having minded her own business, for having given her sister too much space in which to make "her own choice." This is why she vows that she will more freely and openly express her opinions to her surviving sister Nina. She comes to the decision that at least with Nina she will create "an intimacy" that she hadn't sought with her "for the last few years" (25). As a result, she begins to distinguish the difference between Nina and herself. It is not due to her being older, but to their different "temperament." Lei "could endure; I could shut my heart and let Mah and Leon rant. Nina couldn't. She yelled back. She said things. She left" (25). Nina, the postfeminist, is not willing to "eat guilt" (26) as Lei is.

A key passage in the novel reveals the distinction between the two sisters— one, a struggling feminist, the other a postfeminist. Lei admires Nina for wanting "the family to be the last thing on her mind" and having "the courage of heart" to do exactly "what she wanted." On her part, Nina sees Lei as having "peace of heart, knowing [she had] done [her] share for Mah and Leon" (32). To illustrate, on the verge of marriage, Lei does not want a banquet, but Mah does, because of social and familial obligations. Lei sympathizes with her mother's position: "Everybody's always inviting her to their banquets, and she's never had the occasion to invite back" (33). But Nina's position is that Lei is "thinking like her [Mah]," and advises her older sister to "Do it the way you want." Over Lei's objections, she continues to insist that it is easy to do so. "Look, you've always been on standby for them. Waiting and doing things their way. Think about it, they have no idea what our lives are about. They don't want to come into our worlds. We keep on having to live in their world. They won't move one bit" (33).[3]

It requires very little effort at this point to historicize and allegorize Nina's position as the postfeminist attitude about cultural constraints from the past imposed on contemporary women. Simply put, women should do what they want without referentiality to history and tradition. This attitude is neither as new or so shocking as may appear at first glance. As long ago as 1945, Jade Snow Wong represented herself as "trapped in a mesh of tradition woven thousands of miles away by ancestors who had had no knowledge that someday one generation of their progeny might be raised in another culture." And her response to this cultural training of self-obliteration, "suicide in life," is the same as Lei's and similar to Nina's. "Acknowledging that she owed her very being and much of her thinking to those ancestors and their traditions, she [Snow Wong] could not believe that this background was meant to hinder her further development either in America or in China" (J. S. Wong 1993 [1945], 110). The passage preceding these remarks in which Snow Wong's father provokes this response bears quoting, as well:

"[I]t is the sons who perpetuate our ancestral heritage by permanently bearing the Wong family name and transmitting it through their blood line, and therefore the sons must have priority over the daughters when parental provision for advantages must be limited by economic necessity. Generations of sons, bearing our Wong name, are those who make pilgrimages to ancestral burial grounds and preserve them forever. Our daughters leave home at marriage to give sons to their husbands' families to carry on the heritage for other names." . . . How can Daddy know what an American advanced education can mean to me? Why should Older Brother be alone in enjoying the major benefits of Daddy's toil? There are no ancestral pilgrimages to be made in the United States! I can't help being born a girl. Perhaps, even being a girl, I don't want to marry, *just* to raise sons! Perhaps I have a right to want more than sons! I am a person, besides being a female! Don't the Chinese admit that women also have feelings and minds? (J. S. Wong, 1993 [1945]), 109–110) [Emphasis in the original]

The differences between Snow Wong's, Hong Kingston's, Tan's, and My- enne Ng's representations of their characters in terms of gender asymmetry is that the postfeminist Nina consciously refuses from the beginning to take tradi- tion into account and acts on that refusal: " 'I know about should. I know about have to. We should. We want to do more, we want to do everything. But I've learned this: I can't' " (33). Here Myenne Ng in the character of Nina has en- tered into dialogue with Hong Kingston and Tan, telling them that their resolu- tion does not work for her.

Although Myenne Ng undeniably shows intertextuality with her predeces- sors, especially Tan's *The Joy Luck Club* and *The Kitchen God' Wife*, Tan's works end where *Bone* begins. Myenne Ng sees a dilemma for her characters in familial relationships: how to weigh what one owes to loved ones against what one owes to oneself. This dilemma is evident in Chinese American women's literature, at least since Snow Wong's *Fifth Chinese Daughter*, as I have just shown. Once again in Myenne Ng we will see a continuum of women such as we have seen in *The Kitchen God's Wife*, but this time in allegorical relationship to the system of gender asymmetry. And once again, open rebellion has too steep a price. For in *Bone*, Myenne Ng depicts Nina from the beginning as al- ready having "lifted off," already having soared free of the shackles of tradition. On a literal level, she lives in New York, at three thousand miles distance, and is therefore physically unavailable to her family. The price is that she lives away from and is distanced from them. This is the price of independence for her as well as for her relatives. Figuratively, she has "taken flight" from her group, her "bones," her ancestry, tradition, and culture.

LEON'S TRANSFORMATION AND ITS ALLEGORICAL MEANING

Lei tells us that Leon "never finished anything he started" but delights most in "making old things work" (13), which is a paradox. Thus she reveals the global allegory of the system that inheres in such a representation of his charac- ter. He never finishes anything, but he fantasies, he dreams, he imagines possi- bilities, and then is always disappointed and disappoints others when his projects don't pan out. He is also always involved in one "get-rich scheme" or another (13). Throughout the text, the elements and symbols connected with him on this level stand for the global patriarchy, as well as its historic identifying character-istics. At the end, Leon's ultimate behavior modification, his "repair job," repre-sents Myenne Ng's revisionary suggestion for undoing this existing system.

We begin where Leon begins—with gender asymmetry in relation to ethnic men of color. According to Goellnicht, "Ruling Fathers" who are white men dominate over other men by forcing them into the missionary position—into "feminine subject positions in work and social situations" (Goellnicht 1992, 197, 207). What happens to Leon in this predicament is what Hong Kingston shows happening to her (fore)father(s) in *The Woman Warrior* and *China Men*, and what Elaine Kim, Katherine Newman, and Hong Kingston perceive as one of Frank Chin's major qualities. Such men, in order to avoid internalizing female acculturation, make themselves "male" toward their women. Thus, Asian Ameri-can men as a group tend "to reassert their lost patriarchal power" by dominating over whatever they consider "weaker than themselves: [their] women" (Goellnicht 1992, 200). I would add "their children," as well. Always Leon resorts when insecure or in a quarrel to bluster and bluff. After Ona's death, Leon offers to put in fluorescent lighting in his wife's business, The Baby Store. Significantly, he leaves the job half done so that his wife has to work "in the dark." The postfeminist daughter Nina describing her father to Lei sees through Leon's response as the pompous, hollow posturing of the time-worn and thread-bare traditional patriarchal party line, which she has the temerity to label "stupid." Indeed, in his battles with his wife and in his threats to Ona, Leon re-veals himself as much like the Wizard of Oz, a timid mortal beneath his fright-ening mask.

She called him a useless thing, a stinking corpse. And Leon had an answer. You know the fortune teller's voice he uses when he's on the edge, like he's giving warning? Well, he swore to jump from the Golden Gate, told her not to bother with burying him because even when dead he wouldn't be far enough away. And then he used that stupid thousand-year-old curse of his, you know that one, something about damning the good will that blinded him into taking her as his wife. (31)

In addition to his liking for "making old things work" (3), which is also an allegorical statement about patriarchy, Leon is loyal to friends and family in the face of trying circumstances. He married Mah after her first husband abandoned her and Lei. This man's name Ly(ing)man Fu (Phooey) contains a significant double entendre in English. After moving with his wife from mainland China to Hong Kong, he then takes her to San Francisco where he leaves her and their infant daughter to emigrate to Australia and never returns or sends for them. Although the intervals between their arrival increase until they cease altogether, Lyman does post letters and funds back to his family.

At this point, the thematic of a young girl being raised by a devoted man not her blood father must be considered as a major thread running through the work of contemporary Asian American writers. Like Ben Loy of *Eat a Bowl of Tea*,

Jimmy Louie of *The Kitchen God's Wife*, and Charley-O of *The Floating World*, Leon will break with tradition. He will raise his wife's child as a loving father and establish family relations with her "because he has chosen" like Ben Loy and the other men enumerated above, "to face reality" (Kim 1987, 110).

Late in the text, Lyman is revealed to have acknowledged his daughter and to have cared about her. In the beginning he even supports her, but eventually sends a letter in which he admits that he has lost interest in his family and asks forgiveness from his wife for doing so. The probability is that he has begun a new family in Australia. Out of hatred for Wen Fu, Winnie in *The Kitchen God's Wife* does not even acknowledge for many years that he is Pearl's father. Only Winnie knows and shrewd Helen realizes the truth. In contrast, in *Bone*, Leon's frequent comment to Lei that " '[I]t's time that makes a family, not just blood' " is supportive and nurturing of her and the family he and Mah have created, as well as indicative of his willingness to carve out a nontraditional family like Jimmy Louie of *The Kitchen God's Wife*. That Leon is the first one Lei tells of her marriage to Mason Louie after living with him "four, five years, and it was time," signifies her deep attachment to her stepfather.

After Ona's death, Leon seeks escape from his inner civil war in long sea voyages and by taking up bachelor's quarters in a run-down hotel. It is Lei's opinion that Leon is seeking the same thing as Ona—escape—only in her case it is through suicide. Lei "always felt that [Ona] had the most to lose. She was too sensitive, too close to Leon" (171). Characteristically, Nina had advised Ona to just " 'say whatever Leon needs to hear' " while proceeding to do whatever she wants, but Ona refuses to lie. Instead, she tells Leon she loves Osvaldo. At this point Leon makes his crucial error by threatening "to disown her. 'You will not longer be my daughter. I will no longer be your father' " (172), he rants. Lei feels that "after those words came out of his mouth, it was all over. Forbidding Ona was like daring her" (172). But "because she was Leon's target, she didn't have an out" (173) the way Lei does with her husband and Nina does when she removes herself to New York into a separate life.

Myenne Ng here exposes Leon to the reader as pathetically vulnerable under all his bravado, while at the same time as she also exposes the credulous Ona as taking Leon too seriously. As a result, she does leave, while Leon is left to look after the retreating car "as if he was watching everything he'd ever hoped for disappear" (175). Sadly, it does.

Myenne Ng's portrayal of Leon is perhaps the finest, most believable, three-dimensional representation of a male character in contemporary Asian American women's literature. To a point, he is much like Hong Kingston's male characters in *China Men*. Like them, he is "strong and vocal." Like them, he exemplifies a "reconciliation of the contemporary Chinese American and his immigrant forefathers, nourished by their common roots, strong and deep, in American soil" (Kim 1982, 212). Yet although like Hong Kingston Myenne Ng depicts "with compassion and skill the experiences of both sexes," the younger writer draws Leon differently from the way Hong Kingston draws her male characters, where "reconciliation between the sexes is not complete" (Kim 1982, 213). Leon moves far further toward "reconciliation": toward reconciling "the experience" of the "difference" within from a more postmodern feminist perspective than any of his literary predecessors. In the beginning and throughout the text Leon reads his traditions and his heritage, as well as his own life experiences, from within a Chinese perspective. It is always in relation to the past, to ancient history, that he makes his moves, although reluctantly. Like a sheet of ice, he gradually begins to break up, to flow on into the present and future. To begin with, he believes that all his sorrows stem from his not having kept his promise to Grandpa Leong to bury his bones in China. Consequently, he makes what amends he can in as traditional a manner as he can.

Leon blamed himself. He had this crazy idea that our family's bad luck started when he broke his promise to Grandpa Leong. Grandpa Leong was Leon's father only on paper; he sponsored Leon's entry into the country by claiming him as his own son. It cost Leon. Each time he told us, his eyes opened wide like he was hearing the price called out for the first time. "Five thousand American dollars." Of more consequence was the promise to send Grandpa Leong's bones back to China. Leon was away when Grandpa Leong died. Leon worried about the restless bones, and for years, whenever something went wrong—losing a job, losing the bid for the takeout joint, losing the Ong and Leong Laundry—Leon blamed the bones. But in the end the bones remained here. Then Ona jumped and it was too late. *The bones were lost, like Ona was lost.* That's why Leon shipped out on a cargo voyage. Cape Horn was as far away as a ship could go. Forty days to the bottom of the world. (50) [Emphasis in original]

Leon goes to Grandpa Leong's grave site and does homage to his bones. Nevertheless, as Lei takes pains to point out to the reader, the ceremony he performs there is not about Grandpa Leong, but about Ona, that "he was looking for Ona" (88). Here Leon's psychic search relates to Rimonte's penetrating analysis of violence as "learned behavior" in dealing with stress and in fulfilling one's needs and desires. Violence is therefore chosen, whether the abuser is conscious of it or not. Fortunately, violence can be unlearned. What she suggests is that Leon do what Mr.———(Albert) finally does in *The Color Purple*: "choose again," but this time nonviolent behavior. She suggests as a first step that the abuser "take responsibility" for violent behavior. The same goes for abused women. They too should modify their behavior and summon up the courage to confront the reality of their situation. Rimonte extends this commitment "to the community" (Rimonte 1989, 336).

Although she only addresses herself to the Asian Pacific community, Rimonte could at all points apply her analysis to a global community as well, especially in the key element of her solution to asymmetry—namely, that in order to change culture and institutions, individuals must change. This would not be as difficult as it seems because "adaptability is the hallmark of the survivor species" (Rimonte 1989, 337). Leon eventually enacts this scenario by modifying traditional Asian expectations for males in order to humanize himself and expand beyond role-playing, but only after paying a terrible price, the loss of his beloved daughter. This process begins at his completion ceremony at the Leong family grave site, when Leon uses a seemingly incongruous pack of Lucky Strikes:

Leon stood sadly, with both hands deep in his pockets. Hidden fists. A firm horse stance. What was he thinking? I knew he blamed himself. The misplaced grave, the forgotten bones. Leon gave those bones power, believed they were the bad luck that stirred Ona's destiny. There was no way to talk about it. This was Leon's thing, and I'd learned the only way to respect it was to leave it alone. . . . The pack of Lucky Strikes made sense to me; this was Leon's ritual. The cigarettes were breath. Like the funeral candy that called back sweetness, the cigarettes called back breath. Leon's gestures toward the grave became a part of his own private ritual. This wasn't all about Grandpa Leong. Leon was looking for a part of his own lost life, but more than that, he was looking for Ona. (80)

Through this completion process, having paid his respects to his past training and in his way bidding it farewell, Leon is now ready to admit its limitations. He does not do this verbally, only through his actions. Unlike a younger generation of Asian American men, for example, his step-son-in-law Mason Louie, the immigrant Leon will never verbally express his separation from the system. But his syncretic actions will speak louder than words. From this point on, he will syncretize the old and the new. According to Lim, "[As] each new generation of immigrants casts away its old selves in the fresh American present, so American culture casts away its old self in the presence of new Americans. This political and cultural dialectic has presented to the modern world many of its models of dynamism and continues to invigorate despite its many corruptions and oppressions every other nation and culture in the world" (1992, 19).

All through the book the narrator takes great pains to show that Leon talks the traditional hard line of his immigrant generation, but that underneath all the ranting and raving, he always does come around. His first unwilling movement away from the traditional cultural prescriptions for appropriate masculine conduct can be traced to the period after his wife has shamed him publicly by committing adultery with their landlord and her employer, Tommie Hom. Leon curses her publicly and rejects her publicly, even after she comes begging him to forgive her. But then after Ona (and she is still a child) keeps coming around to him, never letting up, he returns to his wife.

Leon and Mah never talked about Tommie Hom. We all went on trying to be a family, like Mah wanted. But things were never the same. Even their quiet was different. Leon was pensive, sad; Mah's quiet was about being afraid. Any day, I expected to come home and find an itinerary on the table, his duffel bag gone. More than that, although he had shipped out regularly before this time, I have to give Leon credit, though. During that time, he tried to find steady work on land. (160)

The most dramatic movement is when Leon modifies his cultural training to that of a feminist ideal in regard to an appropriate model for masculinity. When we first meet him, we see an old man living alone in the San Fran Hotel, his room a mess. Or as Mah, calls it, a *lop sop*. The mess is allegorical, but not only in the sense in which Flaubert commented on "this grand furnished hotel of the universe." The room reflects Leon as Everyman, as the summation of patriarchy's characteristic relationship with the environment: a botched-up mish-mash of meddling and tinkering. "There was an old-man smell, and junk all over. Leon was a junk inventor. Very weird stuff. An electric sink. Cookie-tin clocks. Clock lamps. An intercom hooked up to a cash register hooked up to the alarm system."

When he had lived at home, his wife had thrown "everything into the garbage" as soon as he would ship out. Nevertheless, Leon continued inventing "on the long voyages. On the ships, his bunk was his only space, so every invention was compact. Leon made a miniature of everything: fan, radio, rice cooker. And he brought them all home" (5). In allegorical terms, Leon as Generic Patriarchal Male is a collector, a pack rat:

Stacks of takeout containers, a pile of aluminum tins. Plastic bags filled with packs of ketchup and sugar. White cans with red letters, government-issue vegetables: sliced beets, waxy green beans, squash. His night stand was a red restaurant stool cluttered with towers of Styrofoam cups, stacks of restaurant napkins, and a cup of assorted fast-food straws. Metal hangers dangled from the closet doorknob. On the windowsill were bunches of lotus leaves and coils of dried noodles. There were several tin cans: one held balls of knotted red string, another brimmed with tangles of rubber bands. The third was ashy with incense punks. (80)

Whenever Lei visits him, Leon would show her "every project he had in progress: alarm clocks, radios, lamps, and tape recorders." He would also read to her from piles of Chinese newspapers from which he "snipped and saved the best stories for his private collection: Lost Husbands, Runaway Wives, Ungrateful Children" (80–81).[4] Leon's garbage, his inventions, his continual, inept tinkering are all incompletions. They molder and choke up his surroundings in the imagery that ecological feminists use to characterize their view of what patriarchy has made of the earth today: littered with the detritus of their inept tinkerings: a "junkyard" as Myenne Ng puts it. Mah, Leon's wife (Everywoman), for example, has "to work in the dark" because Leon cannot succeed in installing modern lighting into her store, The Baby Store.

In contrast, Mason, the supportive, postfeminist male does this effortlessly. This signifies that Mason (note the pun here on Mah's Son) is in no way constrained by traditional male training, as is Leon. Nevertheless, it is Leon who had initiated the idea, who had "suggested" the fluorescent lights for the Baby Store. "Enthusiastic, Mah went with him to Three Star Hardware and chose soft white over bright white. When Leon carried the ladder up from the basement and perched on the top rung to rewire the switches, she held the ladder steady" (49). Mason "called it their first joint project because it was the friendliest thing they'd done together after Leon moved into the San Fran" (49).

Lei is glad for Leon, because she sees this project, his devising the idea of bringing new and improved lighting to The Baby Store as a way of his escaping into something outside himself. "After Ona died, Leon still talked up new ideas, but he hardly ever started anything. Working on the lights, Leon seemed almost his old self, not happy but preoccupied. I was hoping he'd see this project through to the end, but half-way through he told Mason that his concentration was gone, that something disconnected between his mind and his heart" (49). This is precisely what keeps the generation of traditional men like Leon from full self-expression as human beings: their need to keep up their learned disconnection between their minds or lights (the "male" essence) and their emotions (the "female" essence):

Mason offered to put the lights in. . . . [He] dragged the ladder to the center of the store and I pulled the tubes out of the corrugated casings and handed them up to Mason; they lifted away from my hands, as thin as eggshells. Mason snapped them into place, one, two, three. What was wrong with Leon, leaving the easiest part till last and then walking away? I flipped the switch, looked up. The white line of lights flickered and snapped and shot across the ceiling, jagged as a headache. (54)

After Nina takes Mah to Hong Kong, Leon moves back into the apartment in Salmon Alley. Lei discovers that "Mah's not being around helped; her absence lessened the weight somehow, as if she'd taken some of our sorrow about Ona far away" (95). She indulges herself in moving back in with her husband Mason and having good times with him. One evening, when Lei goes back to pick up Leon for dinner, she finds that Leon has made a mess of the apartment. The real reason Leon has returned is not yet obvious to her:

Before I even got inside the apartment I could smell the junkyard odors: old oil and grease and rusting metal. And what I could see in the half dark was worse than what I smelled. I stepped over the piles of junk, old toasters and radio parts, old antennas—dumpster quality, all of it. Something crunched underfoot but I moved on, not caring what I destroyed. The living room was an even bigger junkyard. There was a bare bulb hanging over an old coat rack. In that strange factory light, everything looked dirty and grimy and completely useless. It was a disaster area. Screws and wires and lampshades, the shells of clocks, a bowling ball. But in the middle of all of it was Leon in the American President Lines coveralls, holding a wire coat hanger over a flaming torch. . . . I saw the large metal Singer machine on the floor by Leon's feet. It was all taken apart. On its side like that, it looked like the head of a horse. . . . Mah hardly used the thing anymore. . . . and I didn't like seeing Mah's machine in pieces all over the floor. (96–97)

There is much more here than meets the unreliable narrator's eyes, however. When Leon rejected his wife's reconciliation attempt before her departure for Hong Kong, Mah in her fury had purposely run the old sewing machine without material in it and broken it. The hidden significance of the machine is that Mah had learned to sew from her lover, Tommie Hom, owner of the sewing factory where she had worked for many years. She had risen to become his head seamstress and had grown so talented with the needle that she had reached the level of artistry. By sewing for others, as well as sewing everything necessary for the family's needs, she had earned some of the family income. Now, with her children grown and out, she sells her own creations from her own shop, The Baby Store.

To Leon, the sewing machine and his wife's connection with it always served as endless reminders to him of who it was who had taught her to sew in the first place, of what had grown between his wife and that man thereafter, of

Leon's "green hat" [of his being a cuckold]. Now that he has left her, Mah has purposely broken the machine, a very significant action to Leon. His wife is finally declaring her preference for him. Leon tells Lei when she is expressing her upset at his having taken it apart that the sewing machine is "Broken. I fix him for Mah. Be the surprise" (97). She has not the slightest clue that this action on his part is Leon's reconciliation gesture to his wife. In fact, she is so upset that Mason has to calm her down:

"Hey, stop it."
"The machine's a wreck," I said.
"He's fixing it."
"No one's touched it for years!"
"He's got a week. Let him have his space."
I sure wasn't going to clean up after him this time. I gave Mason a look and said, "I hope you're good with sewing machines." (99)

When she returns from Hong Kong, Mah asks for Leon in Chinese and shows Lei "the new watch she'd bought for him. A fancy, black-faced, many-dialed diver's watch." She then informs Lei that " 'This one works' " (99). In other words, she too wants a reconciliation, and is making a subtle gesture to her husband to indicate this. In fact, Mah has always been the conciliatory one. It is Leon who has been difficult, and with reason. But now with no prodding from his children, with no excuses, Leon concedes. Note Myenne Ng's use of casually phrased but subtly crafted lines to reveal the enormous significance of his conduct:

Maybe Mason was right. I worried too much. Not only did Leon fix the Singer, he polished it. And he pointed one of his lamps at the dark body so that it looked sinister in a bright, shining way. The old floors looked scrubbed and the kitchen and bathroom were so Clorox clean they smelled like the YMCA pool. Leon was clean too, freshly shaved. He was wearing self-ironed dress slacks for the occasion. (100)

All this, in great contrast to the way we have seen Leon live at the San Fran with his tinkering incompletions. In fact, all this is Leon's love letter to his wife, his offer of reconciliation, of a new beginning. Nowhere in the work is the contrast between the traditional training of the Chinese male and the movement forward into shedding that training made more clear than in these lines. Not only does Leon symbolically re-tie the marriage bonds by fixing the symbol of Mah's adultery and self-sufficiency, he cleans their home and himself, something unheard of for traditional Chinese males. It cannot be stressed too much what "a major upheaval" (Yogi 1992, 148) in traditional Asian male-female gender roles Myenne Ng here describes in Leon's actions—all performed in silence. Truly, Leon here "defamiliarizes patriarchal practices by reversing sex roles" (Cheung, 1993, 101), as does Lei's husband Mason Louie who is passive and waits patiently for her for so long.

On the surface Mah and Leon assume their culture's prescribed conduct for an old married couple, but Lei's naive description inadvertently exposes their inner anxieties about each other. They don't say a "formal hello, they just kind of bumped into each other. Leon looked a little shy, Mah, a little scared" (100). They then proceed to go into "a long gossip ritual about the relations. . . . I couldn't follow all this Hong Kong talk. . . . It didn't matter who these people were. Mah and Leon seemed to enjoy talking about their problems almost as if realizing that other people had problems cheered them up. Strange medicine" (100).

"Ritual" is the key word here. The couple is doing a ritual ceremonial approximating everyday typical couple talk after returning from a trip, which actually signals to one another that they are recommitting themselves to their marriage. The facade, "the bone" (of cont[v]ention) remains in terms of their adhering to the surface details of their ancient traditions. But within that context—superficial adherence to the conventional—they conceal the transformation in their relationship to the outside world but not from each other. They do this in order to save face, to make it appear outwardly as if the relationship is still gender asymmetrical.

Additionally, next to the sewing machine, Leon has placed Ona's ashes which rest in a brass urn on a card table where he has made an altar with two teacups, one containing rice, the other water. "He'd found a way to live with his grief. I could hear him say, Side by side, the sad with the happy" (102). Here Leon's revision of the traditional Chinese altar for the dead is reminiscent of Winnie's transformation of the Kitchen God's altar, also done privately. Surely we have gone full circle when a man is represented as "cleaning [his] house" and revising the traditional mourning symbolism for a lost daughter, if only privately and without making public waves.

ONA'S RESPONSE TO GENDER ASYMMETRY AND ITS ALLEGORICAL MEANING

Finally at this point Myenne Ng gives us a sense of Ona. Of the three daughters, Ona had been the most attached to Leon. When he was at sea she would count off each day until he returned. She would stand "at the mouth of the alley, counting the cabs that went by. Every night that Leon was gone, she'd count out ninety-nine kisses to keep him safe, to bring him back" (90). Not only is she by birth the middle girl, but she literally as well as allegorically is put in the middle in terms of her response to traditional gender asymmetry. "Ona wanted to be equally divided about her loyalties to Mah and Leon. But in the end Ona felt disappointed by Leon and betrayed by Mah. Why hadn't Leon seen his selfishness? Why hadn't Mah come to Ona's defense?" (119).

Here Rimonte on domestic violence is again useful in reading Mah's response, that of the reactive, accepting gatekeeper, the unconscious perpetuator of domestic violence and abuse. For one thing, the Asian American woman's male partner comes from the same group to which she would ordinarily turn. Secondly, this group, comprised of relatives and community, have shared beliefs about appropriate conduct for men and women. For these reasons, they do not encourage an abused woman to take the necessary steps toward improving her situation (Rimonte 1989, 330). If they do support her, they often cannot shelter or support her or even appear to do so because "community gatekeepers are interested in maintaining the status quo in order to preserve the culture." Rimonte blames religious authorities because they indoctrinate women into obedience, into accepting individual solutions "for the sake of peace," which again replicates gender asymmetry in ideological terms. She suggests a shelter for these women, while doubting that many of them would take advantage of it because, according to her, they would be frightened by the unknown and have been trained to feel comfortable only in the home. She answers the question of whether abuse and violence would not be more frightening to them than strange surroundings by reasoning that as a result of their training they lack the imagination, the initiative, the capacity to leave an abusive situation, preferring what they know, even if that includes "the certainty of abuse" (Rimonte 1989, 331).[5] For the man, his woman's departure is "a diminution of his status," a loss of face. For the woman, the idea that has choice over whether or not she is a victim "is to challenge the view by which she has always lived, to wit, that as an individual she does not count for very much and that only her roles and functions within the family have any value" (Rimonte 1989, 334–335).

Rimonte makes another interesting point about why abused women return to and/or remain with their spouses, which bears out Myenne Ng's position on the over determined inscription for women regarding the nature of appropriate conduct for them. These women still somehow believe that their children need their father as an authority figure; incredibly, this was one of the primary motivations for their remaining in relationship with their men (Rimonte 1989, 331). Extending this model out into the planet, we can see that in culture after culture a male rules and continues to rule in private and in public, to some extent because women see this set-up as the best and most appropriate family model. As they perceive the men in their family—both in their birth family and later on in families they create—so they perceive government in all institutions. Men should be and are in control, as well as being the source of power and authority. Women and children are to be dominated and subordinate.

Myenne Ng abstracts this world view in Lei's case as her parents' "dependence" on her. This self-imposed burden does not lead to a sense of intolerable inner divisiveness for her, at least not for a long time. On the other hand, Leon, who is the repository and recipient of all the power, begins to feel increasingly that it is "an uncomfortable power, too much control" (119). Ona, the believer, has a "need for them which destroyed her" (119). She felt "betrayed that no one came to her rescue about Osvaldo, that she had to suffer the blame for Ong & Leong's failure" (139). She and Osvaldo, the son of the Ongs, with whom her parents had opened a laundry, had fallen in love during that period. When Luciano Ong had irresponsibly caused the bankruptcy and loss of the laundry, Leon would not forgive the betrayal and took it out on Ona and Osvaldo, the Ongs' son. In Osvaldo he created the repository for the rage he felt about the senior Ong's betrayal of his trust. Frustrated, Leon casts about to hurt everyone around him at the point of their greatest vulnerability, just as Ona had hurt him by continuing her relationship with the Ongs by choosing their son. He blames his wife for the whole relationship with Ong, since it had begun with herself and a friend from the sewing factory, Rosa Ong, the wife of Luciano and the mother of Osvaldo. " 'Your fault. Women's talk, sewing-lady gossip' " (170).

But tragically, he finally turns on Ona in an attempt to vent somewhere, any-where, as close to Luciano Ong as he can, demanding that his daughter "break up with Osvaldo. " 'I forbid you to see that mongrel boy. Crooked father, crooked son' " (172). He thus projects his humiliation and disappointment out on Ona, making her into the pawn between Luciano Ong and himself. Believing him—it is her belief and trust in the patriarchy that causes her "downfall"—she obedi-ently forces herself to break off with Osvaldo when Leon blackmails her with the threat to disown her. In turn, this leads to her taking her life. All because "[s]addled with time-honored prejudice, words have a way of perpetuating patri-archal ideology" (Cheung 1993, 133).

But Leon didn't mean his outward reversion to the traditional father role. He was bluffing: " '[E]ither him or me. . . .' 'You will be disowned, no longer my daughter if you remain with the man I forbid you to go with.' " These are all culturally available clichés for fathers which Leon only mouths in his frustration at having been humiliated and made bankrupt by the partner he had trusted. He takes this route in a vain effort to strike back at his former partner, because he had no recourse in the courts (none of the deal was made in writing); no recourse against Ong who had beaten him up when he confronted him; no recourse but to vent through Ona and through Luciano Ong's son, Ona's beloved, Osvaldo Ong

The trouble is that Ona takes her father at his word. She feels so trapped in the no-win, no-way-out situation in which he places her that she kills herself to end the stalemate within her. She can't live without either man, tied equally by her love for each of them. She does not realize that Leon is all bluster, that his bark is louder than his bite. What Ona, who believes in the Father, who swal-lows the party line, so to speak, never understands is that when Leon threatens her he is pretending for the moment (like Maxine's father in *The Woman War-rior* and *China Men*) to recuperate "the father's worn-out desire to return to male privilege and centric heroism. . . . The desire to employ masculine heroic tac-tics" (Goellnicht 1992, 204). Torn between the demands of the old and the pos-sibilities of the present, Ona is paralyzed, cannot go forward into life, or is unwilling to do so, and therefore does not survive.

In this way, Myenne Ng conveys to her readers that only when men and women, both in the family and in the group, are willing to reject acculturation into gender asymmetry can they continue to survive. Ona was so equally divided in loyalties between her father and her lover (and all they each represented in terms of cultural constructions) that she could not solve the equation. Ona did not fall free when she fell down from a great height to her death. In falling down to death, Ona is simultaneously obeying the injunctions of gender asymmetry (erasure of the disobedient female), as well as attempting to defy it by going to a

great height first before she falls to her doom in order to destroy herself for de-
fying it. Thus she acquiesces to the Father, making Him right by not flying, by
not remaining alive and living her own life, as Nina does. To have lived out a
life of success and personal fulfillment in the face of Leon's disowning her
would prove him wrong, which Nina, again unlike Ona, is willing to do. Had
she done so, Ona would then fly high endlessly without ever falling to where the
Father decrees she belongs: at the bottom. Onas are female Daedaluses; Ninas
fly free; Leis syncretize.

LEI'S RESPONSE TO ONA'S DEATH AND ITS ALLEGORI-
CAL MEANING

The final questions for Lei reside in whether or not she and the rest of the
family will succeed in getting off their respective guilt trips; whether the narrator
will succeed in her effort to stop giving too much of herself to her parents;
whether she will ever realize that she deserves to have her own life; whether she
will learn to live her own life and have her own relationship through distin-
guishing her sense of self from her mother and her mother's marriage to   Leon;
whether she will be able to leave her obligations and responsibilities of the past
to her mother and stepfather and leave them be, even if they suffer, live together,
or apart; whether her "hovering" in a holding pattern is healthy for all concerned.
And what does she owe to the present—to her husband Mason Louie—who is
always there for her? She doesn't even yet live with him. She is still watching
over her mother and caring for her and Leon, for her "Bone." On the surface,
these predicaments are individual and specific, but they are simultaneously
global and allegorical because they are all provoked by gender asymmetry historically and in the present.

Myenne Ng ascribes to Lei the vocation of "a consultant," in which she acts
as a bridge between the classroom teacher and the parents: "getting the parents
involved, opening up a line of communication." This profession projects Lei's
basic personality trait of thinking of others rather than herself, of "selfhood as
relational and identity as the product of commitment to shared accountability"
(Lapidus 1993, 25). Myenne Ng thus creates Lei as a living embodiment of the
"ethics of caring" (Gilligan 1982). This common attitude shared by many
women everywhere is culturally constructed. Myenne Ng believes that it is culturally inscribed in Lei's "bones" so that it has become second nature to her to
give to others to the point of not having her own private life. The author represents her character as like many women globally—constructed and situated as a
bridge—always pulled between one set of obligations and another.

Throughout *Bone*, Myenne Ng shows Lei as seeking a balance, not from the
weight of excess ego as is common in the *bildungsroman* tradition, but from the
opposite end of the human character continuum, from a superfluity of lack of
ego. It could be said, in fact, that the literature of most contemporary Asian
American women (as well as women writers globally) is about the internal quest
of a woman to learn to live and love for herself, to break the bonds of

"caregiving" (Mukherjee 1991, 214) and at the same time to give to herself as well as to others, despite her cultural training. In marked contrast, for most traditional heroes, the problem is set in terms of learning through chastening life experiences how to subdue the demands of the ego.

Now after feminism, the narrator Lei defines a woman's family responsibilities (what would have made sense before feminism) as irrelevant, what she terms "out-of-context." At first, Lei only meditates about "moving back to the alley because Mah couldn't stand living with the question: What could have saved Ona? The blame is what I can't live with: the fear is what I can't get away from" (46). That is, she fears that she may have been responsible, a fear that each family member seems to be living with, except Nina who has chosen to distance herself geographically and psychically and is doubly estranged from the family.

In spite of this, Nina's postfeminist solution is not the solution Myenne Ng would advocate for the problem, but one that will ultimately include what Lei works out. At this point, Lei is still guilt-ridden for not having been there for her sister when perhaps it might have made the crucial difference: "I ask over and over again: If I'd been living on the Alley, could I have had that talk with Ona? If I'd been living on the Alley, would I have said the right word?" (46). She feels that Ona is a mix of Nina and herself and that that was "a dangerous mix"; that "I should have known, that I should've said something that might have anchored her" (51). As the embodiment of "ethics of caring" and like (all) her (fore)mother(s), Lei blames herself: "I want to open my arms wide as a firemen's net; I want to sweep over her whole life and comb out all the sadness that made her do it. Like Leon and Mah, I went over every moment I had with Ona and tried to find my own moment of failure" (106). At the time of Ona's suicide, Lei had been living with her lover Mason Louie and was therefore unavailable to Ona.

How far do family obligations go before we get trapped by them, before we no longer retain our sense of self? Myenne Ng seems to inquire, as if in conversation with Tan's *The Joy Luck Club*. She is showing Lei as at this point possessed of too much compunction, too much self-assumed responsibility for the terrible loss. An undue sense of responsibility for Ona's death and her feeling that she is in a no-win, no-way-out trap as mediator between her parents are the causes of Lei's recurrent back pains. Some illumination, aided by Nina, has to distance her because she believes that "Nina had the best attitude. Leon's problems were his and Mah's were hers, and she hated Chinatown and she was getting out" (170). True to her postfeminist perspective, Nina advises Lei to "Let it go. . . . Ona had her own life. It was her choice" (51).

As long as Lei is caught in her self-made trap of dutiful giving without reciprocity, her tone of voice is one of suppressed rage and impotence—the voice of the "nag." In this tone she expresses "resentments" toward Nina for "her fast move, her safe distance" and toward Leon for his "madness, his blind lamenting to Confucius, his whole hocus-pocus view of the world." She resents Mah; "her stubborn one-track moaning—crying over Ona who was dead, crying over Nina who was gone. Crying over her two lost daughters. I wanted to shake her and ask. What about me? Don't I count? Don't I matter? There I was, the living present daughter, and Mah was hung up on the other two. I wasn't dead. I wasn't gone" (91).

Lei has to learn to stop being a shadow, to live her own life, before she will be treated as a separate identity. When she tells Mason about the possibility that "if the community-relations position opened up, I might think about it," that it entails, "[G]oing into the homes, talking to parents," he responds wryly, referring to her overly dutiful sense of daughterhood to her parents, that she's "got experience" (96). For example, Mah uses Lei as her unwilling "bridge" to Leon, sending him money and food. Even in her marriage to Mason Louie, Lei's soul is that of a "bridge." She resists telling her mother because she feels that then "she'd have to face her bitterness about her own marriages and that's what I wanted to protect her from. Remembering the bad. Refeeling the mistakes" (12). At the same time, she is torn because she wants to give her own life to herself, as well as to others: "I didn't get married just for a name change. I wanted a marriage of choice. I wanted this marriage to be for me" (18). What she is hoping for is "completion: change . . . to [f]inish one thing before beginning another (108); to bring the mourning, the guilt, "the sadness" to an "ending" (106). Until she understands that Ona had free will, could make a choice, but did not realize it, Lei cannot see the similarity between her predicament and Ona's:

It was being pulled back and forth between Mah and Mason. All that worry about Leon. . . . It was worrying about my new job and parking tickets and the crowds on Stockton Street and seeing Nina in New York. . . . Mah's being alone and Mason's waiting for me. The head part was Ona. That's the thing that was in my head. Everything went back to Ona. And beyond Ona there was the bad luck that Leon kept talking about. What made Ona do it. Like she had no choice. (50)

Lei longs "to forget. The blame. The pressing fear. I wanted a ritual that forgave. I wanted a ritual to forget" (54). Myenne Ng is here insinuating that resort to religious rituals is a waste of time, a distraction, "an opiate." What has Leon's loyalty to the "bones" of his past gotten him in the U.S. of A.? Myenne Ng's clever pun for what it hasn't gotten for him is "social security," which Leon does finally get literally and allegorically. In her effort to help Leon get this "social security," Lei goes through his suitcase and finds that Leon has kept everything. "Leon kept things because he believed time mattered. Old made good." Leon holds on to "everything." In this country, however, whatever move he made he is made to feel "rejected": "from the army, unfit," from "A job . . . unskilled," from "An apartment: [that it is] unavailable" (58), and so on. All his various roles and endeavors in life molder in the American suitcase of rejection. Nevertheless, Leon continues to believe that "this country was his place, too. Leon had paid; Leon had earned his rights. American dollars. American time. These letters marked his time and they marked his endurance. Leon was a paper son" (58).

It is at this point that the allegorical level in this text and these characters is fully revealed and must be confronted. The suitcase contains "the meaning of our past, distorted and omitted by racism, from shreds of stories heard in childhood or from faded photographs that have never been explained" (Kim 1987, 103). The suitcase stands for the inheritance of Asian American men and women in terms of their experiences in this country. All the moldering materials in the suitcase allegorize the "real story" of Asian American immigrant experience. This story was first recorded "from poems carved on the walls of the Angel Island detention center, in pieces written by those close to them and, decades later, by their racial descendants who attempt to piece their story together with fragments of documents, legends, and their own powerful feelings" (Kim 1982, 20).

Myenne Ng's use of the suitcase encompasses both literal predicaments and simultaneously "the bones," that is, tradition, the ancestors. As Lei puts it: "For a paper son, paper is blood" (61). Kim here explains that "Chinese who had been able to establish their American citizenship before 1924 [when the Exclusion Act went into effect], perhaps because their papers had been destroyed during the 1906 San Francisco earthquake, could invite their sons or sell their right to sponsor sons to other non-citizens or ineligible Chinese." From 1924 to 1943, no Chinese born man could get into the United States without first proving that he had an American father. Thus "[y]oung men sponsored under the 'slot racket,' as it was called, are called 'paper sons' " (Kim 1982, 297).

When Lei calls herself in relation to this history "the stepdaughter of a paper son," she is using a significant term allegorically. Leon, though long a despised and rejected part of the ruling regime, is ultimately accepted. This happens once Lei finally discovers what Leon needs to receive his "social security" from the American government—his "affidavit of identification." Leon is finally given and does therefore possess an "affidavit of identification" as one of the sons of The Great White Father, even though he is considered a negligible one. In this respect his stepdaughter is "too much like" him, as her husband Mason points out meaningfully. Lei keeps "everything too, and inside I never let go. I remember everything . . . I never forget." As the stepdaughter of this Chinese American man who got into the hierarchical computer illegally, Lei has "inherited this whole suitcase of lies. All of it is mine. All I have is those memories, and I want to remember them all" (61).

Additionally, in having her character use the term "stepdaughter" Myenne Ng is doing what Hong Kingston did in *China Men*: simultaneously disrupting "Chinese and white patriarchy" by drawing "unspoken parallels between the racist persecution of Chinese male immigrants in America and the traditional subjugation of women by these very men." She thereby "enacts a double political move in braiding racist and sexist abuse. She expands her feminist horizon to include men who have been voiceless in historical records, but she resists subordinating her feminist concerns in the name of nationalism" (Cheung 1993, 25).

It is absolutely necessary to remember "the bones," all the bones from the past that link the "stepdaughters" to their "stepfathers" and their "stepfathers" to "the [Great White] fathers." They bear witness to racial asymmetry as well as gender asymmetry. The historical facts in the suitcase are used by Myenne Ng to resonate historically off the page. Joy Ogawa also uses material in letters in a suitcase about the removal of Japanese Canadian citizens from their homes and subsequent internment in Canadian relocation camps during World War II. Additionally, intertextual with Myenne Ng and Ogawa in this respect, Hong Kingston also uses a suitcase for the same purpose in *Tripmaster Monkey: His Fake Book*, as well as a devastating, deadpan factual historic list in *China Men* of disgraceful U. S. laws in relation to the Chinese. Thus, without any overt comment, all these authors use their material symbolically to indict American and Canadian xenophobia.

CONCLUSION

Nina's unreflexive postmodern postfeminist stance, her privatized, "selfish" solution—leaving it all behind to live her own life—is typical of the traditional Western value system, the "narrowly goal-oriented action aimed at individual redemption" (S. Wong 1988, 22) which is so characteristic of the West and American ideology. Lei tries to mediate and to find her own life, while Ona remains caught up in the tradition's/her father's discourse, believing that his traditional masculinist discourse replicates his feelings and actions. Lei wonders whether there is any "end to it. . . . What makes their ugliness so alive, so thick and impossible to let go of?" and then immediately follows these questions by referring to the gender asymmetrical Chinese traditions that have determined the husband and wife's poses and responses to one another and to everything else.

Myenne Ng believes that underneath the hardened outer masks of cultural constraints, "the bones" that have taught them their way of being, their perspective, are now hollow. Contemporary men and women are acting out parts that no longer fit the reality of the current situation. Myenne Ng provides answers as to how we get men and women to separate themselves from their outmoded, ancient social constructions as represented by Grandpa Leong and his "misplaced" bones: to forego obligations and attachments to "the bones" when they no longer serve or nurture individuals, families, and communities—when they become irrelevant, part of the unusable past. She shows how to distinguish which portion of "the bone" of the past to syncretize with the present. For women like Mah who have (un)intentionally collaborated with the system but no longer wish to do so, she suggests a productive response to their cultural regime. She answers the question for all her characters as to whether they need to continue to collaborate willingly or not, consciously or not, with patriarchy; whether they should kill themselves like Ona, or cut themselves off from it entirely like Nina (whose endless affairs and abortions symbolize Myenne Ng's negative response to this solution); or whether they should somehow "bridge" or syncretize between the different options.

She exposes her preference by ending her text with Lei's solution, to bridge to the past and bring it into the present and then leave it be. Lei finally realizes that Mah does love Leon, which frees her to leave her mother and begin to live with her husband. As she drives off, she looks back at her old home in Salmon Alley. "Like the old timer's photos, Leon's papers and Grandpa Leong's lost bones, it reminded me to look back, to remember" (193). Unlike the resolutions of Ona and Nina, Lei is going to syncretize: going on into her own life to an apartment with her own husband as a community relations specialist while remaining in San Francisco and living in proximity to her "bones"—still ever mindful of them, still available to them. Lei's soul is now that of a "bridge" that spans the community.

The book ends with Lei telling the reader about the dinner celebration after Leon's return from his last voyage before Ona's death. During that voyage Leon had met with Lei's biological father, Mah's first husband, and told him about "'Mah and me.' Leon looked over at Mah, who was busy with a piece of crab" (192). To Lei's anguished questions about herself, he replies: " 'I told him that you'd finished school, stuff like that.' He looked at Mah" again. Tellingly, she gives him some fish, and then in response to Lei's continued clamoring about how the meeting with her father had ended, Leon replies in his characteristic blustering, endearing way: " 'End?' He put the morsel in his mouth. 'What else? Shook hands, said goodbye, long life, and good luck.' " Afterwards, recollecting and reflecting about this seemingly minor incident, Lei finally perceives "what Mason had been saying all along: Mah loved Leon" (193). She finds the sounds of their eating together "comfortable, and for a moment, I was tempted to fall back into the easiness of being Mah's daughter, of letting her be my whole life" (192). But finally realizing that Mah does have Leon, Lei then does let go at last and moves on with her husband, to leave Salmon Alley, including "Mah and Leon—everything—backdaire" (193).

As long as Lei, the hovering, concerned daughter—the conscious, concerned feminist—feels that her mother (traditional woman) is trapped and mistreated in a gender asymmetrical relationship—so long will she suspend her own flight to self-fulfillment and remain grounded with her mother. Only when she realizes that her mother truly has her own separate life from hers, that she is willingly in relationship with Leon, and that Leon is capable of and actually does move on to greater equality in relationship, does Lei distance herself to lead her own life, but not too far away. Unlike Nina, Lei will still hover in flight nearby.

Myenne Ng thus establishes her distinction between the feminist who leaves the past behind when it is appropriate, and only after much soul-searching, and the postfeminist who ignores it by fleeing it entirely. Lei is not going away to turn separatist and to solve problems as an individual for herself alone, as Nina, the postmodern postfeminist does. For Nina, "Leon's problems were his and Mah's were hers, and she hated Chinatown [traditional training] and she was getting out" (172). Whereas Tan ends both *The Joy Luck Club* and *The Kitchen God's Wife* with the bridging concept between mothers and daughters, Myenne Ng sees such a stage as preliminary. Bridging the generations, she feels, is too strenuous. It causes suffering. It demands too much giving up of one's own life, as signified in the beginning of the work by Lei's separating herself from Mason to return to the family apartment to hover over her mother. In contrast, in the end Lei will stay nearby as a loving witness to the past, but at a remove. Her over-solicitous attitude has changed. She no longer sees herself as having to be a bridge, a mediator between tradition-bound husband and wife, incapable of moving out and onward.

The "bone" of the title ultimately means "memories." Remembering the past gives power to the present to leave the past, "the bone," "backdaire." Memories do add up. "Our memories can't bring back Grandpa Leong" (the traditional past) "or Ona" (the casualty of that past who didn't make it past the present) "back, but they count to keep them from becoming strangers" (89). Myenne Ng's solution to gender asymmetry builds on Hong Kingston's and Tan's: to accept the previous generations; to understand where they stand; to see the differences without upset. One must remember and never let go of tradition, memories, history, "the bone," the past. One must also accept that it has died and turned to dust and go on.

NOTES

1. See "The Cricket," "Social Connections," and "The Golden Toothpick" for examples, in Roberts (1979), 6, 73, 150. An identical predicament is noted in a real-life letter "typical of the many expressing anxiety about parental or other forms of interference with freedom of choice in marriage" (Hsu 1981, 52). Also, buildings do not traditionally include a thirteenth floor.

2. From the Chinese perspective, Nina is considered a prostitute by her parents, rather than a liberated woman. As "a distinguished visitor to the United States from Taiwan" put it, according to Hsu, such "girls" who think they are "emancipated and equal with men" have "in reality . . . become objects of public recreation" (Hsu 1981, 57). Whose "reality" is "reality"? The men's, or the "girls," or both? Hsu does not question the "distinguished visitor's" assumption that the male "reality" is the sole "reality." Therefore, presumably, the "girls' " "reality" does not exist, only the males' "reality."

3. It may be recalled that Nina here raises the same issue that Tan resolved in *The Joy Luck Club* and *The Kitchen God's Wife* when she moved the daughters toward historical understanding of their mothers' contradictory qualities.

4. Note that Leon's tastes in narrative discourse are similar to the anonymous mother's in R. A. Sasaki's *The Loom*, as well as those of the gatekeepers in Chinese American literature. As discussed in the previous chapter, all these characters are reinforcing the morality tales by which they had been trained in their childhood.

5. When I worked in a battered women's shelter, I was frustrated by the large numbers of women who left prematurely to return to their husbands. It was too difficult, too late, these women claimed, to change the grooves of their training and experiences. This bears out Rimonte's point, as well as mine. The problem of gender asymmetry is global, because the system of patriarchy is global, as well as local and specific.

Chapter 3

Gish Jen, *Typical American:*
The Rise and Fall and Rise
of the House of Chang

Slavoj Zizek makes a distinction between "imaginary" and "symbolic" identification. According to him, "imaginary identification is identification with the image in which we appear likable to ourselves, with the image representing 'what we would like to be,' and symbolic identification, identification with the very place from where we are being observed, from where we look at ourselves so that we appear to ourselves likable, worthy of love" (Zizek 1989, 105). The questions he asks that relate to Jen's meaning when she uses the term "typical American" are "for whom is the subject enacting this role? Which gaze is considered when the subject identifies himself [*sic*] with a certain image?" (Zizek 1989, 106). In the chapter that follows, I will address Zizek's questions in terms of what Jen's use of the term "typical American" signifies and from whose perspective. I will analyze the major characters as created in relation to the concept of the "typical American." This group is depicted as all in the process of becoming "Americanized" or "typical American." They each concern themselves with the issue of what is and what is not "typical American." In doing so, they serve as vehicles for Jen's project to address herself to the American success mythology in relation to a group of immigrant Chinese in the United States immediately after World War II.

THE "TYPICAL AMERICAN?"

Ralph Chang

Jen's major character is (Li Feng) Ralph Chang. Jen traces his life trajectory from his birth and early youth in China to his rise, followed by failure and then by a (different) rise again. Ralph achieves tenure as an assistant professor of mechanical engineering at an East Coast university (Columbia?). When he is tempted to abandon academia for the lure of the "profit motive," the "making it big" aspect of the American dream, he nearly loses everything in life that he cherishes. This plot outline seems influenced by Henry James's *The American* (1877) and even more so by William Dean Howells's *The Rise of Silas Lapham* (1884). Both Christopher (as in Columbus) Newman—what is "the typical American" if not a new man?—and Silas Lapham end up suffering financial and personal setbacks, but become "refined" ethically. Both James and his friend Howells represent their characters as evolving in terms of "natural nobility." Influenced by Rousseau's idealization of "the noble savage," they projected for white lower class American men *sui generis* a natural, inborn capacity and a loftier sense of ethics than any European, Native American, other ethnic men and men of color, or anyone else on earth, in fact. Through reversals of their earlier naive expectations, they are purified and rise spiritually, and Ralph is cast in their mold.

In *Typical American*, whoever and whatever is "typical American" is not ultimately the issue, as much as how its pursuit disempowers Chinese American men and women. Even more sadly, whether they become Americanized or not, women collude in their own disempowerment, both in terms of Chinese mainland traditions and Western customs. This being the case, the question arises as to whether Ralph is meant by Jen to be the "typical American." The first lines would certainly lead us to think so. "It's an American story," Jen begins sardonically. "Before he was a thinker, or a doer, or an engineer, much less an imagineer like his self-made-millionaire friend Grover Ding, Ralph Chang was just a small boy in China, struggling to grow up his father's son" (3). In this statement, Jen encapsulates her opinion of the Chinese immigrant pursuit of "the American dream," of becoming "typical American" in terms of materialistic consumerism, as contrasted to traditional Chinese values.

Before he ever gets hooked by the negative aspects of the American dream, Ralph tries to emulate his mandarin father who is successful on three counts—as an "upright scholar" and as an "ex-government official" (4) who also owns "the only car in town" (3). The importance of the car as symbol for male success, both in Chinese and American culture, can be seen throughout this work.[1] It is the ultimate masculine dream machine. It is used for joy rides to materialist orgies and as a consumerist icon in terms of women, much as Tan used it in *The Kitchen God's Wife* when Wen Fu runs over and kills a girl whom he has invited out for a joy ride. Ralph ultimately runs over his sister with a car he uses as a vehicle to dominate women.

In keeping with his basic characteristic of being "Intent on the Peak," Ralph describes himself as "a man with a mission" (11), originally to do what is "right" as a student. Even before his arrival in the United States, while on the boat, Ralph composes a list of virtues to guide his career objectives, first as a student and then as a professor. Ralph's list is a parody of Benjamin Franklin's *Autobiography* (1791) and Jay Gatsby's in F. Scott Fitzgerald's *The Great Gatsby* (1925). In order to reach his objective, Ralph, like Franklin and Gatsby, essentializes projects of self-improvement and transcendence as masculine activities. These exclude women as The Other, an obstacle in a man's way. Also, as with

Emerson's and Thoreau's Transcendental discourse, Franklin's, Fitzgerald's, and Ralph's creates a binary dichotomy between masculine efforts at success and earth-bound, frivolous, irrelevant females. In Ralph's words: "I will on no account have anything to do with girls" (6).

Because his father had requested him to make his brilliant older sister Theresa his model, "observing everything she does, and simply copy her" (4), Ralph's feelings for her become a complex mix of humiliation, envy, resentment, and competitiveness intermingled with love. He calls her "know it all" and wishes that he could have been his sister, or that Theresa could have been a man. In other words, had she been Ralph's brother, gifted with the same qualities as Theresa, his father's admonition would not have insulted him. For the rest of his life, Ralph never misses an opportunity to invalidate Theresa as a woman: her size (5'7" compared to his 5'3"); her big feet ("that entered rooms before she did"); and her walk ("like a man because she used to play baseball . . . with her father's permission") (47).

One of the stereotypical qualities of Americans that Jen depicts Ralph as buying into whole-heartedly is his enthusiasm for self-improvement fads. When reviewers of *Typical American* laud Jen's acerbic humor in her use of such postmodern techniques as punning, pastiche, and paradox mingled with "wise cracks" and common Chinese sayings, the elements in Ralph's character that lend themselves to these devices are no doubt uppermost in their minds.

Jen's seemingly playful humor is in reality bleak, used to mock and deplore the degradation of two great philosophies. Whenever she meditates on the American appropriation and debasement of inspirational spiritual experience for materialistic ends, whenever individual self-fulfillment and self-aggrandizement are pursued at the expense of one's interconnected obligations to family and community, Jen employs this technique. By this means she exposes both the perversion of the ideals traditionally identified with "the American founding fathers" and the Transcendentalists, as well as those of Ralph's Confucian fathers. According to Jen, traditional American and Chinese values have deteriorated into an efflorescence of consumerist materialism characteristic of the postwar period in the United States, the years covered in her text. Jen employs Dale Carnegie's and Norman Vincent Peale's teachings to illustrate the degeneration of Emersonian Transcendentalism. When his thesis adviser gives him a copy of *How to Win Friends and Influence People* (1936) by Carnegie, Ralph is galvanized into "believing he could do anything!" From this key text he goes on to many others of a like nature, such as "*Making Money. Be Your Own Boss! Ninety Days to Power and Success*" (198), titles that resonate off Carnegie's text and Norman Vincent Peale's *The Power of Positive Thinking* (1952).[2]

The traditional Chinese dinner set up by Janis Chao in Helen's and Janis's aborted effort to match Theresa with Grover Ding provides Jen with the opportunity for a take-off on Ralph (as well as Helen, Ralph's wife) that is intertextual with Shakespeare's comedy of errors in *A Midsummer Night's Dream*. It is Ralph who first "stepped forward, as though to be presented" to Grover. Moonstruck, he completely forgets that it is Theresa, his sister, whom Grover is there to meet, not himself: "Head tilted, mouth slack, [Ralph] looked for all the world like someone in love" (95), Jen tells us, describing Ralph's infatuation for American material success mythology in the person of the rich American-born entrepreneur and quintessential "con man," Grover Ding, who will nearly undo Ralph and his family. Jen ironically labels this chapter "Love at first sight," reminiscent of Shakespeare's lucid re-formulation of couples in *A Midsummer Night's Dream.* Not only does Jen's title reflect Ralph's attraction to Grover, it also reflects Old Chao's' to Theresa, as well as Grover's inappropriate reaction to Helen, Ralph's wife, who is far gone in pregnancy. Such a reaction foreshadows what readers will later learn about him—that he is amoral and does not even attempt to conceal it by appearing to abide by ordinary civilized codes of conduct in public. He winks three times at Helen broadly with "a gleam in his eye" (93) and in a "rakish" manner. But when Helen proves unresponsive, Grover then "simply turned and winked once more, at Ralph" (96). Later in the evening, he commandeers both Old Chao's new car and Ralph. Even the colors of nature hint at Grover's Satanic, infernal referentiality:

He [Ralph] was captive. What could he do but watch Grover drive? Ahead the moongate stretched wide, just as a cloud cover lowered itself out of nowhere. Lower, lower. It hovered above them like an attic ceiling. The town ahead, squashed, became all broad, bright horizon; and when the clouds went gold, it seemed to Ralph that the buildings kindled violently. Such live reds and oranges! And now, as though on cue, it all turned—in an instant—to writhing cinder. Ralph felt smoldery himself. Yet Grover drove through the whole grand catastrophe undistracted, as though the torching of a place simply did not matter to him, or as though it were no more than some histrionics he'd ordered up. Background, say, for some large drama. (100–101)

Grover is driving the captivated, ensnared Ralph into hell. He tempts Ralph where he is most vulnerable: through his tendency to "instability, divergence, distraction": all that the Confucian ideal of balance, order, and harmony militates against. When Jen writes that "they were driving through forest" the reader may resonate with the echoes of Dante's opening lines to *The Inferno*, where Dante's persona enters the tangled forest of his life's errors. These lines are also intertextual with Hawthorne's "Young Goodman Brown" (1835) (itself influenced by *The Inferno*) in the passage where Goodman emerges from his first venture into the forest, already corrupted by curiosity and doubt. As Helen puts it, Ralph returns from his wild ride "ungrounded." Ralph (like Young Goodman Brown and so many other "typical Americans") has sold his soul to the devil in Jen's eyes. This is revealed when Grover stops at a roadside restaurant, which we later discover he owns. Here he mockingly leads Ralph in a wild orgy of gluttony:

They had dinner, then lunch, then breakfast. . . . "Nobody eats a burger naked." He [Grover] piled on top [of Ralph's hamburger] ketchup, mustard, relish, a tomato slice from his own cheeseburger super deluxe, a few rings of onion, five french fries . . . and when Grover ordered a black-and-white ice cream soda, Ralph shyly did too. And when Grover ordered a fried clam plate and a Salisbury steak, just for fun, Ralph ordered a list of side dishes—onion rings, potato salad, coleslaw. Plus a chocolate milkshake. "What the heck," said Grover approvingly. Ralph laughed. They ate at whim, taking a bite here, a bite there. When their table was full of plates, they moved to another one, where they ordered desserts—apple pie, cherry pie. Black forest cake. Ralph groaned. "I'm full." Grover roared, "I say we order more!" "Nonono," Ralph protested, thinking, fleetingly, Typical American wasteful. But when Grover ordered bacon and eggs, Ralph did too. It was a game. French toast. English muffins. German pancakes. (102–103)

This is reminiscent of the famous scene in Henry Fielding's *Tom Jones* (1749), when Tom is seduced by the prostitute after foreplay with a gargantuan meal, except that Jen creates a triangle with Grover the seducer having violent sex with "the waitress" afterwards in the kitchen, to which Ralph is forced to listen. Indeed, Jen always accompanies seduction scenes with the wolfing down of fattening, greasy American food. Grover, of course, shows no appreciation for the traditional Chinese feast which Janis has prepared earlier that evening with such care. To be fair, Jen does reveal that the Chinese feast is also a glutton's delight. When in the mood, as here, Jen will call a plague down on both houses, equally. For the most part, however, she represents Chinese culture and customs as superior to American ones. Food associated with the United States, especially restaurant and fast food, always stands for the sins of material greed and lust associated with the temptations of hell:

Meanwhile, in the darkest booth of a deli, over double cheeseburgers with everything, Grover was chummily confiding how he'd been wrongly charged with burying barrels of stolen grease. . . . Ralph ordered another double cheeseburger. Grover lit a cigarette. . . . It had been his error of judgment, Grover explained (over a quadruple-decker club sandwich deluxe), to have once done business with the lunatic owner of a fried chicken takeout counter, who now claimed to have had his grease stolen several times. (188, 189, 192)

One day, Theresa, happening into her brother's home office finds "an entire wall of it papered with inspirational quotes" whose purpose is materialistic, not spiritual: "ALL RICHES BEGIN IN AN IDEA./ WHAT YOU CAN CONCEIVE, YOU CAN ACHIEVE./ DON'T WAIT FOR YOUR SHIP TO COME IN, SWIM OUT TO IT./ FOLLOW THE HERD, YOU END UP A COW./ YOU CAN NEVER HAVE RICHES IN GREAT QUANTITY UNLESS YOU WORK YOURSELF INTO A WHITE HEAT OF DESIRE FOR MONEY" (199). Theresa's first reaction is that these are very much "like cheng yu—idiomatic sayings, the Chinese had a lot of them too. . . . But no, these were different" (198), she realizes sadly. Jen then describes Ralph's fall in terms of its being a shocking violation of the Confucian veneration for scholarship when Theresa wonders where "the Ph.D." was that her brother had "worked so hard for. Helen had taken it to a special place to have it framed, Theresa recalled. Now it languished on a high shelf, under a box full of cash register tapes" (199). Ralph "Yifeng—intent on the peak" (4) in the spiritual sense is now buried under "cash register tapes."

Under Grover's influence, Ralph takes a leave of absence as a professor and enters into a deal with him to purchase a fried chicken franchise. Its current owner is threatening to expose Grover as head of a criminal ring that has been stealing barrels of waste lard placed outside restaurants. But Ralph chooses to ignore this warning. Instead, he passes on his new-found convictions to his girls: "Got to keep eye on the big picture. . . . And you know what's the important thing in this country? . . . Money. In this country, you have money, you can do anything. You have no money, you are nobody. You are Chinaman! Is that simple" (199). His "money worship," as Theresa disapprovingly puts it to herself, causes him to turn dishonest. With Grover's coaching and constant prodding, he daily takes the proceeds from the store and "[e]very night he rang, rang, rang, making a new register tape to replace the tape for the day" (201).

Ralph's philosophy and experiences, his life trajectory, represent the perverted extension into the middle twentieth century of that philosophy of which Jen considers Ralph Waldo Emerson to have been the "typical" exponent. Ralph's schoolmate and later colleague, Old Chao, whose Anglicized name is Henry, has a love-hate relationship with Ralph, much as Henry David Thoreau had with Ralph Waldo Emerson. Ironically, where Thoreau and Emerson once used Transcendentalism as a powerful argument against money grubbing, Ralph now manipulates Transcendentalism, as well as his Confucian training, to justify and rationalize it.

Jen describes Ralph as if from within his ruminating consciousness and only enters into the thought processes of those characters who orbit around Ralph, primarily his wife Helen and his sister Theresa. Jen thus creates "polyglossia" in Bakhtin's (1986) sense of the term: the addition of multiple perspectives through the use of different voices, which adds dimension to this tale of a Chinese immigrant family's quest to "Americanize." Through the use of a concatenation of voices, paradox, and ambiguity, as well as in her descriptions of the pivotal character of Grover Ding, Jen juxtaposes Chinese values with the term "typical American." She also provides alternate additions to traditional mainstream meanings of the term "typical American." Ralph and the other characters, recent immigrants, gradually become bicultural, gradually syncretize. Only Grover, born in the United States, has lost his "Chineseness" altogether and become a "typical American." Significantly, he cannot speak Chinese and has no familiarity with or use for things Chinese. But Jen's caustic, mock-heroic tone distances her alike from the characters whose ruminations she exposes and those whom she describes, like Grover. To be "typical American," Jen reveals, primarily through Theresa's thoughts, decent Asian-born immigrants do not repudiate their ancestral inheritance and mimic native-born citizens. By linking their private birth repertoire with the received public one, they imbibe the external characteristics of Americanness. However, once this complex interchange gets under way, it is impossible for the influence not to go in both directions, to become syncresis. Thus, "typical American" becomes Chinese American (or indeed any and all hyphenated American) interpellations into the stereotypes inherent in the semiotics of "typical American." As Maxine in *The Woman Warrior* points out, it is very difficult to separate the strands: "Chinese Americans, when you try to understand what things in you are Chinese, how do you separate what is peculiar to childhood, to poverty, insanities, one family, your mother who marked your growing with stories, with what is Chinese? What is Chinese tradition and what is the movies?" (6)

In all this, on the surface it is difficult to ascertain whether feminist theory comes into play at all; whether Jen's notion of "typical American" is linked in any way with gender asymmetry; whether she represents it as an issue, as an essential ingredient of the component elements of that complex that comprises "typical American"; whether she conceptualizes gender asymmetry as irrelevant, even nonexistent in terms of the concept "typical American[ness]." The odds are, however, that Jen's cluster of meanings around the term "typical American" is not just one more example of traditional masculinist discourse in the service of "the cultural regime," as the book blurbs would have it. Never have I seen so many blurbs introducing a novel that place so much emphasis on its treatment of "the American dream."[4] Reading them, one would think that gender asymmetry has nothing to do with "the immigrant experience," or with anything at all in this text, despite the fact that the term "typical American" is in fact traditionally used as descriptive of a singular male, and Jen's major character is a male. It remains for Amy Ling to question what it means when Jen and other women writers choose to "cross the gender barrier" (Ling 1990, 142) in order to assume the perspective of their male characters. My question here is related to Ling's—that is, whether any review writer felt the least bit wary about so seemingly gender neutral a title as *Typical American* when used by a Chinese American woman writer.

In Jen's text, both male and female immigrants mock certain aspects of Americanness from their Chinese perspective, yet at the same time they all still struggle day and night to conform to what they each think of as being "typical American." To them, at bottom, "everything modern, new, different came to signify the West" (Mutman 1993, 182). Since the group of characters orbiting around Ralph includes female characters, what they see as desirably American for themselves will consist of whatever they gather from the media of the period as "typical" of American women. Jen depicts Helen as covertly poring over American women's fashion magazines and hiding them under her mattress. She longs to acquire whatever she sees in them as ideals of American womanhood. In situations like this, Jen takes the Chinese concept of a "typical Chinese" acculturated woman and opposes it to that of a "typical American" acculturated woman. On the surface of the text Ralph, the major male character, is intent on having inhere in himself those traits that will make him a "typical American." The man's attainment of a specific complex of signs that convey a given form of manhood as "typical American" is conceived of as higher, of greater standing and significance in the value system than those "frivolous" fashion and consumer products that Helen pores over in the women's magazines. Ralph and his womenfolk conceive of women's role as subsuming themselves to serve him in his goal of becoming a "typical American." Ideal American women's values are perceived and positioned as a different set of values from those for men and as apart from them.

Every member of the group that is formed around Ralph comprises a working unit exactly like the Confucian family. Ironically, the organization of the family members surrounding Ralph replicates the structure of the traditional Confucian family system because it is embedded in its structure. In this traditional manner, all function together as one unit to achieve Ralph's goal—to become a "typical American." Supposedly, only Ralph strives to be its embodiment, as I have pointed out. Even so, women and female children still internalize for themselves the "typical American" values meant for men. It rubs off on them. Indeed, most people, no matter what culture, wish to become consumers like Ralph and his family of all the material pleasures which their culture has to offer, especially in the United States where they are continually bombarded by the media: the radio, the glossy women's magazines, which Helen reads, and the American success mass mythology publications that inspire Ralph. Theresa alone seems immune to these material temptations. Hers are of a different kind—of the flesh.

Ralph's and his family's process of becoming "typically American" (so very Confucian in its methodology) and the traditional mainstream American ideal of "family values" do not differ much. But Transcendentalism does differ from Confucianism in one key way. In Transcendentalist discourse, everyone else in the family and community is subordinate to the individual, and the individual is assumed to be male. Emerson himself provides the most convincing proof of this gender asymmetrical perspective. He essentializes his gendered position as universal, as do all the Transcendentalists, except Whitman. Emerson isn't even conscious that he speaks from within a male psyche distanced and separate from the female (as well as everyone else) when he proclaims, for example: "Say to them, O father, O mother, O wife, O brother, O friend . . . hitherto I am the truth's. . . . I shall endeavor to nourish my parents, to support my family, to be the chaste husband of one wife" (Emerson [1841], 1990 1522). On the other hand, in Confucianism, the traditional Chinese man is supposed to include his family's interest in all his calculations. Nevertheless, in many cases, as in Ralph's, the family is subsumed into the male's needs, as though his needs and theirs are one entity. He then defines whatever he wants and whatever he does as best for his family. It would appear therefore that the Confucian ideal in terms of gender asymmetry is identical to Transcendentalism's, as well as that of the contemporary advocates of "family values" where wife, mother, and children are subsumed by, revolve around, and serve as subordinate(s) to the needs of "the head" of the household, the breadwinner, thereby perpetuating the system. Globally, this is exactly how most cultures define marriage: as "two becoming one and that one the husband," as can be seen in Milton's *Paradise Lost* (1623) and Cokewood's primer of English law that the European Americans followed as their legal model from the seventeenth century onward.

In Confucianism, a hierarchical ladder continues upward to the emperor. The individual male is subordinate to his superiors according to class, but dominant over all those beneath him in rank. As Ralph puts it, China is "a terraced society" where people are concerned about "one's station." Knowing this, people know how "to treat each other" (177). There is "a different understanding . . . in practical, can-do, down-to-earth America" where it was even "an industry," not with what, but "in mystery," with "who they were." He uses this tenuous argument to rationalize that in becoming a criminal and a fraud in America he is testing what his "limits [are], and . . . impulses, what evil and what good he had it in his soul and hands to fashion" (178). Even though he reminds himself that he had "once wished, achingly, ardently, only that no revolution should ever take his wife from him. . . . He took his own wife, his own family, his job, his house, and gambled as though they were nothing to him—as though, indeed, his whole life weren't his. What sort of thing was that for his father's son to do?" (179). Here as elsewhere in the text Jen does not mean readers to see Ralph's relation to his own family only on a literal level, but as in Myenne Ng's *Bone*, to stand for broader relationships, as well. Thus, Ralph's fall is also related to the immigrant generation's values and those of "the motherland," China's value system. As Tan says of China: "It is the motherland I inherited from my ancestors. . . . All Chinese people are family to one another in some unexplainable way" (Tan [1987] 1992, 269).

If we go by the stereotype for a "typical American," then, it might very well be Ralph to whom Jen confers the title. Emerson's discursive structure, as I have pointed out, erased women from consideration of what constituted a "typical American." The female statue in New York harbor may symbolize liberty, but it is the depiction of Uncle Sam, who wants the viewer to join him body and soul, that embodies a "typical American." Emerson's vision was similar to that of Ralph's in his youth, of rising above all worldly distractions (and women are considered one of them) in pursuit of his individual calling, or "vocation," as Thoreau puts it. For a long time, Ralph uses whatever insights he has achieved through meditation on his own and the human condition in general and applies them only to his drive for wealth. He even gives up his career as a professor of mechanical engineering to buy a fried chicken restaurant. The business symbolizes his demeaning of the term "peak" in his name into "making it big, into climbing to the top" in terms of economics, rather than what the term means in traditional China and Transcendental Concord.

Grover Ding, The Tempter

If Grover is the "typical American," then Jen is being even more sarcastic than she would be if she were playing Ralph off against the most stereotypical generalizations about the character and conduct of a "typical American." This is much like what Mark Twain did with Hank Morgan, the arms manufacturer in *A Connecticut Yankee in King Arthur's Court* (1889). Morgan starts out as a "typical American" entrepreneur blessed with an abundance of "good old Yankee ingenuity" and ends up, like Adolph Hitler, an insane megalomaniac in a bunker. Jen describes Grover as "the entrepreneur." A "self-made man," he has gone "from rags to riches." He too shares with Ralph a belief in Carnegie's hucksterish message. Further, in order to ensnare his victim's soul—just as the devil is depicted as doing—Grover makes himself into a replica of the sinner in regard to his/her "typical American" dreams. With great subtlety, Jen has him damn himself as soon as Ralph mentions Christ, which should have served as yet another warning to Ralph:

"I'm a millionaire. A self-made man. What do you think of that?"
"Millionaire! Self-made man!"
"In America, anything is possible!" . . . "Understand me, I was already the can-do type."
"Doer type. I got you."
"I had the correct attitude. Very important."
"Positive attitude, right? Use imagination?"
"You got it."
" 'I can do all things in Christ who strengthen me,' " quoted Ralph.
"Well, I'll be damned. The engineer's done some reading."
" 'Prayerize,' " said Ralph.
" 'Picturize,' " said Grover. " ' Actualize.' " (106–107)

In addition to Satan, Grover embodies in human form the qualities of the Monkey King of Chinese folklore. Both occasionally display the ability to entertain abstruse metaphysical and philosophical speculations. Initially endearing and charming like Monkey, Grover is ultimately only evil incarnate. Actually, though, his manipulative and underhanded ways are more like many Eighties Yuppie "entrepreneur" white collar criminals than those of the Forties and Fifties, the ostensible period covered in the text. Historically, self-promoters, wheeler-dealers and con-artists like Grover have been a feature of American life and literature since Dickens's *Martin Chuzzlewit* (1843) and Melville's *The Confidence Man* (1857). Grover's character is also intertextual with a type that goes as far back to the serpent in the Old Testament and as far forward as Goethe's *Faust*. Grover's successful temptations of both Helen and Ralph resonate with the temptations traditionally associated with Eve and the serpent/Satan and Dr. Faust with the devil. As such, Grover represents the corrupting and corrupt essence of the material, the fleshly, devoid of moral checks and balances of any kind. The first two letters of his name, "Gr" are time-honored representations of a growl and "Rover" is a "typical" dog's name. Further, Jen uses his surname Ding as Kant, in his *Critique of Practical Reason* (1791) used the term *das Ding* as a "pathological Thing. . . . [T]he most familiar name for substance, *das Ding*, and the Real since Freud's *Civilization and Its Discontents* is the *animal*" (Wolfe 1995, 65).

All these associations with the character Grover are used by Jen as commentary on those elements of the American dream that disgust her because they signify excess, running wild, disharmony, imbalance. Grover is all this, a violation in his essence of the primary ideals of Confucianism. Significantly, he has no family, no kin. He raids others, as does Monkey. His appetites know no bounds. He flirts with and tantalizes vulnerable, gullible men such as Ralph, whose weaknesses feed Grover's sadism so that he can replicate them as a mirror opposite. Continuing with her gluttony imagery, as well as with undertones of vampirism, Jen describes Grover as chewing Ralph up and spewing him out—as gorging on his victims until he has had his fill. Grover acts and thinks outside the paradigms of the norm, while reflecting precisely what the secret desires of his victim are: in this case, the evils of material and fleshly excess for both sexes. For Ralph and Helen who become infatuated with him and all he stands for, this is the dark side of their dream of becoming "typical American."

Ralph succumbs to Grover even sooner than Helen—and even more disastrously. To punish her adultery, Ralph hurls Helen through the living room "picture" window and terrorizes her. Also, in a reversal of the ride on which Grover has taken him, Ralph takes Helen for a ride in his car, there to threaten her with her death and his suicide if she does not tell him the truth about her relationship with Grover. This scene is intertextual with the intended suicidal sleigh-ride on which Ethan Frome takes Mattie Silver in Edith Wharton's *Ethan Frome* (1911) when he despairs of ever freeing himself from his wife. Both Ethan and Ralph purposely aim their death missiles—in one case a sleigh, in the other a car—at a huge tree in their path. Although Ralph makes Helen suffer for her fall, no one ever pays him back in kind for his weakness and gullibility. He considers his humiliation payment enough for his having been fooled by his own folly in the guise of Grover Ding. Ultimately, he comes to philosophize about Grover's cruelty as a spiritual chastening rod, as payment for his past mistakes. Here he is closer to the spiritually risen but financially fallen Silas Lapham at the end of Howells's *The Rise of Silas Lapham* than he is to the wealthy Christopher Newman of James's *The American*, or Jay Gatsby of Fitzgerald's *The Great Gatsby*. Silas and Ralph lose only their materialistic temptations, whereas Christopher and Gatsby lose the only thing in the world they value, their beloved women. Lapham, the "typical American" of his time (the Gilded Age), never falters in his courtesy and kindness to his wife or to any other women, nor do Newman and Gatsby. In contrast, Ralph uses his wife as a punching bag, the passive object of his need to vent, as was customary in his home in China where his father beat his mother. Ralph's betrayal of family loyalty, harmony, and the ideals of decency are never punished by his womenfolk, and never seem to diminish the respect, love, trust, and dependence on him exhibited by all his female relatives. On the surface of the narrative, therefore, it would seem that the system of gender asymmetry remains securely in place throughout the text, even to the last page, in the form of an efficient, well-running Confucian family with Ralph, as ever, at its head.

Following Amy Tan's daring critique and subversion of this global family model in *The Kitchen God's Wife*, Jen here includes in her meanings of the term "typical American" that the family's and the society's well-being and productive functioning include the running over or crushing of women—the laying of them low and on their backs. At this point, two questions arise. The first, is whether readers will find relief anywhere in this text for the indignation and rage the putative hero of this book, as well as Grover Ding, provoke. Secondly, there is the unresolved question as to whether or not these unsympathetic Chinese American male characters will get away with what Wen Fu of *The Kitchen God's Wife* does in China: to die a natural death like him, at a ripe old age, surrounded by a loving family and friends.

Theresa Chang, Sainted Sister

It is in the trope of "Theresa's falling and breaking" in her various encounters with her brother that we come to see the "goodness" of Theresa, her "self-sacrificing" nature, the "saintliness" encoded in her name in Western tradition past and present. Theresa acquiesces to her subsummation by her brother into the traditional family structure. Theresa, the saint, and Helen, the beauty, both serve to forward Ralph's agenda, never their own. They perform their sacrifices for the Confucian family good, harmony, well-being, and smooth function. These values are primary in Chinese culture (as well as in American and most other cultures). No wonder, then, that critiques of this entrenched form of gender asymmetry have come up against seemingly insurmountable barriers from institutions in every culture that have everything to gain and nothing to lose by keeping gender asymmetry in place in the family, as everywhere else.

If we turn to Theresa, more brilliant and humane than Ralph, to act in the capacity of "a woman warrior" against gender asymmetry, our hopes are dashed. After Ralph comes to the realization that his sister is indeed more brilliant than he and becomes ill as a result, she dutifully subordinates her needs to his wounded ego. By choosing to appease her brother's ego and lie to him about her scholarship to medical school, Theresa even goes so far as to reject this "top Ivy League" school's offer to her in order to assuage Ralph's bruised ego. As a result, she causes her family and herself great personal and financial loss. The contrast in the means by which Theresa achieves her MD, between Theresa's "rise" and her brother's, should also be noted. Her goal is continually interrupted, because she always takes everyone else's opinions and feelings about her into account. Indeed, it could be said that she attains her professional success in spite of her continual self-abnegating deferrals and deferences to her inferior brother. But Ralph at once joyously arises from his bed of psychic illness, as soon as he learns that Theresa has been unsuccessful, thereby matching the other literal ways in which he "runs over" his sister. He does it three times in all. The first incident is when they were children, with a seesaw. The second time he runs over her is with his own body at the moment of their first reunion in this country: when Theresa discovers Ralph at the lowest point of his life, starving and a hopeless failure. The result of his greeting foreshadows the future results for her, when "[I]n springing up to welcome her, he knocked her over, so that she fell to the sidewalk and sprained her ankle" (46). Finally, late in the novel, he crushes her with the symbol of the American dream of mobility, his car. Ralph is always running over women, not only Theresa. Readers of *The Kitchen God's Wife* are here inevitably reminded of Wen Fu's wild joyride with a girl that ends with his running her over, crushing her to death, and getting away with it! None of the women seems to mind the gender asymmetry encoded by the author in her use of this metaphor. For months Theresa lies in a coma in the hospital. Only then does Ralph come to his senses and the family begins another kind of "rise," one based on genuine love and support for one another.

Jen also gives readers the clearest of signals in her naming of Ralph in Chinese "Yifeng" as to just how bicultural, if not global, is one of the exclusively masculine signifiers for American success—"Go to the top." She is also corrosively ironic in so naming him in terms of Transcendentalism, where the name Ralph resonates for Americans. To attain transcendence through meditation is the goal to which Buddhists and Transcendentalists alike both aspire. In their sense, this is what "the peak" means, not the materialist meaning to which it has degenerated in contemporary American culture. Throughout the text Jen revels, as she does here, in such postmodern punning; in her ludic play of dichotomies in creating her philosophical variant on the traditional concept of yin and yang. By means of this subtle contrast between Ralph's and Theresa's characters, Jen shows the difference between Theresa's complex, communitarian drive to the top of her capabilities, as opposed to Ralph's selfish and individualistic moves "to the top." Theresa's career moves reflect the need to fulfill her talents and serve others; his are the moves of a lone wolf ranging about for material success. Motivated by her desire to serve others, Theresa shares whatever she earns with her brother and his family, whereas he expects his family to serve him, as I have pointed out earlier.

By the time Ralph runs his sister over for the last time, readers are still left with no resolution of or solution to this bleak state of affairs. Ralph rules supreme in his bailiwick; Grover goes from one victory to another; Helen, made a fool of by Grover, remains satisfied with being her husband's and family's subordinate and servant. Theresa, who has left the family for a while to complete her internship and go on to become a practicing MD, has returned to become once again part of the Chang family's support system financially and emotionally. In contrast to a male doctor, she also provides additional domestic services to Helen and Ralph, as well as sexual services to Old Chao as his concubine, but not exactly as in China. Again, no protest is registered by any female character in this text to so palpably asymmetrical a treatment of a female doctor and a single woman. This is because none of the female characters seems to have a developed sense of self-interest, such as all the male characters possess. Theresa strives to achieve this, but her unselfish love for her brother, for her sister-in-law who is also her best friend, for Janis, Old Chao's wife, and for her two young nieces outweighs any personal considerations. Theresa has been trained in China where taking herself into account routinely—her wants and needs—fits nowhere into the equation of a choice between herself and her family, especially her brother's needs. In fact, she doesn't count herself of any significance at all, as illustrated by the red shoes she buys to meet Grover when he is being considered as a possible match for her. Jen represents her as guilt-ridden, feeling like an impostor in them. She is more comfortable in the worn-down, worn-out gray shoes she always wears, which "fit" her image of herself. And this is also the way she takes a lover, as a hand-me-down from another woman. From birth, according to Jen, female children are taught to assume subordinate positions until it seems natural and normal to them to suppress their needs and desires in favor of others. Used to swimming only in gender asymmetric currents, their sense of self-interest suffocates quickly after they are hooked and beached in childhood. Many never even realize that they have a self to serve. Like Helen, they are caught before they swim, or like Theresa, they try to swim at the same time as sacrificing themselves in favor of the "bigger fish" in the sea, their "[br]others." Before they even start out in life, Helen and Theresa have totally internalized gender asymmetry. Under these circumstances, it is a miracle that Theresa gets as far as she does, and then only to immediately take whatever she earns to diminish herself to fit the Procrustean bed of her brother and his family's needs.

By telling Theresa's story so that on the surface of the text no subversion is evident, Jen's process itself becomes its own indictment of gender asymmetry. All is not what it appears to be, as Shirley Geok-Lin Lim explains: "Younger Asian American women writers have inherited the scene. While they are not pioneers in the sense that . . . older writers were, they are striking new notes and registers in their exploration of subjectivity as gendered. . . . " (Lim 1992, 12). Accordingly, Theresa is not totally the pliable product of bicultural prescriptions for women. Even when accounting for her concession of almost all personal gains in favor of family security, Jen represents Theresa as smoldering with suppressed anger over the humiliation of her family's attempts to find her a man: "about having to parade herself through parks in August. Or what about that dinner? Her indignation came to her in English, even as she recalled a Chinese saying, Lao xu cheng nu—constant shame becomes anger. . . . Her heart was indeed a fist, just as it was described in the [medical] texts [she studies]" (142). Theresa broods "about being a spinster" (141), mourning her apparent fate: to be alone for life. In this way, Jen takes the opportunity to make a feminist statement valorizing the significance of anger for women in the face of traditional prohibitions against its expression by them. One of the first stages toward awareness of the power of gender asymmetry is anger. In fact, anger about gender asymmetry should be considered another common thread uniting contemporary Asian American women writers with women writers globally:

Years later, she might have recognized anger's place in her life to be like that of a poison color in needlework. . . . She might have seen it to be the garish shade that could bring a planned composition to life. Now, though, she tried to box herself up. She had always been nice about her morals; she grew nicer still. How dangerous a place, this country! A wilderness of freedoms. She shuddered, kept scrupulously to paths. Once she had allowed other [medical] residents to wink at her, and had sometimes even winked back. Now she stiffened and turned away. (142–143)

A certain tone of voice in their speaking and writing—an ironic, sarcastic, raging tone—is characteristic of contemporary Asian American women writers, other ethnic women writers, and white mainstream feminists. All are angry, and justifiably so, as Brenda Silver eloquently explains:

The anger I feel is real and has its roots in the circumstances in which we experience our private and professional lives. . . . I know that the battles I set out to fight, including the battles about critical authority and institutional change, are far from won and that the sense of urgency I feel is shared by women who differ from me in significant ways. . . . When the anger born of these differences [between women] threatens to subsume my own anger and my voice, I can also acknowledge that all these angers, all these voices, are necessary to feminist critique today. For just as there is no one feminist criticism, there is no one feminist anger, and no one tone of voice appropriate to its ends. (Silver 1991, 970)

This last point, about accepting diverse tones of voice, is perhaps most significant, since tone of voice in Asian American women, in ethnic and women of color, in women globally is one of the most successful ways in which we have been policed and suppressed from an early age onward. Our tone must always be rational, unemotional, impersonal, subdued, abstract, scholarly, or we will be dismissed as "hysterical." Our society considers an ideal citizen as universal, impartial in perspective as signified by flatness in tone. Any other way of being or speaking is deviant and inferior from this "civilized," "ladylike" or "gentlemanly" norm. The "fundamental animating principle of modern patriarchy . . . grounds its claim of power in the view that (elite white) men's 'knowledge' is universal and that of others contingent" (Stivers 1993, 417). Therefore, women are "silenced, inauthenticated" by "rules of politeness and rationality that govern social dialogues." It then becomes "impossible to say what needs to be said by making certain topics impolite, certain tones of voice or emotions irrational, or simply defining topics as psychological and not political." This process needs to be reversed; for "[h]owever difficult to name, however hard to write . . . the angers that continue to animate feminist consciousnesses and critiques may well be the most compelling source of our strength" (Silver 1991, 970).

I can conjure up many better sources of strength for women than anger. Still, anger at global asymmetry, at "the missionary position" has been the single most influential source of inspiration for the most powerful feminist critiques, as well as the work of the contemporary Asian American women writers in this text. Anger has nourished them by providing them with the motivation to fight inequity, injustice and oppression. They feel that to disguise this, to suppress it, to be made wrong and bad for expressing it, is to submit themselves once again to another constraint on women in yet another form. In addition, rather than viewing Asian American women writers' anger as marginal to feminist strategies for destabilizing and dissolving asymmetry, it should be included as yet another equally viable response. Anger, as Silver points out, should be viewed positively as the forceful byproduct of much meditation and illumination; it should be seen as a political tool, because "[t]o become angry, to recognize that one has been angry, to change what counts as being angry, becomes a political act. Moreover, one is not just angry, one is angry about—and the difference can be crucial." Thinking along the same lines, the African American feminist June Jordan's meditations about "the problem of gender identity" includes anger as a solution:

Usually we push for things to change in our favor . . . but usually we push in the most courteous and reasonable and listening fashion imaginable. Rarely do we ever "enter the realms of righteous rage" . . . so that whoever opposes or impedes or ridicules our demands will understand that if he does not get out of our way and/or rid of that smirk he will be the one in danger; he will be the one in pain. Hardly ever do we make it clear that by quote rights unquote we mean power: the power of deterrence and the power of retaliation and the power to transform our societies so that no longer and never again shall more than half of every people on the planet beg for dignity and safe passage and political and economic equality. (Jordan 1993, 9)

Jen also represents Theresa from a feminist perspective in terms of what is difficult for her about being a single woman, During her internship Theresa is refused separate facilities on the grounds that she is the only woman in the group. Accordingly, she is forced into a "dank, little room" with the other interns—all men. Jen thus leads readers to wonder if the same rule would have held true if there had been one male intern and the rest had been female. What is hardest for Theresa is not the "horror" of the tragic deaths and smell of the emergency room, "not the hours . . . not the responsibility, or the pain, or the patients, or the politics, or the masses of information tumbling and reeling in her head like cars on a circus ride. It was not the mnemonic devices, as hard to recall as the facts. . . . It was not the fatigue":

What was hardest about training, for Theresa, was having to sleep in that dank, little room the interns all shared, with men. "If there were more women . . . " someone had explained, with a shrug. Now, as weary, she headed that way—finally, finally done—she thought about how soundly the men slept. She thought about how the men snored and tossed. They cried out. They moaned. They farted. They scratched themselves, and worse. Even the still ones, who slumbered soulfully, who curled up neatly, even they disturbed her; she could feel their radiant presence, against which she had to stand guard. Maybe they bothered her most, the sweet ones. So peaceful, but what dreams they might stir up in her if she slept, all throbbing, and sliding. A spinster's hot heaves; how pointed her needs were, it was impossible to sleep. It was impossible to think about people witnessing her sleep. What if she moaned, and cried out, and scratched herself, or worse? (147)

But Jen goes even further in the tradition of Hong Kingston and Tan in the use of a female-centered perspective. Theresa proposes to have her sexual and romantic fulfillment cake and eat it too in a culturally subversive way by accepting and enjoying love where she finds it—in the arms of a married man, Old Chao. From a feminist perspective, appropriating another woman's man for oneself is disloyal. In the following chapters, we will see the lonely postfeminist Jo in *The Loom and Other Stories* also doing this. But in Cynthia Kadohata's *The Floating World* when this issue arises, as soon as Jack's mistress realizes how his wife must feel, she breaks off with him.

The family's fall begins to reverse itself, as illustrated in Helen's growing appreciation of Theresa (who stands for everything opposed to individualism and materialism). Rallying around the beloved Theresa during her coma allows the family "crack" to heal: "Now, now, Helen realized: Theresa had made that world possible. She must have, for her absence made it impossible. In one thing, Grover had been right—Helen had understood nothing about love. She had understood nothing about how people could come to mark off her life. For example, she had considered the great divide of her self's time to be coming to America. Before she came to America, after she came to America. But she was mistaken. That was not the divide, at all" (288). And when Ralph hears the news of his sister's awakening from her long coma, he experiences an epiphany about a beautiful childhood day they had once spent together. Again, the globally significant motif of the male causing his sister to fall is brought in by Jen:

> Once, as a child, he had slid too quickly off his end of a seesaw. He remembered now how his sister hurtled to the ground; how she lay on her side like an upturned vase. Then she righted herself. They trod back to the house silently, along the path they knew better than anything anyone had ever taught them. He remembered how the gravel crunched underfoot, how they hopped the first step onto the bridge. Their footsteps beat then, on the wood, as though on the skin of an old, deep drum; they stamped to augment the effect, and swung their arms, and on the other side gave a two-footed jump back onto the gravel, running the rest of the way. Through the giant peonies, elaborately staked; racing. His sister won, of course, and at the end they dug up some stones they'd buried the day before. These were just to hold—cool to the touch, though the day was hot. He remembered holding the stones to his cheek, murmuring with pleasure; his sister did it too. . . . Such was the simplicity of childhood, he thought now—events vanished, wordless. (294–295)

Daringly, Theresa permits Old Chao to openly visit her in her room in the family home, an unimaginable option in China for a respectable woman. In some considerable measure she gets away with these heresies only because Ralph's excess of materialistic ambition and criminal bungling have brought the family to their now-straitened circumstances. Once her financial contribution to the family becomes vital, Ralph can no longer be the actual sole head of the household. Theresa is no longer an inferior to him, but a necessary, fully functioning part of the family. Jen is here making a statement about the positioning of women in gender asymmetrical economics: when women's economic contribution matches or surpasses that of their men, women can then rise from beneath their men to working beside them, a rise that then affects so much else, including revision of sexual codes.

Another gain Theresa makes is that she is the one who shapes her relationship to Old Chao as she wishes. His friendship and concern are all for her and her best interests, not Ralph's, although they were once classmates and later colleagues. As chair of the Department of Engineering, he assists Ralph in achieving tenure only in order to make Theresa happy. Previously a virgin, although we have seen how much sexuality she has suppressed, Theresa finds that she is compatible with Old Chao. Yet despite her lover's publicly avowed preference for her over his legal wife, Theresa at the end of the book has still not married him. When she could have it all, she again takes less so that everyone's needs can be served to the fullest extent possible all around. All along, Theresa

has wanted to be part of Old Chao's family, even fantasizing her formal adoption
into it, as was sometimes done in China (and Japan and India, as well as other
cultures) for favorite mistresses:

> How had she come to where she was? She hardly knew. And what did that mean,
> that Janis was getting used to the situation? Impossible. Yet in the weeks since Helen
> first mentioned it, the idea had put on girth in Theresa's imagination, until now she could
> almost begin to envision a future in which she and Old Chao were reconciled with Janis.
> It was too much to hope for. Still . . . she did. No more closeting; she could have one
> part of Old Chao, Janis and the children another. The arrangement would be open. Ac-
> cepted. Why not? In China, there were concubines—not what she wanted to be at all,
> but which proved human nature capable of different sorts of marriage. Maybe there
> could be a ceremony whereby someone like her was taken into the family; just thinking
> of it made her prickle with happiness. A string of fireflies flashed on the lawn, as though
> with kindred enthusiasm. Why not, they blinked, why not, why not? (279)

Theresa creates a kind of female-centered, extended family that is most reminiscent of the one which Alice Walker creates at the end of *The Color Purple*.
In order to do so, she becomes Chao's concubine and endures the public and
family disapprobation, while Janis maintains public respect by retaining the legal
title of wife and full financial support for herself and her children. Married traditionally, trained only as a wife and mother, Janis has no marketable skills,
whereas Theresa has had no man, but everything else. Together, Theresa and
Janis hammer out a compromise. Together, they shape a "different sort of marriage." Theresa's and Janis's set-up is like the traditional Chinese way on the
surface, except that it is what Theresa and Janis have chosen to best fit their
combined needs. Theresa is taking the less preferred woman into account, at
least in Jen's eyes, right down to refusing to deprive Janis of the fulfillment of
her sexual needs. That is, providing Old Chao can and wishes to satisfy his
wife's demands, and providing Janis still wishes to make those demands on him.
Under this set-up, Janis can look for and turn to another man if she so wishes.
Thus, Janis, although deprived of her legal husband's love and fidelity, is yet
deprived of nothing she had before. The only difference is that she is sharing her
man's body with her friend, while nothing else is taken from her. Actually Old
Chao has never loved Janis. Theirs was an arranged marriage. As the man in
question, he represents patriarchy, ordinarily a privileged position. But in this
case, Jen does not represent him as getting what he wants.

Instead, Theresa gets what she wants, something she has never had before: a
caring, concerned, loving male partner. By the end of the book she is just start-
ing out as a doctor in her own practice and can at last financially support both
herself and Ralph's family. She makes enough to need only psychic support
from her lover: her one best friend who is on her side and her side alone. Ordinarily, it is winner take all in such a situation, while the loser gets nothing. Jen
seems to approve of Theresa's conduct, to see her as extraordinarily kind and
considerate to Janis, the loser. Theresa syncretizes both traditional Chinese po-
lygamous as well as Judaeo-Christian American monagamous marriage tradi-

tions. Again, Jen seems to view this revisionism as a postfeminist subversion with which she seems to identify. According to feminist ideals, however, a free woman does not compromise her ethics, especially to a "sister's" disadvantage. A true "sister" never intrudes into other women's (or men's) preexisting relationships. She always excludes from her consideration any men (or women) who are not equally free. Naming Ralph's sister and Helen's sister-in-law "Theresa" in a text in which Jen has chosen the other names of her characters with utmost care for their associative connotations indicates that the character Theresa clearly is intended to represent "sister"(hood) literally and symbolically, and in many ways she does. Nevertheless, her takeover of Janis's relationship to her husband is a hostile one and thus creates an ironic play on the term "sister." This is not how sisters conduct themselves, whether by literal blood ties or according to feminist ideals. Secondly, since her name is that of two "sisters of the cloth" who are universally considered to be saints, Theresa's ultimately selfish sexual revisionism prohibits her from consideration in their ranks, despite her "saintliness" of conduct otherwise. In the spiritual sense therefore, Jen is also employing the name "Theresa" ironically. For these two reasons, it is difficult to imagine that Jen could consider Theresa as a candidate for the individual she has in mind when she titled her book *Typical American.*

Helen Chang, Seduced and Abused in the Suburbs

Even harder to imagine as the title's referent is the character of Helen. Jen represents her as likable and a devoted friend to Theresa, as Theresa is to her. They lived together before ever Ralph came on the scene. Each is capable of valuing the other for who she is, for her unique combination of qualities. After Helen fixes the boiler in their first apartment, "Theresa mused all night, and the next day too. She'd always respected Helen, but she had never felt the kind of overwhelming admiration for her that she did now. What different kinds of intelligence there were in the world! Who was to say which mattered most? One couldn't say, couldn't begin to say, although this much was certain—what mattered in China was not necessarily what mattered here" (81).

To some extent, Helen's and Winnie's friendship in *The Kitchen God's Wife* could be said to have influenced Jen's representation of this relationship. In this text, however, Helen and Theresa are from the same class. Both of these women have always formed a cushion of support for Ralph—like three parts of a marriage instead of two: "That's the way they were, they slid, bound together with some old rope—their overlapping history, their parents' relationships" (52). Also, they are never abrasive to one another, at least not outwardly:

Things in common, that made it easier to talk to each other than to strangers, but hardly meant that when they did they would agree. And they didn't agree, though after a few near-arguments, each did her part never to let that show; so that they grew at once closer and lonelier, like colors that, when knit together, gleam all the more distinct. Every day brought compromise so basic neither one would talk about it, as though such prideless [sic] friendship belonged to a realm past conversation. (52–53)

Helen is generous, compassionate, a fine wife and supportive mother. She cooks and cleans for the family. Secretly, however, she tinkers with machinery, has mathematical abilities, is strong and energetic. Helen's being "handy" is what in American culture is traditionally lauded as "good old Yankee ingenuity and know-how." But such a combination of qualities is far from typical for women of any culture, let alone that of an "upper class" girl. She also discovers to her amazement—this upper class, hitherto inactive, "proper Shanghainese-girl" (77)— that "working was enjoyable" (76) to her, a discovery which she keeps "a secret" about herself. She still retains the traditional Chinese female training for women that "enormous circumspection" is necessary to avoid humbling her husband's ego, that is, rocking the gender asymmetrical boat:

She made curtains; she made bedspreads; she rewired Ralph's old lamp. She couldn't help but feel proud. Too proud, really—she tried to bind that feeling up—recognizing still, though, that in her own way she was becoming private strength itself. She was the hidden double stitching that kept armholes from tearing out. And all because she'd discovered, by herself, a secret—that working was enjoyable. Effort, result. . . . She knew how tiny she was too, how unmuscled in the arms; she appreciated, as if in a mirror, that she was amazing. And that mattered, the way it mattered that she be busy but not busy at the same time—that, while competent, she be a Chinese girl. (76–77)

Helen deploys other strategies and solutions besides concealment and circumspection in the face of opposing demands between the individual woman's personal needs and talents and the family's and external community's decrees. Covert conduct is perhaps the most common solution globally, especially for women of color because they are concerned, like Helen, with survival and "[s]urvival as a woman and as a minority group member, is in itself a form of resistance" (Mazumder 1989, 20). Private forms of resistance such as Helen's are ineffective because they often go "unnoticed." This is due to the power of prevailing myths such as the "passivity" of Asian American women. Actually, as we have seen in the works of Hong Kingston, Tan, and Myenne Ng, "portraits of resistance" are not unknown, whether individual or "collective political forms." What she conceals from others, Helen vents privately—in a safe space with another woman, Theresa, who is doubly safe. Theresa has already been publicly ostracized by Ralph for an unthinkable thing in China: becoming Old Chao's mistress.

Working is yet another strategy for Helen and for women, in general, a strategy that has "changed the balance of power between the sexes," especially work that "contributes to the family income" and work that is done in a "family business" (Mazumder 1989, 21). In *The Woman Warrior* Brave Orchid performs extraordinary feats of strength in the laundry she operates with her husband. The anonymous mother in R. A. Sasaki's *The Loom* and the grandmother in Cynthia Kadohata's *The Floating World* both help in their family's boarding houses, although this is expected of them, since both are from the lower classes. In this text Jen brings a feminist perspective to one of the rare liberatory elements connected to the semiotics of what would seem closest to the concept of "typical

American" for women. That is, she expands the concept of women's work in relation to the traditional Protestant work ethic to include ethnic immigrant women. When elements in this American success mythology conflict with the constraints of their patriarchal culture, these women take the opportunity to syncretize the two cultures to express their own talents. The elegant, high-born Helen has been trained in China that women of her class do nothing physical—that they are decorative items of "conspicuous consumption," in Thorstein Veblen's term. She gradually comes to revel in her skill with her hands, although not what happens to their appearance, after she and her young daughters end up working long, hard hours in Ralph's fried chicken franchise before it collapses. Doubtless, Helen's ancestors would turn in their graves at this turn of events.

Helen is also "attentive": "She sensed when a guest needed more tea before the guest did, expressed herself by filling his cup, thought in terms of matching, balancing, connecting completing. In terms, that is, of family, which wasn't so much an idea for her, as an aesthetic. Pairs, she loved, sets, and circles"(56).

Because Helen was fussed over as a child by her family due to her "sweet nature" as well as "a disabling illness," "her life ambition was to stay home forever" (61). The metaphors Jen uses to explain the difference here between Chinese and American training is that between "a skating rink, a walled-in, finite space" where words "inevitably rebounded," and an enormous world, "all endless horizons" where Helen's communications "arced and disappeared as though into a wind-chopped ocean" (85). Here Jen takes the opportunity in her own voice to compare and contrast Americans unfavorably to Chinese, as is usual with her. Americans are movement and bustle, whereas the Chinese "love to hold still; removal is a fall and an exile" (61).

In the beginning, Helen resists Americanization, but gradually she succumbs to the American consumerist acculturation of women that has influenced the globe:

She also developed a liking for American magazines, American newspapers, American radio—she kept her Philco in the corner of the living room nearest the bedroom, so she could listen nonstop. She sang along [with Gordon Macrae in *Oklahoma*, a quintessentially American musical comedy and great hit of the mid Fifties]: "The corn is as high as an el-e-phant's eyyye" (63). Unbeknownst to Ralph and Theresa, she spent large parts of her afternoons listening to the radio, or reading the magazines she kept under her mattress. She loved the advertisements especially, so gorgeously puzzling. . . . Also she liked the insights into American home life—the revelation that most Americans showered every day, first thing in the morning, for example. This amazed Helen, who took occasional baths, in the evening. (77)

Helen develops a complementary material obsession to that of her husband: she longs for a home in the suburbs with a dining alcove for the family, as opposed to the cramped apartment they rent in a poorly maintained building. Again, Jen's imagery here is symbolic of the Asian condition in the United States and of their drive for "upward mobility," according to Sau-ling C. Wong, who rightly sees this theme as one of the major elements in Asian American literature.

Certainly this could be said of *Typical American*, except that Jen critiques such projects. In her view, both the Chinese immigrants' materialistic motives and the system within which they flourish are corrupt. This is why she represents both the janitor and the apartment building in which the Chang family live—management as well as ownership of the American value system—as metaphors for its corrupt, rotten, deteriorated condition. The landlord (none other than the infamous Grover Ding) and his representative, Pete the super, are only out to milk the property for all it is worth and get rich quick.

In many quarters such an attitude as Grover's and Pete's is considered to be an identifying characteristic of the U. S. colonialist government and enterprise. At the very least, it reflects the predominant philosophy of the Reagan-Bush era when Jen was writing the novel. Jen obviously detests this aspect of the West and of the United States which Paule Marshall calls "the monolith" (*Daughters*). Like Marshall, she condemns the West for exploiting the resources and population of emerging and Asian countries and people of color. Theresa, here as elsewhere, represents Jen's position: "She'd seen how poor people were treated in the hospital; they died waiting. And to be nonwhite in this society was indeed to need education, accomplishment—some source of dignity. A white person was by definition somebody. Other people needed across their hearts, one steel rib" (200).

The Chang family is likewise exploited, as they later realize, and this, too is "typical[ly] American." Significantly, their first apartment is in Harlem, which extends Jen's critique to all people of color as exploited, not just Asians who intend to become Americans. Racial and ethnic prejudice is in fact not just an American issue, but a global one. For example, the Japanese have been charged with xenophobia, particularly against whites, although they do not regard Blacks, Chinese and Koreans highly, either. And in Vietnam, according to a Vietnamese witness during the American occupation and war against the North Vietnamese, "Times were very hard after the departure of the Americans. There were lines for everything. . . . It was especially hard for people who were ethnic Chinese. There was much prejudice against them. All the ethnic Chinese schools had been ordered closed. Businesses and jobs were taken away" (Lee and Oberst 1989, 105).[5]

The justified and well-warranted emphasis on the racism exhibited by the white race against people of color has caused many feminist, women of color feminists, and ethnic writers and scholars to tend to omit or elide the fact that racism is also exhibited by people of color toward other people of color, as well as toward Caucasians globally, and vice versa. In fact, all groups discriminate against other groups by difference of skin color and even by cultural difference. Amazingly, they do this even where there is no racial difference, as the Philippine critic E. San Juan, Jr. astutely observes: "Denying racial difference will not exclude nor eliminate racism. . . . '[T]he Jewish holocaust in Nazi Germany involved an ethnic group of the same racial stock as their killers, who were motivated by an ideology of racism despite the lack of objective racial differences between their victims and themselves' " (San Juan 1991, 217). The anti-

Vietnam demonstrations offer another example. Asian American male discrimination against Asian American females accords with that shown by many African American males toward their own women in the Civil Rights and Black Power movement struggles: "[Y]oung Asian American women, particularly on campus, walk[ed] picket lines, march[ed] in demonstration, [took] notes at meetings, [ran] duplicating machines, [made] coffee, support[ed] Asian American men, and then remain[ed] silent as the men departed with non-Asian women" (Lott 1989, 354).[6]

Courageously indicting her own characters on this score, Jen reveals that objects of racism (and sexism and class oppression) too often replicate racist, sexist and class oppression when they themselves discriminate against both blacks and whites alike as their Others. Jen represents racism as not only infecting whites, but Chinese, as well. When Ralph is a graduate student, he conceives an infatuation for the white secretary of the department who makes a fool of him. His Chinese friends refer to his experience as "falling for foreign devils" (32). And when after Ralph marries Helen, the family moves to "a run-down walk-up north of 125th Street," the couple's initial response is that they are surrounded by "So many Negroes! Years later, they would shake their heads and call themselves prejudiced, but at the time they were profoundly disconcerted" (65). When Old Chao's wife Janis proposes a possible suitor for Theresa, Helen learns that "he's completely American." Her response to what Japanese Americans call "ghosts" and "hakujin" is the same as that of Maxine's mother in *The Woman Warrior* and the anonymous mother in *The Loom*. "A foreign devil?' . . . A long nose?" (85) Helen sneers. Thus the potential suitor is disqualified, leaving Grover to fill the vacuum. That part of Grover which is "American" is also described pejoratively: "A short, American-born, English-speaking businessman—with no degree" but with "a maid . . . think of it—no housework! (86)" Janis exclaims, exhibiting class elitism, as well as ethnocentrism.[7]

Like Theresa, Helen is the embodiment of "the ethics of caring" over abstractions about justice. She gives meaning and substance to her family. Like most women globally, especially after achieving motherhood, nurturing is so deeply inscribed into her psyche that it is like an instinctive reaction for her. In naming her Helen, Jen is also making a commentary on the gender asymmetry of Greek mythology: "Theresa picked the English name Helen for her delicate friend. Like Helen of Troy, she explained: also it sounded like Hailan, her real name, Sea Blue" (52). In the Greek myth, the possession of Helen's fleshly embodiment is used as the sign of masculine power and supremacy over other men in an economy of conflict and war. Women were objectified as commodities to fight over. Today when many men are not literally fighting each other, they do it with equivalents for "arms." When many a powerful man wishes to signal his supremacy socially, he hangs a beautiful "trophy wife" (the equivalent of Helen of Troy) from his arm. "Femaleness" is still a site for economic and military domination and conquest, locally as well as globally. This is how Ralph views Helen: as necessary to forward his efforts to become rich through his own agency. She is subsumed, as is Theresa, to Ralph's goals.

Interestingly, it is Helen, not Ralph, who purges Grover Ding from all their lives. Jen wittily puns on this when she has Helen throw out "the love seat" which Helen had once so coveted as an item of conspicuous consumption. On this love seat Grover had seduced her. Subsequently, he appropriated it whenever it took his fancy to stay overnight. Although initially she had disliked him, for a long time Helen is complicitous with Grover. What causes her fall is her desire to be desirable; to be treated romantically and sexually like her Greek namesake as an object of male passion and desire, if not of combat and warfare. Grover does with Helen as he has done with Ralph: transforming himself into a mirror reflection of all that she desires: ardor, romance, extravagant courtship talk and actions—above all, the feeling that she is not taken for granted: " 'Anything else, my dearest?' How he talked! You have to know how to talk, her mother used to say; Helen understood now what she meant" (213). Grover brings into her mundane world, as he had into Ralph's, a sense of play, the unexpected, glamour, and mystery.

Frequently in the work of Asian American women writers, the wife/mother of the family is tempted to commit adultery for the same reasons as Helen. Their married life is set up by their culture's demands in so monotonous and service-related a grind that it provides no outlet for their need for fantasy and romance. In contrast, when Grover begins to court her, Helen finds "her apron pockets full of sugar" (214) and "on the sole of her shoe, a heart drawn in pencil. There were words in the middle. She held the shoe up. It read, Don't tell R." (215). At first she is "Chagrined." Then, she is "secretly delighted" (215). How he did it, if nothing else should have warned Helen that he was "full of the devil." Nevertheless, when she finds "the mailbox full of lilacs, her heart flooded," even though right after that Helen finds "one of her small bushes stripped! She trimmed the broken twig ends, so that the cuts would be cleaner, less apt to harbor disease" (216). Jen's genital pun in Grover's stripping of "one of her small bushes" is also an instance of foreshadowing here.

As Old Chao's actions on Ralph's behalf are motivated by his passion for Theresa and not his friendship with Ralph, so Grover claims that what he does for Ralph is only motivated by his love for Helen:

"You were made to be loved."
"Ralph loves me."
"Ralph!" Grover snorted.
"And you don't love me either."
"Now how do you figure that, miss? What do you know about love? What you read in magazines? Why do you think I set your husband up in business, eh? Why do you think I got involved?" (224)

Here Grover might as usual be mixing truth in with his brazen lying. For it is only after Helen rids herself of him that Grover ruins Ralph (and thereby his family). But even the sinking of the business is not the nadir of the family fortunes. This comes about when Ralph beats Helen and throws her out the picture window, another one of Jen's ironic puns on American success mythology, both in terms of domestic architecture of the Fifties and of the "picture perfect" marriage. Actually Ralph starts abusing Helen early in the marriage: "Sad refinements: Ralph knocked at Helen's skull. 'Nothing to say? Anybody there? Come on, open up.' Knocking made Ralph feel fierce, but it made Helen go blank—which made him knock more" (73).

According to Chinese custom, Helen has brought dishonor to the family by having an affair with Grover, as has Theresa before that when she took up with Old Chao. It is Helen who has done the heretical deed that traditionally would result in her death, not Grover's. Here it must be recalled that Ralph was also seduced by Grover in every way but sexually. By comparison and in Confucian terms Ralph's seduction and fall are worse than shameful and dishonorable. It has brought his family to the brink of bankruptcy. In this connection we see another thread that runs through the texts I have covered so far, as well as in Hong Kingston's *The Woman Warrior* and *China Men*, and Sasaki's *The Loom and Other Stories.* Asian American male characters are frequently betrayed by their business partners. That Helen was seduced by Grover; that Ralph was gulled and betrayed by Grover (cuckolded by him and cheated financially), that he gave up his academic career to go for the gold as embodied by Grover—all these actions signify that Jen is attempting to write a cautionary tale for Chinese immigrants to the United States. In her opinion, those who blithely cast off their traditional value systems to become "typical American" only become inferior human beings.

In any event, only Ralph's pride is battered, whereas Helen and Theresa both wind up physically battered in the hospital. Only the threat of Theresa's possible death awakens Ralph from his maniacal pursuit of the "American dream." It is the context of the situation (traveling the false path) that bothers Ralph. It is not the content (battering of his womenfolk), for "to discipline" wives for errors was the norm in traditional China and in most cultures worldwide. In China, when Ralph's mother wished to discipline him, she would do it by bribing him with sweets and money. She would also admit to him that if he did not obey her, she would be held accountable, not him: "*Do you realize your father will beat me too?*" (4), she demands of Ralph [Emphasis in original]. Also, Ralph (like Leon in *Bone*, but without the excuse of financial necessity) is never there for his wife before and during the birth of their children. In American culture, such an absence on the husband's part is considered shocking and reprehensible, but not by the Chinese, nor in many other cultures globally.

From a feminist perspective, one wonders what Helen gains from all her sufferings. True, she has her little fling, with her ego and sexual needs completely satisfied for once in her life, as are Theresa's with Old Chao. Again, as in Theresa's case, Ralph does not ask her to leave the family domicile. Filled with resentment, he acts as if he has something over her, even though he is the one who has brought the family to ruin over his infatuation for Grover who rejects him. Helen's infatuation was brief, by comparison, and she rejects Grover. Again Jen is here consciously setting up gender asymmetry as so all-pervasive that readers see the situation in the way she does. She provides no opening for any other conclusion than that her female characters are confined within the constraints of a monolithic patriarchy. Once again, what she shows rather than tells her readers will so upset them that there is no need for her to spell out for them that gender asymmetry has to be destabilized, transformed, ended. Her material speaks for itself. It is, after all, Jen who manipulates events so that conscious awareness of gender asymmetry is absent from the surface of her text. She does this to make it appear as if the novel has everything to do with the question of "typical Americanness" and nothing to do with gender asymmetry while blazing it out from the lines themselves, as well as from between the lines.

Here Jen's work is intertextual with Charlotte E. Perkins Gilman's classic *The Yellow Wallpaper* which exposes gender asymmetry in all institutions, especially marriage, as from within the pattern of old wallpaper in a room once used for a nursery. This critique is done as Jen does it, without any overt discourse about gender asymmetry from the author. On the surface, the allegory has everything to do with a woman's increasing insanity and nothing to do with gender asymmetry. But the tale has everything to do with this problem from the moment the young "Everywoman" bride Jane is driven by her "Everyman" husband Dr. John (as in "all men prescribe for all women") through the rusty gates into the decrepit mansion and then forced into the old nursery. All these sites symbolize the hoary patriarchal institution of the prison house of marriage and the enforced solitary confinement of motherhood on women. The horror lies in the allegorical unfolding of the effects of gender asymmetry on women. It is not at all supernatural, or Poesque, as Howells believed, unless woman's entrapment in marriage and then enforced imprisonment in that institution and in motherhood can be so considered, as Gilman did, at least in her first marriage. True, Dr. John specifically refers to a popular society women's doctor of the period whom Gilman believed deprived women, especially new mothers, of their rights to be themselves and pursue their own interests. But Dr. John also represents the male hierarchy and all the complex societal institutions—i.e., the patterns in the wallpaper with which he papers the nursery wall like so many bars behind which Jane's imprisoned *doppelganger* is crouching. In Gilman's eyes, he and his cultural gatekeeper "sister" Jenny who colludes with him in the perpetuation of gender asymmetry are the cause of every problem for women.

Poe's influence on *The Yellow Wallpaper* in creating a mood of suspenseful dread and horror into the issue of gender asymmetry is also evident in *Typical American*, but only in relation to the issue of spiritual corruption, not gender asymmetry. In "The Fall of The House of Usher" Poe used the symbols of "cracks" in the doomed house and in the brother and sister to signify the incest and madness that will bring down the last of the Ushers. In *Typical American*, Jen uses the "crack" in the wall of their house to symbolize the spiritual bankruptcy of the House of Chang whose house and chicken franchise literally "crack and fall apart" from the pursuit of material wealth, from the obsession to become "typical American."

At first, the family had lived in an apartment with plumbing and heating problems and a "crack in the back bedroom wall" (66). Handy Helen had ingeniously covered it up by hiring a plumber, by scraping "the loose paint so it wouldn't hang, and [by] walk[ing] Ralph's file cabinet into the back bedroom to hide the crack" (66). All this foreshadows the family's spiritual downfall. Ominously, after Grover's successful divisive manipulations this seemingly external phenomenon of a crack both in their apartment and in the apartment building in which they live (both owned by Grover) is carried over into the family fault line in terms of their business. The restaurant is built on "unstable and unbuildable land" and the roof addition that Ralph designs and builds under his supervision falls in.

All these are Jen's somber puns on the American value system and on Chinese immigrant efforts to rely on it by means of obsessive striving for upward mobility, to "reach the top." Before the establishment collapses, however, it gives ample, Poesque warning of the weakness of its foundation. The interior first "developed several fresh, fine cracks; it looked as though someone had drawn a few pencil lines from the new wood paneling up to the new suspended ceiling" (242). In the chapter with the punning title of "Watching the Overhead," the suspense builds as the crack does. With sinking hearts, but outwardly optimistic, the family calls the crack "the settling." Ralph, Helen and Theresa have "compromised" themselves: have "settled" in different ways by the point in the text where the structure falls in. Jen's tone is in its way eerier than Poe's. Hers conveys a surrealistic ordinariness, a false cheeriness characteristic of her.

FURTHER USES OF THE TERM "TYPICAL AMERICAN"

Previously I have shown how Jen uses the term "typical American" through her representation of characters, and ultimately the syncresis they create between their original culture and the "American culture" and the ways in which this interaction impacts on the characters in terms of their gender. As an additional way of reflecting Jen's critique of what is "typical American," I will now focus on how Jen's characters use the term "typical American."

When Theresa, like Winnie in *The Kitchen God's Wife* makes up her own rules, the result is a variant of the Western and Chinese patriarchal institutions of marriage. This act involves a syncresis on Theresa's part of what she considers to be the best of the Chinese and American concepts of gender roles in relationship. Of course, the very fact that a woman character is represented by Jen as tinkering with a traditional Chinese institution is heretical, much as is Tan's representation of Winnie as creatively transforming the meaning and message of traditional Chinese religious mythology in *The Kitchen God's Wife*. "To know that there is both a Chinese and an American way to be 'feminine' is to deprive each of absolute claim, thereby deesentializing femininity. . . . [P]itting Chinese patriarchal rules against Euro-American ones . . . splinters the force of both Chinese and white cultural authority" (Cheung 1993, 99). Both culture's claims on Theresa and her family ultimately "splinter" them to the point where they become syncretic: re-working ancient Confucian values whenever American values do not work for them.

Again, Jen chooses Theresa to illustrate this when she represents Theresa as the first character to add a new dimension to the term "typical American." Hitherto, she and her family had used it as an epithet to express contempt and ridicule. Suddenly Theresa concludes that there is no such thing as "typical American," only "just a person" underneath the stereotype. "We're wrong to say typical American! Over and over she explained that Pete [the building super] was just a person, like them, that Boyboy [his beloved dog] was just a dog" (74). Pete, the crude American super often fantasies about a career such as Ralph pursues and achieves through much hard work in order to become a professor of engineering. The difference is that Pete, slovenly, undisciplined and lazy, contents himself with sitting in his office and daydreaming about what Ralph is doing, of having a better future for himself. The family, in their contempt for him, label him "Typical American unreliable!" (78).

On the other hand, Jen also shows the family becoming "typical American" themselves. The chapter "Chang-Kees" puns on Twain's *A Connecticut Yankee in King Arthur's Court*. In this tragicomedy whose techniques and message anticipate postmodernism, Twain made a prophetic call to his age (one of many) about its neglect of ethical and moral values in the single-minded pursuit of material wealth and technological advances (from which he himself was not immune). If Americans continued in this direction, he predicted, we would end up on a scale of military destruction and devastation inconceivable to previous generations. Following Twain, Jen is tragicomic in a perversely ironic tone beneath the surface of her surrealistically slapstick humor. With historical accuracy, she reveals the response by the typical "Yankee fans" (as American as "hot dogs") to the family's sole attempt as new Americans to enjoy their adopted country's national pastime. Since as "typical Americans" they wish to consider it as their own, they decide to "go to a game," the American "game," the American "national sport." The tragic result was that "[P]eople had called them names and told them to go back to their laundry" (127). "They in turn had sat impassive as the scoreboard. Rooting in their hearts, they said later. Anyway, they preferred to stay home and watch. 'More comfortable.' 'More convenient.' 'Can see better,' they agreed" (128).

Such face-saving rationalization in the face of racist rejection also parallels William Boelhower's (1982) and Werner Sollors' s (1987) observations about the immigrant experience. First the immigrants (primarily uncritical and eager) consent to Americanization. Then a second generation is assimilated. Finally, a third generation emerges. A "nostalgic" group, it attempts to link what it feel is most valuable about its ancestry with what is valuable in its new world. Sollors sees these three generations as going "from consent to descent." But as Sau-ling C. Wong puts it, such "ethnic scholars' theories" are all well and good, except that "certain ethnic groups, as a result of racism" (such as Jen describes at "the American ball game") will "never be able to enact" integration into "the cultural regime in full" (S. Wong 1993, 41). Also, Jen in *Typical American* describes a much more rapid time frame for the process than Sollors's lengthy period of three generations. The Chang family quickly moves from consent to descent in their own immigrant generation. Mona and Callie, Ralph's and Helen's daughters, are first generation Americans and daily observe as they grow the syncretic processes of their parents' generation. In fact, both generations go from consent to dissent—the children through their parents, as through a glass darkly. The children, however, although they retain the bicultural sensibility of the previous generation, do so with a diminished grasp on the ancestral language, culture, and customs of the motherland, a situation which we will see reflected in Sasaki's and Kadohata's depiction of immigrant and first generations:

They celebrated Christmas in addition to Chinese New Year's, and were regulars at Radio City Music Hall. Ralph owned a Davy Crockett hat. Helen knew most of the words to most of the songs in The King and I, and South Pacific. It was true that she still inquired of people if they'd eaten yet, odd as it sounded; Ralph invented his grammar on the fly; even Theresa struggled to put her Chinese thoughts into English. But now she had English thoughts too—that was true also. They all did. There were things they did not know how to say in Chinese. The language of outside the house had seeped well inside—Cadillac, Pyrex, subway, Coney Island, Ringling Brothers and Barnum & Bailey Circus. Transistor radio. Theresa and Helen and Ralph slipped from tongue to tongue like turtles taking to land, taking to sea; though one remained their more natural element, both had become essential. (124)

To prove their accelerated syncresis, after a time the immigrant family can critique itself and its original notions of "typical American": "You know why we used to say typical American good-for-nothing?' Theresa said at supper. 'That was because we believed we were good for nothing.' 'You mean *I* thought I was good for nothing.' Ralph could laugh about anything these days" [Emphasis in the original]. In the next sentence, Jen describes Theresa as "tactfully" nibbling "a slice of stir-fried hot dog" (126). Characteristic of her sardonic humor, Jen uses the bicultural food combination as yet another means of depicting the syncresis going on in the family at this point.[8]

Still another negative use by the family of the concept of "typical American" is shown in the difference between how Chinese and Americans are socialized to hold conversations. For Chinese Americans it is like playing a game without a partner when they are dealing with "Americans": "In later years, when Helen taught the girls how to talk, she'd teach them when not to continue, as she put it. It was a polite way of making a point, she said, but the way she said it, the girls knew that by point she meant barb. How come, though, when they fell silent, no one seemed pricked? 'American kids, their mothers teach them nothing,' Helen said. '*Typical American*, what can you say' "(135) [Emphasis in the original].

When the family moves to a house in the Connecticut suburbs, Theresa learns more things about America, enough to make them understand that "We didn't realize." Then in an example of the polyglossia characteristic of postmodern authors, all the family's voices sing out in turn, each in harmony, to the tune that although they lived here, they "actually knew nothing"(157). When compared to their former life, American suburbia seems "radiant with truth and discovery . . . A paradise . . . An ocean liner compared to a rowboat with leaks . . . A Cadillac compared to an aisle seat on the bus" (158). Comparing Chinese to American soil unfavorably, Helen even equates her first lawn with America: "It was the great blue American sky, beguiling the grass upward. It was the soil, so fresh, so robust, so much better quality than Chinese soil; Chinese soil having been prevailed upon for too many thousands of years. . . . After all, this was top-quality grass, grown out of top-quality soil" (159). She relates her own family to the new lawn: "Just as a top-quality family was growing out of a top-quality house." But then Jen ominously and caustically adds, "or so Helen believed" (159), to remind us once again of the parallel with Poe's "Fall of the House of Usher."

Jen also uses the title "typical American" to critique the single-minded pursuit of economic success under the combined rubric of religio-secular progress to which the immigrants of the world aspire. Grover embodies this "heresy" when he seduces Ralph. As in this example and in many other instances throughout the text, Jen exposes her real conviction: this is a siren song and infernal, at that, for Grover immediately blows "a smoke ring" (193) after singing it: "[T]that business of his could be the start of a real success story. This could be the start of a self-made man." (195). Ralph, seduced, converts wholeheartedly to this new secular religion. To Jen, the ways of capitalistic entrepreneurship are criminal when ungrounded by the ethical anchors that Confucianism and Transcendentalism provided. Like a typical amoral, postwar American capitalistic entrepreneur, Ralph learns how to drain the proceeds from the chicken franchise he buys:

First he and Grover put a lock on the door; then Ralph began to spend an hour or so in there alone, every night.
What was that noise? A certain wha-ingg! over and over.
"A cash register," said Helen.
"But why would he be ringing a cash register?"
It was very mysterious. Every night he rang, rang, rang, making a new register tape to replace the tape for the day. (201)

CONCLUSION

Outraged by this disease of "money worship" (200), Jen agrees with Chaucer (citing I Timothy 6:10) that money is the root of all evil, because too many Chinese immigrants suppress their spiritual and ethical training in obsessive attempts to become Americans only in terms of acquiring wealth. Thus Jen's resolution for the House of Chang is neither the headlong rush into "typical American"(ness) that splintered them as a family and nearly destroyed them, nor the clinging to the old mandarin class system containing the Confucian ideal of the family and rigid hierarchical order. At the same time, she does not advocate a cultural amalgamation or a melting pot whose purpose is to homogenize everyone into "Americanization." Instead, she advocates a syncresis that contains an "idea of identity expanded beyond its customary limits . . . a synthetical identity of the oppressed that resolves all the competing elements of experience" (Uba

1992, 41). From a feminist perspective, syncresis is the "ability to hold same-ness and difference in suspension . . . [that] is identified with resistance to as-similation by dominant forms of power" (Newton and Stacey 1993, 64).

Perhaps the best summing up of both the positive and negative aspects of syncresis in terms of the writers under discussion in this text is what has been used for contemporary Chinese American poets: "[T]hey suffer from a lack of attachment, but they also gain the advantage of being able to choose commitment to either culture. They have the frustration of lacking connections to society, but they can more easily adopt a critical distance vis-à-vis that society. . . . The ne-cessity of embracing, but at the same time distancing themselves from, their cultural roots give [sic] their works unique tension." (Wang and Zhao, 1991, xxi).

Shirley Geok-lin Lim uses irony in "Dedicated to Confucius Plaza" to convey this dual consciousness:

> The city [New York] is a mountain
> Also, made of Asia,
> Europe and Africa.
> They call it America.
> Every morning I practice li,
> Perform my wifely duties,
> Watch color television,
> And eat pop, crackle, snap.
> It is not hard to be
> An Asian-American Chinee. (Wang and Zhao 1991, 134)

In contrast, in *Typical American*, Jen ultimately represents her characters as having mellowed, having learned to live through "cooptation" and "monologic dominance" into a productive syncresis:

No longer isolating themselves in their enclaves, these [characters] demonstrate their desire and ability to integrate into the mainstream, as their ultimate goal. Yet for these people integration does not spell cooptation or monologic dominance by the host culture. Rather, by merging with the mainstream without repressing their nostalgic dreams, native heritage, and distinctive voices, they can assert their identity and participate as Americans in the enrichment of their new country's pluralistic culture . . . in [a] polyphonic post-modern discourse. (Tran 1992, 283)

Like Hong Kingston, Amy Tan, and Myenne Ng, Jen represents her female characters as by cultural training and temperament the successful syncretizers who in Nellie Wong's words "move the anger out, from self-expression to ac-tion,/ from individuality to community, from compromises to demands, for the right to live as women, as a people" (1989, 207). Hong Kingston's, Tan's, and Jen's male characters go off or represent the deep end. Their female characters, if and when they do, quickly regain their equilibrium and balance. Ironically, this is an ideal of Confucianism.

NOTES

1. The influence of Younghill Kang's *The Grass Roof* (1931) might be considered here in relation to the use of a similar motif: the importance of the hero's achieving the key to his American car.

2. He happened to have influenced my own immigrant father who took and graduated from the Dale Carnegie course. Since I picked up and pored through all the reading matter my father left lying around, including Carnegie's and other self-help books, it could be claimed with some justification that Dale Carnegie also influenced *this* text. Other similar highly influential and successful inspirational texts of the period that Jen satirizes here are Fulton Sheen's *Peace of Soul* and *Life is Worth Living*; Harry Overstreet's *The Mature Mind*; Joshua Loth Liebman's *Peace of Mind*; Gaylord Hauser's *Look Younger, Live Longer*; and Norman Vincent Peale's and Smiley Blanton's *The Art of Real Happiness*.

3. The term "Old" does not always signify age, but seniority in rank and class, as well. Although Old Chao is Ralph's age, he is slightly ahead of him in school and has risen higher in their profession, having become chairman of their department. In this text, therefore, the term is used by Jen as a common honorific, signifying respect for his rank.

4. The publisher does this on the front cover—"Gish Jen has done much more than tell an immigrant story. . . . She has done it more and in some ways better than it has ever been done before (*Los Angeles Times Book Review*)"—as well as on the back cover—"The immigrant experience will never be the same . . . a comedy . . . a tragedy . . . a pure delight (*The Boston Globe*)." And in the first pages we open, fully two and a half pages are devoted to extravagant praise, such as "A dream. Compounded by heartbreaking humor and exhilarating tragedy, it rings true as the stories my own relatives would recite in hushed tones around the banquet table" (David Henry Hwang). Or, "Heartbreaking . . . Sidesplitting . . . A rich addition to the ever-growing body of immigrant literature, lovingly imagined, thoroughly satisfying (*The Washington Post Book World*)." Or "*Typical American* is indeed an American story, and Gish Jen's immensely intelligent, thunderously funny, truly heartbreaking novel is perhaps the best story of contemporary immigrant experience ever to grace our literature (Jayne Anne Phillips)." "The brilliance of Gish Jen's novel is that it operates so deeply, yet so entertainingly, and at so many levels at once. . . . She has created that rarest achievement in fiction, the profoundly comic novel (*San Diego Union*)." *Kirkus Review* predicts that it will be compared to *The Joy Luck Club*. The *Library Journal* hails it as "Truly an American story. . . . Immigrants coming to terms with the possibilities of America. . . . Poignant and deftly told. . . . Filled with humor and sympathy." *Entertainment Weekly* lauds the book's "discerning comic touch." The *Arizona Daily Star* prefers *Typical American* to *The Joy Luck Club* on the basis that it is "grander" and "more moving" than Tan's book. The *San Francisco Chronicle* sees it as a "saga" of "disillusionment and discovery, of romance and betrayal." Publishers Weekly, also paying tribute to Jen's "wry . . . compassionate . . . darkly humorous" perspective, sees her as "a virtuoso raconteur of the Chinese-American experience." This conclusion seems strange in view of the fact that except for Grover (the exception in all things), Jen's major male characters are Ph.D.s and Theresa is an MD. In fact, in China their ancestors have all been Mandarins.

5. Elaine Kim's and Janice Otani's *With Silk Wings* contains further proofs of the universality of xenophobia. For example, Sook Nam Choo, a Filipina, records that

"school was a struggle for her. Japanese American children had called her 'kurombo' or 'darky,' and white children outside her new school called her 'Chink' or 'Jap.' She gained acceptance only by being an exceptionally good student." (62). Also, the North Vietnamese-American Le Ly Hayslip makes a similar point at great length *in When Heaven and Earth Changed Places*, 21–22.

6. See Calvin Hernton, *The Sexual Mountain and Afro-American Women Writers* for a detailed examination of this subject in relation to African American men discriminating against African American women in Civil Rights organizations.

7. Here and elsewhere Jen refutes the common contention that Asian American women are less class elitist than their American counterparts. See my Conclusion for further discussion of this point.

8. Sau-ling C. Wong in *Reading Asian American Literature* identifies alimentation as a major theme in Asian American literature, as well as that of the *doppelganger* or "racial shadow," as she puts it. Also, Shirley Geok-lin Lim plays a variation on this moment when she writes in "Modern Secrets," "Last night I dreamt in Chinese./Eating Yankee shredded wheat" (In Wang and Zhao 1991, 132).

Chapter 4

R. A. Sasaki, *The Loom and Other Stories:* "There Has Got to Be More to Life Than That"

LITTLE WOMAN

In *The Loom and Other Stories*, the narrator's name is Jo, an intertextual reference to the major character of Louisa May Alcott's *Little Women* (1868). In American literary history *Little Women* is perhaps the most popular of all narratives about girls and women in a family community, and Jo March is its most beloved character. Like Alcott's character Jo, Sasaki's Jo is plain. By the time she reaches the fifth grade, she already feels sorry for her mother on the grounds that the poor woman deserved better than to give birth to a "horse-faced daughter whose picture was full of teeth" (4). She then "considered the possibility" that she would not make it "as a Mouseketeer" (her childhood dream); that "[l]ooks would never be my meal ticket. I would have to develop other talents" (4). In this "self-belittling" way, which puns on Alcott's title here and throughout the text, Jo justifies how she was originally motivated to take up her future vocation—writing.

We also learn in the first chapter that one of the narrator's three sisters, Cathy, goes mountain climbing and falls to her death. The lofty goal of the activity, followed by the fall of "little women," is a motif we have seen in *Typical American*. Sasaki may here be fictionalizing a real-life tragedy. In 1984, a Japanese American woman was part of an American team that attempted to scale Mt. Kilimanjaro. She would have been the first woman to have ever performed this feat successfully. However, she fell to her death near the summit after having tied her gear in a faulty manner. I have often wondered since then how much of what happened could be attributed to the culturally internalized gender-asymmetrical prescription that scaling heights is literally and figuratively for men to do and women to observe. As the female climber came ever closer to the summit, the psychic stress of committing a forbidden act—of simultaneously "going to the top" and "going up against authority" might have been too much for her, to the point where falling became a self-fulfilling prophesy. She strove for "the top," for success, but failed as "little women" are programmed to do. Falling may well have been a culturally internalized safety valve of obedience.

Such a tragic downward trajectory illustrates the "fall-out" of gender asymmetry as a projection and abstraction onto women of traditional masculinist discourse and conduct. In this discourse, only men are conceptualized as performing physical and psychic activities that physiologically and psychically equate with male social and worldly positions of height. Whatever is deemed "high" in terms of "dominant" and "successful" is naturalized as allocated to men by cultural norms and standards. It should be no surprise then when "climbing" of any kind—from ladders to mountains—becomes difficult or impossible for women globally. In *The Loom*, in the mother's life trajectory we will see how Sasaki uses the metaphor of "the falling woman" to illustrate a less spectacular "fall" then Cathy's, that is far more common for most women. These falls are downward slides to private obscurity, to "little" lives in "little" houses.

Throughout the text Jo exhibits one of the major characteristics of postfeminists. She mocks her mother's traditional ways, her petty "little" preoccupations, her concern about "what people will say." Jo describes her mother as cutting her daughters' hair off very short in order not to "give people the wrong idea" (15), or as going into "a frenzy of cleaning" before going away on vacation because in the event of a fire or a break-in the *yoso no hito* [strange people] would "have to come in" (15). Jo sneers that it was unclear to her family on whose behalf—"the firemen, the police, or the burglar"—her mother would be so "mortally shamed if her house were not spotless" (15).

Unlike her unreliable narrator, Sasaki meanwhile takes pains to carry her readers back to the past, to describe how the mother came to be so "up-tight" in the present, as Jo might put it. The mother has internalized the need to always do everything right, to always be the good girl. She perceives all other human beings as her judges. "They" are her authorities. She holds all other heads higher than her own. This is why she is concerned about the "They" who might be judging her housekeeping abilities and finding her wanting. "They" entirely run her, from "the way she cooked" to "the clothes she chose" for her daughters only because " 'They' were wearing [them] these days" (15).

Her postfeminist daughters profess not to know or care how their mother came by her intense drive to obey the "They" who make the rules. It is a source of condescending humor to them. They can afford to luxuriate in all the gaps they experience between their values and perspectives and their mother's. They can afford to label her motives and her conduct "idiosyncrasies" that frustrated them, but to which they "were more or less resigned" (16). Fortunately for them, the feminist movement has intervened between their mother's "regime of truth" and the one in which they are acculturated. Whereas the mother did not have the advantage of the technology of organized feminism and its way of looking at things, her daughters take the benefits of feminism's advances entirely for granted. As Dorothy Cordova points out to Elaine Kim in an interview: "Who would understand today what the people of my generation went through? . . . In those days it was almost a crime just to be Filipino. People would not sit next to us on the bus. I remember waiting timidly in line with my merchandise for 30 or 40 minutes while the salesclerk would wait on everyone but me. I was afraid to say anything because I didn't want to draw attention to myself. So I would just stand there, wishing I could die" (Kim 1983, 62).

The mother's first response to her daughter Cathy's death reveals the central core of her rules for living—adaptation and obedience. If you follow the rules and regulations, you will survive, you will endure, you will even succeed. Cathy "had broken the rules" (16), the mother claims, not even permitting herself to cry, until after the news has been broken to her husband and he cried "as children cry who have awakened in the night to a nameless terror, a nameless grief" (16). "Only then" had the mother finally exposed her emotions, "but it seemed almost vicarious, as if she had needed their father to process the new stuff of life into personal emotion. Not once since the death had she talked about her own feelings" (17). What societal force(s) can be so powerful as to take the individuality out of a woman to the point where she expresses no emotions without permission, not even grief at the death of her daughter?

It is not so much that Sasaki represents the mother as in accord with "the rules," the "They." It is that she does not see past them, as we have seen the feminists in *The Kitchen God's Wife* and in *Bone* finally succeed in doing after many struggles. The mother of *The Loom* sees rules as to be followed. She believes that the culture gives her assurances that if you play by its rules, then you will be rewarded. You endanger your chances for survival, for acceptance in the human race, if you step out of line in any way. Here Sasaki enunciates a theme identified with her predecessor Hisaye Yamamoto in her great classics "Seventeen Syllables" and "The Legend of Miss Sasagawara." Yamamoto's unforgettable female characters are destroyed because they are different and follow "a different drummer." One writes haiku; the other is a sensitive former ballerina who is misdiagnosed as insane in a detention camp for Japanese Americans during World War II. Interestingly, Yamamoto, and Wakako Yamauchi, as well, including the Chinese American authors covered in this text, all use young, unreliable narrators, a popular device with postmodern writers.

So strong is the mother's acculturation that she actually becomes detached from her own feelings about the death of her daughter. The mainstream feminist Carol Gilligan defines this indoctrination as "the ethic of caring and compassion": to do as told, to detach oneself from one's own ego and needs and concern oneself only with others' needs. For the mother, everything has to do with rules kept or broken, or her husband's suffering, never about herself. Like Yamamoto again, Sasaki represents the stultifying effects of the cultural constraints of gender asymmetry indirectly, without comment; without naming its cause(s); without judging; without vilification. Sasaki also exposes the results of gender asymmetry after feminism's organized efforts to undo it. In representing differing attitudes and behaviors by women before and after the feminist movement, Sasaki thereby adds her voice to the indictment of gender asymmetry. She elicits the reader's indignation through indirect means, perhaps more powerfully than if she had done so directly. She does this through disconnected but eventually incrementally powerful descriptions. At first, the reader does not realize where Sasaki is going with these seemingly aimless flashbacks, until they begin to reveal a pattern: her representation of all the ways in which the fearless child that the mother had once been was stunted.

The mother's postfeminist daughters attempt to rectify the situation through individual suggestions designed to re-instill into their mother a sense of self and self-volition. At first, as in *Bone* after Ona's fall to her death, they also try a change of scenery for their grieving mother, persuading her to visit with one of her daughters, Linda, whose husband is stationed in Heidelberg. At the airport, her daughters see for the first time what has become of her "outside the context of their house. She had always been there when the children came back from school; in fact, the sisters had never had baby sitters" (17). Now they wonder about "this person," "so small and sweet," "this little person . . . their mother" (17). They wonder who she really is. Sasaki's punning variations on the "little" in the title *Little Women* are always unobtrusive, as in this instance. But Sasaki's repetition of this meaningful word throughout the text also creates an incremental increase of anger, again in terms of the author's theme of female diminution and desiccation due to the constraints of race and gender asymmetry.

Using the daughters' curiosity and concern as the vehicle toward deconstructing the forces that diminished and shrank their mother, Sasaki undertakes to expose how the cultural system worked in relation to the mother. She shows how "They" took a female child and made of her a totally self-alienated individual to the point where all her energy has dwindled down to her weaving a "muffler." The neck covering symbolizes both her lack of self (interest), which has been muffled, and her drive to protect her family from "the elements," that is, the racist and sexist environment.

Initially, racism creates a "duality" in the child, a "double discourse," or in DuBois's famous term, a "double consciousness." The mother is second generation Japanese American, a Nisei. According to Sasaki, "there was no common thread running through both worlds"—Japan and the United States—so that "the duality was unplanned, untaught" (17). It all began on the very first day of school when the mother found that she could not understand the teacher and was called a "Jap" by another child. Until then she had been sheltered within her own group. All she had known of life hitherto was that her mother had taken in boarders, Japanese men without their families whom "she accepted as her world." She had never before had "to sort out her identity." As a result, she had met life headlong and with the confidence of a child" (18).

Psychically, the mother had begun life whole enough—even daring and adventurous—as her daughter Cathy was to become later on. However, Cathy's experience reverses her mother's doubly to a deadly point in relation to the mother's accident at the age of five while roller skating. Instead of just going to the corner of her block she [had] continued "down the Buchanan Street hill," gotten "all the way to the bottom, cheeks flushed red and black hair flying, before shooting off the curb and crumpling in the street. Her hands and knees were scraped raw, but she was laughing" (19). Never again will she react with the joyous, triumphant laughter with which she originally greeted her falling down as a result of violating parameters set for her. After the first day of school she internalizes how another child had expressed contempt for her and her group by calling her "Jap" and then by pulling up "the corners of her eyes at her" and "sneering." From that moment on for the rest of her life, "[a] kind of radar system went to work in her" (20). She pulls herself in. She curbs whatever is unique in herself and different from others, "blending like a chameleon for survival." Ever "[a]fterward" she opts for conformity in every way, acting "with caution in new surroundings." The mother's goal becomes "to blend in" everywhere to the point of obsession. The racial insult has traumatized her forever. She never forgets the name of the little girl who called her a "Jap" and she never cries again. Her psyche has become colonized; a result that has been deplored in postcolonial literature and criticism as the internalization of "the master's script," as I have pointed out previously and will discuss again in the Conclusion in my analysis of the feminist movement in relation to Asian American women writers.

Here Jo's mother is represented as entirely reactive, possessing none of the resistance or skepticism of the feminists Winnie of *The Kitchen God's Wife* and Lei of *Bone*, or the postfeminists Nina of *Bone*, and Olivia of *The Floating World*. The mother of *The Loom* is as much of a casualty of the colonial and colonizing American racism and ethnocentrism in San Francisco as was any Indian girl in Calcutta during the British raj. Already at this early age of five she has internalized accepted external opinion. The "They" her daughters blame for her timidity decree that she should not be, is not, and can never be more than a faceless nonentity. Despite her different appearance from the other children, she strains always from that moment on and into old age "to be as inconspicuous as possible." If she doesn't understand the teacher, she copies the other children. She listens "carefully" to the teacher and attempts never to "provoke criticism." Now and forever after she is convinced that she couldn't stand out because if she did, it would be accompanied by harshly negative consequences: "[S]he at least wanted to be invisible" (20). This is the same internalized prescription to which I was referring in my analysis of the causes for Cathy's deadly fall—(and most women's fall to obscurity)—that invisibility is safest, even safer than smallness.

According to Amy Tan, one of her sisters "who now lives in Wisconsin also wanted to be a writer. But then, the sister mourns, " 'when I was growing up, they told me I could not do so many things. And now my imagination is wasted and no stories can move out of my brain' " (Tan [1987] 1992, 271). Given the same hostile, external environment as their sisters, I am puzzled here by the difference between Hong Kingston's and Tan's courageous responses to negative feedback and those of the silent and silenced little girl who is Maxine's *doppelganger* in *The Woman Warrior*, Tan's sister, and the mother in *The Loom*. Why do a few female children rear up and go into mortal combat the rest of their lives against causeless insult and injury due to such extrinsic factors as race, class, and gender, whereas most do not? As Barbara Kingsolver puts it: "[W]hy do so many people turn inward on their own pain, shutting down even their empathy, while others turn outward and engage their anguished hearts with the anguish of the world?" (1994, 26).

Jo the narrator says of her mother that "[s]he succeeded" in every way in her ambition to fit in, muting "her colors and "[g]oing quiet" (20), so that from her days at school onward the other children easily got used to her. Some even treated her nicely. But Jo wants to know how her mother could ever really become "a part of their world" when "she was not really herself" (21). Worse, after going to the public school the mother became no longer "comfortable" with her parents' language which seemed now to her more "like a sweater that had been well washed and rendered shapeless by wear. . . . She would never wear it outside of the house. It was a personal thing, like a hole in one's sock, which was perfectly all right at home but would be a horrible embarrassment if seen by *yaso no hito*"(21). In *Hunger of Memory*, Richard Rodriguez recalls that he had the same response to the Spanish spoken in his home, a result of the same process as the mother in *The Loom* undergoes: indoctrination in the demeaning of difference from the norm, even one's own difference.[1]

Whenever the mother goes into the *hakuyin* world she employs an internal censor to edit out any "Japanese words and mannerisms when she spoke" (21). As a result, she became stilted, artificial, "muffled," like her "formal, carefully chosen and somewhat artificial words" (21). The reason she gave to herself for not conveying "what she really felt, what she really was" should not be surprising when she confesses that she now views herself as "unacceptable" (21). Jo describes her mother's internal "watchdog" as "a tyrant" when it comes to her "behavior." Another source for the mother's internalization of the low opinion held of her is the media: what she reads in the "popular novels" and sees in "Hollywood" movies. As in Toni Morrison's *The Bluest Eye*, as with the millions of readers of Harlequin novels and contemporary viewers of soap operas and *telenovelas*, female characters are depicted as holding themselves as high or as low as others hold them. The mother calls her response "respectability," which she desires to uphold "at all costs."

In this regard, most Japanese immigrants to the United States were different and differently motivated than Chinese immigrants. The Japanese "admired and tried to emulate Americans. Very few felt hostile or resentful." "Some" like the mother, although the child of immigrants and not an immigrant herself, "responded to rejection and discrimination by trying to modify their own behavior" (Kim 1982, 125). She "would never acknowledge," never admit to any "weakness" or "peculiarity." She determines to be "irreproachabl[y]" American. Ashamed of her background, she suppresses and denies her preschool memories of "young men lounging in the doorways of her home and drinking in the back room with her father; of their gambling and philandering . . . [of] immigrant women who came to her mother desperate for protection from the beatings by their frenzied husbands" (21). The latter too had internalized the inferiority and undesirability of their own kind. All these early experiences of the mother's were in the greatest contrast imaginable, Sasaki tells us in a tone dripping with sarcasm, to the mother's new influences in school—the books she reads about "the drawing rooms of Jane Austen" and "the movies she views about the virtue and gallantry of Hollywood" (21). These influences on the mother remain today most women's deepest influences: the reinforcers of their fondest hopes, dreams, and desires.

During the Depression, her father's business had been "done in" by a dishonest, absconding "*hakujin* partner" and they had to get along "on piecework and potatoes" (21).

Her mother organized a group of immigrant ladies to crochet window-shade rings. They got a penny apiece from the stores on Grant Avenue. Her father strung plastic birds onto multi-colored rings. As they sat working in the back room day after day, they must have dreamed of better times. They had all gambled the known for the unknown when they left Japan to come to America. Apparently it took more than hard work. They couldn't work themselves to death for pennies. Entrepreneurial ventures were risky. They wanted to spare their sons and daughters this insecurity and hardship. Education was the key that would open the magical doors to a better future. Not that they hadn't been educated in Japan, indeed some of them were better educated than the people whose houses they cleaned on California Street. But they felt the key was an American education, a college education. Immigrant sons and immigrant daughters would fulfill their dreams. (22)

For as Kim tells us, "[a]s the years passed, the immigrant Japanese relied increasingly on his [*sic*] children to vindicate him, to prove that his sacrifice and his decision to leave Japan had been worthwhile after all" (Kim 1982, 128). The mother's dream was thus a continuation of her parents' dream, expressed above, to validate their struggles: "To succeed, to be irreproachable, to be American. . . . A smart career girl in a tailored suit, beautiful and bold—an American girl." Notice that all the adjectives which the mother uses equate with approval. Further, she sums up her family as like herself in that "[t]hey did everything right" (22) in describing their efforts to assimilate into American culture just prior to the Japanese bombing of the American fleet at Pearl Harbor on December 7, 1941. The mother's family illustrates the immigrant trajectory of upward mobility, with the second generation pushing ever onward and upward to higher education:

Through watchful community judgment of individual performance and actions, the nisei were guided by a sense of collective obligation. Parental emphasis on duty and responsibility and the use of shame, guilt, and gossip pushed the nisei towards academic achievement. Appeals were made on the basis of ethnic pride: children were exhorted not to fail or misbehave, lest they reflect negatively on the entire group. Parents continually reminded their children of the sacrifices they had made for their education's sake and demanded that the children show their gratitude by making the most of their opportunities. (Kim 1982, 129)

Accordingly, the mother went to UCLA, class of 1939. However, not one of the mother's group, "[t]he Nisei Students' Club . . . about sixty" strong would get anywhere by "clerking in Chinatown shops or pruning American gardens . . . because it was 1939 and they had Japanese faces. There was nowhere for them to go" (23). Jo attributes her father's business failure to racism, also. "America was creating a masterpiece and did not want their color" (23). After Japan bombed Pearl Harbor, the United States instituted its infamous racist policy (for which it did not apologize and make reparations until 1982, and then only after intense pressure). Up to this point in time Japanese immigrants were more highly regarded than the Chinese, despite Japan's invasion of China as far back as 1931, long before it invaded U. S. territory. Only after that point did the Chinese became our brave allies, a positive propaganda effort that began to resonate in favor of Chinese Americans, while responses to Japanese Americans fell commensurately.

The American government immediately rounded up and interned Japanese Americans in camps, while respecting the civil rights of German, Spanish, and Italian Americans, as well as other ethnic white Americans whose countries of origin had become fascist. Approximately 200,000 Japanese Americans like the mother's family were taken to detention camps. Their first prison was Tanforan Racetrack, where they were forced to cram themselves into the horse stables. Sasaki shows how this experience reinforced the mother's internalized low self-esteem. Upon viewing "the dirt and manure left by the former equine occupants," she communes with herself about white Euro-Americans and for the first time realizes what they think of the Japanese, which makes her feel "shame." Again, it never seems to occur to her to resist or differ with this view of her. In college she and her Nisei friends had "believed" they were "accepted," had allowed themselves to glow with "foolish confidence" based on their assumptions and "unfounded dreams" (24). She now realizes that they "had been spinning a fantasy world that was unacknowledged by the larger fabric of society" (24). "The aura of Berkeley" had carried her away to the point where "she had forgotten the legacy left by Eleanor Leland" [the white child who had traumatized her on her first day of school by making a face at her and calling her "Jap"] (24). After a year the family was shifted to the Topaz Relocation Center "in the wastelands of Utah. Topaz, Jewel of the Desert, they called it sardonically" (24) because of its awful dust storms. The same harrowing experiences are documented, to list a few of many examples, in Monica Sone's *Nisei Daughter* (1953); in Jeanne Wakatsuki Houston's and James D. Houston's *Farewell to Manzanar* (1973); in Mitsuye Yamada's *Desert Run: Poems and Other Stories* (1988); and in the riveting factual accounts by Peter T. Suzuki, Michi Weglyn, and Minoro Yasui in *The Big AIIIEEEEE!* (1991).

During this period the mother married a Kibei, a Japanese born in the United States but taken to Japan for his education when he was eight. Like the mother, the father is never named. Once the name Keiko is associated with the mother, but it is unclear whether it is her sister's name or hers. Perhaps Sasaki wishes us to see the mother as a kind of "generic Everywoman" in her shaping experiences, while minimizing the father through the use of anonymity. Or, perhaps, Cheung suggests, by using only "honorific titles," "the narrator" may thereby be transforming "individual family members into archetypes (Cheung 1993, 123). Returning to this country after ten years, the mother's future husband had spent the interval working during the day and going to school at night until he went into the Army. The American government created yet further trauma and turmoil for American men of Japanese ancestry and fighting age when they were given the option of serving in the armed forces as an alternate to the camp. Many eagerly took the government up on its offer, both because as Americans they wanted to fight an American enemy and as Japanese Americans they wanted to prove their loyalty. But those men who refused were called "No-No Boys" and were ostracized by their own group for arguing that if their own country could destroy their lives by throwing them into detention camps, then they should not fight for it.

After the war, the mother became busy with the couples' babies, "one after another, all girls." Sasaki uses the word "absorbed" for how the mother perceived herself in relation to her children, but "obsessed" seems a more appropriate word to describe her preoccupation with "their nursing and bodily functions, in the sucking, smacking world of babies" with "diapers to be changed and washed, bowel movements to be recorded, and bottles sterilized" (26). At this time, the mother first begins to ponder how she could ever "pick up the pieces of her past selves [and] weave them together into a pattern," which foreshadows how she will ultimately do so—through weaving

Sasaki does not touch on the subject of sexuality in relation to the mother, so that we have no idea what her attitude is toward the quick succession of four daughters in almost as many years, only that she became extremely busy and preoccupied as a result of their birth. Also, Sasaki never intimates that the mother's bearing and raising of children impacts in any way on her health. She describes the mother as welcoming the activity, that it keeps her joyfully occupied. She has no time to brood about the fact that her professional future was cut off after graduation from college when she and her family had to suspend their lives after being shipped off to the relocation camps. The Isei generation lost their homes and occupations and businesses, the Nisei, their future, and both groups lost all continuity in their lives from all they had once known.

We also discover that the mother's friends had been shocked and annoyed at her decision to marry downward to a young man who had not graduated from college and apparently never would. Later, we learn that her future husband had completely won her over. Thus we can assume that Sasaki in an indirect manner is conveying that the mother consciously chose her husband because she wanted him. Sasaki does not inform her readers whatever it was—his driving ambition, and/or personal traits that attracted her. Moreover, the mother's parents do not figure at all in the decision, or Jo makes no mention of them in relation to it. At any rate, Sasaki does depict the mother's sacrifice of self in marriage and motherhood as her expression of service to her own family.

The mother projects herself entirely into her daughters, narrowing her horizons down according to their needs. After her own parents' deaths in quick succession, it is significant that all she chooses to retain from their home is her college yearbook "from Cal." This document is the reminder to her of the most expansive movements of her life. After marriage and before her children come, she lives a "[s]ealed off" life "in her little house," in aptly termed "fog-shrouded Avenues" in which her past "seemed like a dream" to her. All her friends have scattered, or have "married and [been] sealed off in their own private worlds." Thus does Sasaki describe as "sealed off" the harsh period after World War II when the ideal was "the nuclear family" with its home-bound, sealed-in-and-off homemaker mother who has completely internalized two cultures' prescriptions for women. Accordingly, the mother immerses herself in her daughters without any "sense of loss."

As she has been as a student, so she becomes as a mother, "without fault." She projects onto her children the same goals as she had set for herself and as her parents had envisioned for her, even expressed in the same terminology; that they would be "irreproachable." She has emerged from the war years with a hearing problem contracted at Topaz from the violent dust storms there. But she will not admit "such a deficiency" at the PTA meetings. As she was as a child when she could not understand the teacher, so now she "pretends to hear when she didn't, nodding her head and smiling." This is because of her overriding de-sire for "things to go smoothly; she wanted to appear normal" (28). Because her ego is sunk so deeply into her offspring, she perceives the girls' school days "as a happy time, the happiest time of her life." In contrast, once the girls grow up, after the house empties, she would "let the telephone ring, pretending not to be home," making the only exception her sister with whom "she would exchange news on the phone for an hour."

"She came alive" only when her daughters came home to visit. When they did so, they were critical of her. Cathy, for example, was annoyed with her for not getting a hearing aid. In contrast, the mother approved of her daughter. From her viewpoint, Cathy had "interesting friends, *hakuyin* friends, whom she sometimes brought home with her. Cathy moved easily in all worlds, and her mother's heart swelled with pride to see it."[2] When Jo came home and was writing, her mother would madden her by giving her bits of information. At these times, Jo would gradually gather up her thoughts from "far away" to even-tually focus on the little figure of her mother," so important did her dreams seem and so insignificant, in contrast to them, her mother's "chatter." Jo's dismissive thought about her mother that "she had led such a sheltered life" (29) is ironic proof of her unreliability as a narrator because she herself has had no experience of life, especially of suffering, although in her youthful postfeminist arrogance she imagines otherwise. Given the actual traumatic situations that the mother has undergone, this is ignorant condescension on the part of a young woman who is actually the one who has led a sheltered and even privileged life. Her sense of wholeness, free choice, and limitless possibilities are still very much intact.

After the mother returns from Germany she talks about it for a week. Then Germany became one more "loose thread in the fabric of her life." Note that Sasaki's choice of weaving imagery here becomes ever more a thread itself in the strand of her impressive use of this metaphor. The next time Jo sees her mother, approximately two months later, she is "once again effaced, a part of the house almost, in her faded blouse and shapeless skirt, joylessly adding too much seasoned salt to the dinner salad." In a letter to Linda in Germany, Jo complains to her sister that she has had to leave home and has moved to New York because "the last time I went home I found myself discussing the machine washability of acrylics with Mom. There has got to be more to life than that" (30).

At this point, Jo's mother visits her in Greenwich Village where she meets Jo's live-in boyfriend. Predictably, she reacts with shock and "disappointment," wondering what "Daddy" is "going to say." Here she sounds very much the collusive gatekeeper of traditional ways. Within two weeks, however, she moves from "guarded assessment to tentative acceptance." For one thing, Michael cooks breakfast for them all every morning. She begins to relax at a little round table over her morning coffee by the window, remembering as she does so "her first trip alone": "As the train hurtled from Topaz to Chicago, she had been alone in the world. She remembered vividly the quality of light coming through the train window, and how it had bathed the passing countryside in a golden wash. Other passengers had slept, but she sat riveted to the window. Perhaps the scenery seemed so beautiful because of the bleakness and sensory deprivation of Topaz. She didn't know why she remembered it now" (32).

As she was then, so she is now—going through a rite of passage: the same rite of passage that she sees reflected in the next generation, especially in her daughter Jo. In Jo's apartment, which reflects a postfeminist lifestyle, the mother is beginning to experience a fleeting sense of freedom that she has not had since those moments on the train long ago. Her daughter's attitude toward life can also be added to the causes for the mother's new-found sense of expansiveness, of possibility. When Jo returns home the next year, however, she feels that "the house, or whatever it was, had done its work" on her mother. The house represents the mother's burden, whereas her daughter's apartment represents Jo's freedom. Domesticity's constraints, its demands for a loss of self-identity on her part weight the mother down. "Her mother was again lost to her, a sweet little creature unable to hear very well, relaying little bits of information." So Jo gives up, because "[w]e seem to lose ground every time. We dig her out, then she crawls back in, only deeper." Jo is well-meaning, but she has no comprehension of or sensitivity to the lengthy acculturation process of self-dehydration that her mother has undergone over a lifetime of obeying cultural prescriptions. Since she has had no way in which to weave out her dreams, the mother has buried herself in her homemaking, in being a perfect wife and mother, in reflecting "[s]ocialization goals and processes which favor the family and community over the individual; the cultural emphasis on silent suffering versus open communication of needs and feelings . . . cultural norms and values that directly or indirectly sanction abuse against women and tend to minimize it as a problem in the community" (Rimonte 1989, 328).

Linda defends "the fortress of 'refuge' "for her mother in her robot-like existence, but Jo advocates wanting to break through. "Like shock treatment. . . . It's the only way to bring her out." Once again, Jo reveals that she is not a reliable narrator, because she is insensitive toward the past, as we have already seen. Alternatively, Sasaki herself may here be consciously taking a postfeminist

stance in depicting Jo's unawareness of the past. She may well be influenced by
the technique of "polyphonic interpretation." She may here be refusing "to provide the reader with any unified, linear history . . . as either progressive or re-
gressive event, for such a master narrative would conform individuals to a
universalized subjectivity and effectively erase the specificity of their experien-
tial history" (Smith 1993, 403). If indeed this is what Sasaki is aiming at, then
she succeeds in the character of Jo.

     At this hopeless juncture, Sharon gives her mother a loom, a perfect gift for a
woman who views her life as so many disparate threads that do not come together, that fly past her. Once involved in the craft of weaving, the mother
brings to the art the same perfectionist stance she had taken toward her work as a
student and then as a mother. She goes to weaving classes and takes "detailed
notes," then follows them "step by step, bending to the loom with painstaking
attention, threading the warp tirelessly, endlessly, winding, threading, tying"
(32). For the first time in her life, she finds herself in control of something, a
capacity she has never hitherto employed or enjoyed. The first year she weaves
samples in muted shades, reflecting the way she has always lived, except for
brief moments, such as on the train going from Topaz to Chicago. She feels
"new excitement, threading the warp with all the shades of her life" (33). She
uses the shades from her mothering days because she views herself as having
been like an artist in life in mothering and housekeeping. Now she is just as ear-
nestly intent on transferring to the loom a perfect expression of art from the elements of her domestic life, the canvas upon which she had hitherto worked. All
her weaving colors poignantly repeat the colors of her confined domestic life.
The mother makes of repetitive domesticity a work of art:

[B]rown, the color of the five lunch bags she had packed each morning with a sandwich
cut in half and wrapped in wax paper, napkin, fruit, and potato chips . . . or dark brown,
like the brownies they had baked to make Daddy come home from business trips. Sharon
and Jo had believed he really could smell them, because he always came home. . . .
White, the color of five sets of sheets, which she had washed, hung out, and ironed each
week—also the color of the bathroom sink and the lather of shampoos against four small
black heads; blue, Cathy's favorite color. (33–34).

     What Jo perceives about a significantly termed "brown muffler" that her
mother gave her is what fascinates the mother about the "advanced techniques"
of weaving:

One could pick up threads from the warp selectively, so there could be a color on the
warp that never appeared in the fabric if it were not picked up and woven into the fabric.
With this technique she could show a flash of color, repeat flashes of the color, or never
show it at all. The color would still be there, startling the eye when the piece was turned
over. The back side would reveal long lengths of a color that simply hadn't been picked
up from the warp and didn't appear at all in the right side of the fabric. (33)

     This is at once the metaphor for her suppressed life and the organization of
the threads of her life. She had brought meaning and beauty to "the back side,"

the dullness and boredom, the private burdens of "the house" and domesticity. She had suppressed her dreams and ambitions, creating a sense of passive futility about external events that ever floated past her. Now the mother can pick out the color and the pattern of the material according to how she has been moved or touched by the colors which equate with those elements significant for her. A "muffler" covers up and protects. It also symbolizes the mother's "sealed in" or "muffled" life. Jo points out about the muffler that it contains "Mom's colors."

This is the first time that something identifiable and uniquely hers is connected to her. The quality of the muffler reflects the mother's essential self for Jo when she puts it on: "[A]s she moved toward the light, hidden colors leaped from the brown fabric. It came alive in the sunlight. 'You know, there's actually red in here, she marveled, and even bits of green. You'd never know it unless you looked real close' " (34–35). This means that deep beneath the surface conformity, the need to do everything according to the rules and regulations for women, still ran the little girl's wild, free, exploring spirit. The mother now pours it all into her weaving, into the colors she uses and the way she weaves those colors into the fabric, as well as the perfectionism she had employed in putting her whole soul into studying and mothering.

When Jo returns from Japan where she works in the American consulate, she sees that her mother stood next to her father "leaning slightly toward him as an object of lighter mass naturally tends toward a more substantial one. She was crying." The mother has always accepted this position, which serves as shorthand for racial and gender asymmetry combined, and she has shaped her life always within their confines. But now the loom represents her self-expression. Through the threads she can give meaning to her life, to what she did with it. She can make it epic, timeless, monumental, eternal: "Amidst the comings and going of the lives around her, she sat, a woman bent over a loom, weaving the diverse threads of life into one miraculous, mystical fabric with timeless care" (35). Given the limitations of the mother, this is a line that resonates ironically with the Greek concept of an immortal goddess who through weaving controls the length of human life.

In a world in which women are assigned the trivial, routine tasks to keep life going, one of the solutions that the mother chooses is to simply take the assignment and make of it a romantic and glorious thing. In this way the mother is an essentialist, having linked herself only to the material, the fleshly, the "natural," the domestic. She accepts the binary division of the genders into male worker/female nurturer and male dominant class/female subordinate or lower class. She becomes an incredible shrinking woman in the process. Like many members of the Nisei generation, the mother is only concerned with racial asymmetry between Americans and Japanese. She never questions gender asymmetry in American and Japanese culture. It could be said of her what Linda Schulte-Sasse says of the great filmmaker Leni von Riefenstahl in Nazi Germany:

[There is a] split self engendered in women by Western [as well as Eastern] culture as comprising a "female" side that is surveyed by others and a "male" side that constantly surveys the self being surveyed. . . . [Y]et only with the help of relatively recent feminist analysis has the complicitous function of these contradictory roles been articulated. . . . [T]his very dual role . . . does not necessarily "play along with," but naturalizes and relishes the objectified role of women in patriarchy. (Schulte-Sasse 1991, 138–139)

THE INFLUENCE OF YAMAUCHI AND YAMAMOTO ON SASAKI

The division of labor between the sexes with the father as remote authority figure is made to seem fixed and natural, rather than the prescription of a cultural regime that can be questioned, modified, transformed. Yet the only asymmetry the mother sees and deplores is American racism against the Japanese people. All her life, instead of confronting racism or battling it, the mother has acceded to it and allowed it to guide her in her goal of becoming "irreproachable" to the master Americans. Here Sasaki represents the Nisei mother in her role as a "bridge" in the sense that Kim uses it to refer to Asian American Nisei writers. Because of oppressive racism, she contends, publishers of that period were not receptive to "criticisms of problems in American society." What they wanted for their "predominantly white readership" were "expressions of self-contempt and self-negation." Limited as they were by such a climate, and often by their own ignorance as well, these early Asian American writers, like Sasaki's mother, "accepted the 'cultural bridge' role while at the same time expressing their ardent desire for acceptance in American society by any means necessary, and under almost any conditions" (Kim 1982, 59). Within the constraints, therefore, of the American racist and sexist and American and Japanese sexist parameters for women, the mother expresses her own personal drive for self-fulfillment. These are represented by the red and green colors in the warp. She sublimates her drives into the "threads," which run into acceptable channels for her race and her gender in her time. She remains on the surface "the stereotype of the Japanese mother whose make-up includes tenderness and an infinite capacity for self-sacrifice and self-effacement as well as an iron will and physical stamina" (Sato 1992, 247).

In the stories of Wakako Yamauchi and Hisaye Yamamoto, women's "striving to realize ambitions" contradicted traditional roles. "[A]lthough marriage afforded Issei men greater control over their lives, for Issei women it meant the transference of obedience from parents to husband. An Issei woman's primary concern was to provide for the well-being of her family. In this context, Issei women's efforts at self-fulfillment outside the boundaries of family and community necessarily become rebellions against cultural standards (Yogi 1992, 131). Sasaki does not go this route, but she is intertextual in that she shows the mother, a Nisei woman, as still in the same predicament as an Isei woman. What Sasaki chooses is to have the Nisei mother remain within the cultural constraints and have the Sansei daughters expose and mourn the price. If the mother told her own story, we would tend to get "melodrama or self-pity" (Yogi 1992, 131). By having the daughter Jo tell the story, we do not "discover the Isei women's defiance" as we do in Yamauchi and Yamamoto. We get the results in the shrunken (world of the) Nisei mother from the Sansei daughter's perspective with the same result as in Yamauchi and Yamamoto, where the Isei mothers violate and subvert the cultural standards. In Yamauchi's play *The Soul Shall Dance* a married woman dares to plan to return to her Japanese lover and in Yamamoto's "Seventeen Syllables" the mother becomes an alcoholic when deprived by her husband of her creative escape route, writing *haiku*. In Sasaki, the Sansei daughters' perspective gives readers a contrast and therefore a better sense of the constraints that affected the Isei grandmothers' and Nisei mothers' lives. Simultaneously, as in the earlier writers, Sasaki reveals "the transformation of the very standards" the earlier mother characters "violate" and by which the mother of *The Loom* lives.

There is no sense of any tension between the demands of the cultural regime and the mother's drives. It could be because she is blessed with enjoying those demands. She loves school and learning genuinely and not just as a means of achieving teacher and parental and community approval. In addition, she genuinely loves mothering, apparently every minute of it. Chronologically, Sasaki the author is of Jo's generation in contrast to this mother character. She is interpreting and representing the mother from a daughter's perspective. This role of mother is as rigidly encrusted with ideological iconography and protocol as those of a figurehead monarch. Most cultures have very similar onerous demands for motherhood, all of which the mother is depicted as meeting with relish. She seems to want nothing more in her life than mothering her four daughters. Thus, when her daughters leave her, all the life goes out of her, according to the author. Only when they return briefly on visits does she reawaken from her psychic coma. She is never depicted in her relationship with her husband, or he with her. When the children grow up and move away, the author depicts the mother in the house as if there is no one with her. Again, this is a limited view, characteristic of a child's perspective. There is no attempt by Sasaki to even handle the relationship between husband and wife, or to show the mother as more than a one-dimensional representation of a life of giving in which any personal threads are handled by creative projection into weaving bright colors that are concealed by muted colors.

JO'S FATHER AND RACE AND CLASS ASYMMETRY

In the stories that follow, we get to meet Jo's father. He turns out to be an ordinary mild-mannered man. In "First Love" Jo, then in high school, dates an FOB (Fresh off the Boat), Hideyuki Sakamoto, aka "George." Although the boy has been here eight years, her father is shocked because "there was an unspoken law of evolution which dictated that in the gradual march toward Americanization, one did not deliberately regress by associating with F.O.B.'s." Ironically, his own wife, who was already second generation, had endured much criticism from her peers on the grounds that in marrying him she was throwing away her college education because her husband had only graduated from high school in Japan. While certainly not an advocate of this rule for these reasons, even Jo's father does assume that "most people felt this way" (57–58).[3]

Sasaki also makes her subtle testament to the devastation of Hiroshima in "Wild Mushrooms," by having Jo's father pay her a visit while she is living and working in Japan. In turn, he takes her on a visit to Hiroshima, his birth place. His mother had been killed in her home there; his sister had died in 1970 "from disorders caused by radiation." Jo's father, we discover, had served in the U. S. Army, but he never speaks of his past. "He didn't talk much, period" (82). And his daughter won't ask him. When he takes her to Hiroshima in an attempt to visit his old neighborhood, he mentions that he used to hunt wild mushrooms in the hills above Hiroshima. At a *sake* store that he remembers as being run by the parents of a classmate, he attempts to find out what happened, but the new proprietor knows nothing of the former shop and its owners. He had only moved to Hiroshima after the war. A master of understatement and tact, the Japanese shopkeeper, in responding to the Japanese American's query, tells him that "there were no longer any wild mushrooms in the hills around Hiroshima" (86).

The next story, "American Fish," is Sasaki's excuse in dialogue form to indict American racism toward the Japanese after Pearl Harbor. Two housewives meet in the American Fish Market, really a Japanese market. One, Mrs. Hayashi, who was at Topaz during the war, discovers that Mrs. Nakamura had been at Tule Lake "where all those branded 'disloyal' had been imprisoned." We then discover what could get Japanese Americans "branded 'disloyal' "—if they refused to fight against Japan, or if they were Buddhist. Such "[I]ssei were treated as enemy aliens during the Pacific war, and many were pressured into repatriation to Japan. There are many untold stories of such 'ambivalent Americans' and their fate after they returned to their countries of origin (including Chinese and Filipinos who decided to return to Asia)" (Lim 1992, 30). Mrs. Nakamura talks about a Mr. Sato, a Buddhist priest who was picked up by the FBI, " '[a]s if being Buddhist was a crime' "(74). In Yamamoto's "The Legend of Miss Sakagawara" a Buddhist priest is actually incarcerated in a detention camp with his daughter. Ironically, his immersion in his religion makes him impervious to the material world, while his daughter, a sensitive former ballerina, suffers dreadfully, and not least of all from her father's insensitivity to her needs.

Another example of American racism against the Japanese occurs when Mrs. Hayashi's father (like most Isei) was " 'forced to sell his store to the first person who offered to buy. A life-time of hard work, just thrown away!' " It turns out that the reason Mrs. Nakamura was in Tule Lake was that her father wanted to go back to Japan. He had been "a fisherman down in Terminal Island" whose boat was taken away after Pearl Harbor. He felt that " 'the only thing to do was to go back to Japan' " because he did not want to " 'stay in a country that doesn't want us.' " On the other hand, Mrs. Hayashi's family didn't want to go back because they felt that they had been " 'born here. We belonged here. And they wanted the family to stay together.' " Mrs. Nakamura's family felt exactly the same way: " 'That's why we said we wanted to go back to Japan, too—so we'd all be together. Except in those days, that made you disloyal' " (75). But ironically Mrs. Nakamura's father " 'changed his mind when he remembered that they didn't have central heating in Japan' " (76). He was already too Americanized!

JO, THE POSTFEMINIST

Like her mother, Jo's strategy in her "march toward Americanization" is to fit in. When her lower class boyfriend visits her at Berkeley, his days with her are numbered. She is ashamed of his "commonness." After the class in Renaissance Literature, at which as her guest George makes the mistake of opening a psychology book, "Jo was brutal. Why had he come to the class if he was going to be so rude? Why hadn't he sat off in the corner, if he was going to study? Or better yet, gone to the library as she had suggested? Didn't he know how inappropriate his behavior was? Didn't he care if they thought that Japanese people were boors? Didn't he know? Didn't he care?" (67). Clearly in this instance Jo is exposing her similarity to her mother, to the Nisei generation, in her internalization of racist attitudes.

In the final story, "Seattle," after the father's death, readers discover that the mother did have a life with her husband. "When he was alive," the mother "always said she was too busy [to watch TV]. Too much to do around the house; no time to just sit around." Now she watches the Japanese program and is "especially fond of the mother-daughter stories." Jo attempts to watch once, "but the pathos and self-sacrifice drove me from the room before it was even halfway through. I have nothing against pathos, but it has to be done well. I admit I have a harder time with self-sacrifice" (108). These lines are significant because they convey the point of much of the story: the gap between the mother and her daughters, specifically the traditional mother and Jo, her postfeminist daughter. Sasaki attributes this gap, not to the influence of the feminist movement, but to the difference between Japanese culture, Hollywood, the media, and American consumerist culture, in general. Jo supposes that she has seen too many American movies:

In American movies getting everything you want constitutes a happy ending. A satisfying Japanese ending, in contrast, has to have an element of sadness. There must be suffering and sacrifice—for these are proof of love. I've always hated stories where everybody sacrifices themselves and nobody ends up happy. It is a compulsion that strikes me as a form of mental illness, and I don't want to hear about it, much less do it. (108)

Thus speaks the divorced, "Thirty-Something" postfeminist daughter. On the other hand, the traditional prefeminist mother likes the mother-daughter tales from the Japanese program because "[w]hat is always the same is the invisible wires that bind them, the bond of obligation, of suffering, of love—and this is why my mother likes these dramas; because this is the way she would like real life to be" (112).

In each generation, the characters accept different gender roles and move through their lives in those grooves. Sasaki depicts both mothers and daughters responding as individuals to environmental necessities and cues. She never shows why and how their environments came to be different. The mother is represented as one way and the daughters are represented as another way, without reference to specific external events that shaped the generational differences in their attitudes and conduct. Sasaki does show external events as obstacles to be negotiated by the flexible female individual. These external obstacles are abstract and generalized as the "They," the authorities and their laws, rules, and regulations, which are to be obeyed without question. No effort is made by the characters to change, transform, or modify, to subvert or sabotage, only to adapt to all found constraints at any particular historic moment in history.

The postfeminist daughters therefore are in reality no further advanced than or superior to their prefeminist mother. Rather, they are the beneficiaries of living in a time which permits their postfeminism. Contemporary with these younger female characters, the Wayakyama Group of feminists believes differently. They insist that we must have "an understanding of the past before we can have a realistic sense of the future" (Kim 1982, 247). The daughters wish to improve their mother's situation only because their perspective has the advantage of the gains of the feminist movement. From this vantage point the mother's life is viewed as dull, limited, and lacking in possibilities. Sasaki apparently does not agree. She sees nothing but nobility and beauty in the lives of those who have suppressed individual yearnings and drives in order to conform to the demands of the roles set for them by the culture. Since this is a well-known training for women in Japanese culture, it should not be surprising to any reader that Sasaki perpetuates it and then represents the Sansei (third) generation as breezily, nonchalantly Americanized. They have benefited from contemporary race and gender perspectives and accepted these new attitudes as if this were the way things had been forever. This is revealed, for example, by Jo as a high school student, in her retort to her father when he sternly decrees that her boyfriend cannot come to the house with his motorcycle. Her language, tone of voice, and attitude would never have been possible a generation before:

"You tell that guy," her father thundered, "that if he's gonna bring that motorcycle, he doesn't have to come around here anymore!"
"Jesus Christ!" Jo wailed, stomping out of the room. "I can't wait to get out of here!" (61).

Sasaki neither mentions nor acknowledges the source for Jo's easy liberation of spirit and attitude, namely the feminist movement. Nor does she give any historical or political rationale for such an enormous and significant change from one generation to the next. Another example of contemporary freedom that offsets her mother's trauma on the first day of school is when Jo is at the University of California at Berkeley:

"Her English is so good," Ava's roommate remarked to Ava. "Where did she learn it?"

"From my parents," Jo said. "In school, from friends. Pretty much the same way most San Franciscans learn it, I guess."
Ava's roommate was from the East Coast, and had never had a conversation with an "Oriental" before.
"She just doesn't know any better," Ava apologized later.
"Well, where has that chick been all her life?" Jo fumed. (64)

Clearly, as Kim points out, "the messages conveyed by such incidents to Asian Americans are that their racial identities are primary and that they cannot be accepted as genuine Americans. She gives as her example Albert H. Yee, "a third-generation American, a Korean War GI, a Stanford graduate" who is outraged by such statements as "How long have you been in the U.S.?" and "You speak English very well" (Kim 1982, 306). African Americans have the same experiences: "This derisive treatment of the 'Other's' mimicry of civilization manifests, through the topos of 'failed assimilation,' both the need of the native for European culture and his or her immutable inferiority to it" (Hawes 1991, 196).

Still, Jo and her sisters just "go with the flow," without themselves playing a part in change, except to react with conformity and obedience to whatever the status quo is at the time. As Carole Maso comments: "Boundaries, parameters, rules, limitations: all our institutions encourage us to one degree or another to behave, to fit in. Don't go too far, they warn, because how will you ever get back?" (1993, 8). Whereas when the mother was insulted she retreated into a shell of conformity, Jo fumed and told the racist off. This is not because Jo is so courageous, but because the changing "boundaries" of the times permit. Again, nowhere is it made evident what movement has made it possible for the "times" to "permit" in each case. In one generation the Nisei mother suppressed selfhood for conformity. The next generation, represented by the Sansei daughters, expressed selfhood in conformity to the liberated freedom of expression then fashionable, as Jo's use of the word "chick" reveals.

Actually a gap does not exist so much between the mother as woman confronting and bending to societal expectations as it does between mother and daughter-narrator. On the surface, Jo is a contemporary, liberated, enlightened woman who has a meaningful career at the American Consulate in Japan. In contrast to her mother, she leads an exciting, self-autonomous life and is contemplating moving to Japan permanently to marry her lover, a married man with a family. Like Old Chao with Theresa, he wishes to divorce his wife for Jo. In *Typical American*, Theresa Chang is a creative modifier of Chinese tradition, who, rather than permit her lover to divorce his wife and leave his family for her sake, forges an alliance with her lover's wife which gives them both what they want. In contrast, Jo remains in limbo: not all that happy or fulfilled, despite all her freedom. According to feminist values, she is being disloyal to another woman. According to her mother's Buddhist (as well as Judaeo-Christian) values, Jo projects herself as an immoral disruption into a couple's married life. In *The Floating World*, as we will see in the next chapter, this realization comes to Olivia's mother also, to be immediately followed by her solution. Both lead her to break off with her married lover. But in *The Loom and Other Stories,* the text ends with Jo still undecided about what to do.

She and her sisters bypass gender asymmetry as if it does not exist now and never existed in their mother's youth; as if separate roles oppressive to one gender where the other gender makes all the rules were never and are not now an issue; as if any problem other than racial oppression were private, internal problems; as if all of it were unconnected: "[A]lthough the nisei might have raged against discrimination, they had other concerns as well, and although everyone was affected by prejudice and discrimination, they were also preoccupied with their economic and social lives, the relationships between parents and children and between men and women, their friendships and their urges toward freedom and creativity. These concerns were not completely determined by external forces" (Kim 1982, 157).

The mother's daughters now move freely and are accepted and accepting in a variety of venues, and with whites, as well. They do not question the set-up of the society, even when it is unjust, as in its racism and oppression of its own Japanese American citizens. They are postfeminist in that they merely accept the benefits to themselves that accrue to them by virtue of the hard work of millions of feminists who struggled to win those benefits in the years when these young women were still children. Kim's interview with a woman doctor illustrates this gap between the Nisei mothers and Sansei daughters:

"Today's sansei are different from us nisei. We straddled two worlds, the Japanese American world and the white world. We grew out of discrimination, and our whole lives were mobilized against it. The sansei have only one world; they only look Japanese. They have access to education and employment we didn't have, and their values are not different from mainstream values. But no matter how assimilated they are, they will face a rude awakening one day. Eventually, they too will confront the gnawing question: 'What am I? Why am I different? Am I really accepted as equal?' And they too will need to be in touch with their heritage." (Kim 1983, 49)

CONCLUSION

Although Sasaki has several stories in which the father plays some part, as in Tan's characterization of Jimmy Louie in *The Kitchen God's Wife,* it is the mother who easily dominates the work. Her character and personality are constructed (or, rather, deconstructed and reconstructed) to be diminished and muted. Her daughters attempt to "put her back again," but she has been brainwashed, robotized. She never questions the sharp division of roles for each gender. This poses no problem for her. What she finds she embraces and lives by. She is the gatekeeper, the caretaker, the colluder in the system of gender asymmetry, but somewhere at bottom she is still not altogether at peace. On the surface, however, she embraces the subordinate roles prescribed for her all her life. Sasaki represents the mother's solution to race asymmetry as struggling as hard as one can to blend in, to become as American as possible. Since she neither observes nor acknowledges gender asymmetry, it must be assumed from the way she lives her life that the mother takes the same position in relation to gender asymmetry as she does to race asymmetry: acceptance of what is found externally in the culture without questions.

Only through "the loom" does the mother finally get to indirectly convey her unfulfilled longings and dreams—the life unlived, as well as the life of dedication she had lived out in the narrow "ethic of caring." Her daughter has a long way to go. Despite Jo's smug sense of superiority toward her mother's narrow life of "pathos and self-sacrifice," her own personal, private life is in turmoil. Whereas her mother was a martyr and a masochist and trained as such by two cultures, Jo the daughter is an unthinking opportunist, self-centered in many ways. She is not yet balanced, as the narrator of *Bone* finally becomes— demanding of life that it go both ways: giving and getting in return. Jo's mother's life of eternal giving without ever asking for a return causes suffering only for herself; Jo's attitude of taking without giving in return causes suffering for other people and for herself. In describing "pathos and self-sacrifice" as comprising the major qualities of her mother's life that she rejects with contempt, Jo, as Sasaki's narrator, insists upon a discontinuity or disconnection between herself and her mother and grandmother, whereas we will see Kadohata's young narrator Olivia in *The Floating World* struggling to reconnect. Jo is a liberated Sansei who loves both Japan and the United States and may probably be returning to Japan, but as an American who cannot even speak or understand Japanese. She feels the beauty and the evocativeness of her ancestral land in a romanticized, nostalgic way.

As I have pointed out elsewhere, Werner Sollors has seen patterns in three generations of immigrants and their descendants very much as Sasaki tracks her characters. He shows a move from descent to rejection to assent. According to him, the last phase is not so much a recreation of the ancestral homeland, as a revisionary return. The first and second generations are busy pursuing conformity to American ways. The first generation struggles to gain a foothold. The second benefits to some extent from that struggle, but is preoccupied with approval, acceptance, and blending in. On the other hand, Sasaki's predecessors, such as Yamauchi and Yamamoto wrote of Nisei women, the second generation, who "reject the subjugation of women dictated by Issei culture" (Yogi 1992, 146) but who fail in their efforts at freedom.[4] Sasaki seems to show no movement in her Nisei mother forward and away from the Isei women whose values were subservience, obedience, and loyalty, especially to husband and family. However, the mother's preoccupation, "to blend in," to be "irreproachable," does move the ideals for Isei women out from the family and into the racist culture, transferring responses based on Isei training to that hostile culture. A Nisei woman, Kesaya E. Noda, sums up the Isei response concisely, revealing a sardonic self-reflexivity which she represents the Isei as lacking:

A third-generation German American is an American. A third-generation Japanese American is a Japanese American. . . . "Weak." I hear the voice from my childhood years. "Passive," I hear. Our parents and grandparents were the ones who were put into those camps. They went without resistance; they offered cooperation as proof of loyalty to America. "Victim," I hear. And, "Silent." . . . Our parents are painted as hard workers who were socially uncomfortable and had difficulty expressing even the smallest opinion. Clean, quiet, motivated, and determined to match the American way; that is us, and that is the story of our time here. (Noda 1989, 245–246)

The Sansei, the assimilated third generation, reaps the benefits from the first two generations' efforts. It luxuriates in difference and sense of identity that the reconnection with the ancestral homeland brings. It is a "rootedness" that in Kim's view "keeps us in touch with who we are and prevents us from succumbing to either of the pitfalls [Cornel] West warns us of—'ethnic chauvinism' or 'faceless universalism.' Thus grounded, we can work toward transforming hegemony, revising the very notions of culture and identity" (Kim 1992, xv). In the "work toward transforming hegemony" that Kim envisions through "revising" notions of "culture and identity," I would include revising notions of gender as asymmetrical, as well.

NOTES

1. Mitsuye Yamada makes the same point: "Most Nisei who grew up before World War II will remember that the pressure to learn to speak American English 'like a white person' was very great. In fact, some Nisei have deliberately resisted learning Japanese in order to be 'more American.' Some of us tried to give up our original language because we were told, hanging onto it would hamper our progress in learning 'perfect' English. For us, cutting away the Japanese language from our consciousness seemed a simple way of casting our lot with the American majority. By disassociating ourselves from 'alien languages' spoken by our parents and newly arrived Asian immigrants, we believed we were freed of the complex issues of identity that plagued our parents. We were embarrassed by our mothers who, it seemed, were either incapable of learning or refused to learn to speak English." (Yamada 1990, 138–139).

2. At this point, the 1970s, there were many young Asian Americans who would not have so admired Cathy. They considered "[i]ntermarriage between whites and Asians . . . as evidence of racial conquest and cultural genocide rather than social acceptance and success for the Asian minority." Writers contemporary with the mother, such as Mitsuye Yamada, "armed with a new-found consciousness of the implications of American racism, exhort[ed] their readers not to allow themselves to be swallowed up by 'white lies' and the urge toward assimilation according to an Anglo-American standard" (Kim 1982, 230–231).

3. For interesting information on the attitudes of such kibei as George, as well as Jo's father during "the internment years" see Kim, 1982, 294.

4. Stan Yogi cites Sylvia Junko Yanagisako about Isei marriages in relation to Isei men's perceptions, as opposed to those of Isei women. But for both sexes, such "marriages were based on the Japanese concept of giri (obligation) rather than love" (Yogi 1992, 147). It is difficult to determine the mother's attitude in this regard, since her Americanized Sansei daughters' perspective mediates their parents' relationship with each other for the reader.

Chapter 5

Cynthia Kadohata, *The Floating World:* "I Like the Diabolical Quality, the Clarity of Admitting I Want"

OLIVIA'S MOTHER

Elaine Kim maintains that "[t]oday's Asian American women are diverse in background and experiences" but that they share "common legacies and contemporary realities that give us a unique collective identity" (Kim with Otani 1983 120). R. A. Sasaki and Cynthia Kadohata illustrate her point in terms of the Asian American women writers analyzed in this text and in relation to each other. The white mainstream populace and the American government's responses to and treatment of Chinese and Japanese Americans differed during the World War II period, as I have pointed out in the previous chapter. Like African Americans and other ethnic groups and people of color, Asian American men and women have been subjected to racism and sexism in the United States, regardless of their diverse countries of origin and reasons for coming to the United States, their class affiliations, and educational levels. All ethnic men of color are doubly devalued by being perceived as and treated by white mainstream men as if they are women. As Frank Chin aptly puts it, Asian men are "emasculated" and "feminized" by the West. But ethnic women of color suffer even more. Men in all other groups conceptualize them as ranking even lower than the men of their group in terms of race, class, and gender. Secondly and simultaneously, they are allocated subordinate status by and to their men within their own groups. And this does not even take into account another dimension of suffering inflicted upon themselves by ethnic men and women of color when they internalize these asymmetries and see them as the natural and normal way that things are and always have been.

Sasaki, like the Chinese American authors analyzed in this text, bears eloquent witness to all these issues, especially gender and race asymmetry, whereas Kadohata seems oblivious to any gender issues at all. However, they do reveal similarities to each other and to the other authors discussed in this text in their characterizations and in their representations of intergenerational conflicts, gender relationships, family, and friendships. Notwithstanding these commonalties between the two Japanese American authors, there are basic differences, which I attribute primarily to class differences and political perspectives. Sasaki writes from a feminist perspective, whereas Kadohata is postmodern and postfeminist. Sasaki's Isei and Nisei ancestors are depicted as united in their striving for education and assimilation simultaneously. Kadohata's character Isura, the grandmother of the narrator Olivia of *The Floating World* is an Isei, yet never reveals any interest in the necessity of education or assimilation, although she has six children. Her daughter, Olivia's mother, although anonymous like the mother in *The Loom*, is also a Nisei, but slightly younger. However, unlike the mother in *The Loom*, Olivia's mother is never much interested in education for herself. She does not go past high school, nor does she seem to care that she does not, or even seem to be motivated by anyone else to do so. The jobs she holds before her marriage are "typist, seamstress and maid" (61). The mother in *The Loom* is a college graduate whose parents struggle to make her education possible. In her childhood, she fantasized becoming a glamorous American "career girl." Before marriage, she works only briefly (due to the disruption of World War II and her incarceration in a relocation camp). At that age and even later, Olivia's mother is only interested in sex. She falls in love with a married man, known only as Jack, and has a child by him, the narrator Olivia's "real father." Then she marries another man, Charlie-O, whom the narrator loves and relates to as her father. Here Kadohata is intertextual with *The Kitchen God's Wife* and *Bone*.

During her pregnancy, Olivia's mother is forced to marry Charlie-O by her mother, the narrator's formidable Obasan (grandmother) in the "picture bride" tradition. This incident indirectly reveals that Olivia's mother is subject to her mother. In case the fact that she does not defy the marriage may strike readers as odd, it is important to be aware that, as Stan Yogi, citing Yuji Ichioka, points out, " 'To refuse [a picture-marriage] would have been an act of filial disobedience, a grave moral offense' "(Yogi 1992, 132). All his life Charlie-O treasures the picture of his wife that he had originally received from his prospective mother-in-law. In this way a rare reference is given to what would hitherto have been a major source of subject matter for conflict resolution, but is now treated as a minor issue revealed to readers in an off-hand manner by the narrator. Yet this topic of enforced marriage takes up much space in the works of contemporary Chinese American authors like Tan and Myenne Ng. Only from this seemingly "insignificant" piece of information supplied by the narrator do we discover that in the past her grandmother had decreed that her daughter and grandchildren be provided with a husband and father for them. Otherwise, no reference is made as to why the grandmother arranges the marriage; no statements are included from neighbors in terms of shame or "illegitimacy."

Indeed, there are only two other indications of any kind of "prefeminist" gender asymmetry and of the anger and frustration that fuel most feminist works that explore the gap between societal constraints as opposed to women's desires. An incident occurs when the narrator and two of her brothers are young children and are being taken care of in Nebraska by a friend of her father's, Isanru, because their parents are having marital problems. According to the narrator Olivia, Isanru is "besotted" with his daughter. When she communicates to her father that she is coming to visit him, he drives the children thirty miles to wait for her at the nearest train station for ten hours. When she does not arrive, Isanru, furious, raging, "turned to us, his eyes ugly and cruel" and calls his daughter "a slut." Olivia makes sure to inform the reader that she does not yet know the meaning of the term. But even so, even though "I didn't know what that meant . . . I knew it was awful" (15).

A second example occurs with Trina whom the narrator befriends. She tells us that she was not permitted to visit Trina's home or play with her because her mother is not legally married to the man who lives with the mother and the family. Only later, after the couple is legally married is the narrator allowed access to Trina and her home. Again, as in Sasaki, Kadohata provides no explanation, no discussion, no analysis, no problem solving suggestions, no rhetoric of discursive opposition. Gender asymmetry apparently does not exist for this young postfeminist postmodern narrator, even though her parents' generation attempts to impose it somewhat, although why this should be so is kept a mystery from the reader.

Like Winnie in *The Kitchen God's Wife* and Mah in *Bone*, Olivia's mother herself has lived with a lover outside of marriage. Certainly Olivia does not seem to live by what seems to her somewhat dim and distorted remnants of an asymmetric past, because later in the text readers discover, again, in the most casual, offhand tone and manner that Olivia's mother, an enigmatic and shadowy figure, has also had a second lover after marriage. Olivia makes it clear that the marriage between Charlie-O and her mother is not in trouble for any of these reasons. In truth, and this is another example of Kadohata's postfeminist perspective, the couple is having problems because Olivia's mother is in love with another man. At least this is the case according to Olivia, who is not necessarily the best judge of the matter.

The observer-narrator as unreliable witness is a commonplace in the work of postmodern, feminist and postfeminist Asian American women writers. Unreliabiliy, as in this case and that of the narrator of *The Loom and Other Stories* also creates an unclarity that the authors deploy to enhance the ambivalent, enigmatic, mysterious personalities of the silent, suppressed mother characters. Later, we find that long after her marriage to Charlie-O (who knows about Olivia's father and has to contend with his complex feelings about him), Olivia's mother has taken a second lover. At the end of the book, after Jack, Olivia's father, has died, his widow asks Olivia to temporarily take over his vending machine servicing route. Charlie-O agrees to "come just until I felt comfortable. . . . I didn't doubt he wanted to help me, but I also thought he was curious about the man he had perceived as a rival: when he married my mother, she still loved Jack. Though she once told me she loved my father [Charlie-O], I wasn't really sure" (185). Again, this is much like Lei's quandary in *Bone*. Charlie-O also knows about this recent second relationship. In fact, the man in question makes a desperate play for the mother:

On the walkway stood a man I'd seen around in Florence, Oregon—a friend of my mother's. At first I didn't know why he was out there, why he didn't come in. Charlie-O went outside to talk to him. While my mother waited, her hands started shaking. . . . I kept thinking of a fight I'd overheard a few weeks before we left Oregon. My mother had been crying, and she said, "I tell you I am grateful. But now—do you still want me?" Charlie-O said he didn't know. "I don't know if you should still want me," she said. "And I don't know if I want you to.". . . My mother was lovely and radiant, and suddenly she reached out to touch his face. The touch was sad, and also loving, sad because loving but not in love. (74–75)

The mother's conduct here, not just when she is being stalked by a former lover, is habitual with her, one of *gaman*, a quality generally identified with Isei more than Nisei: that is, the habitual " 'internalization of, and suppression of, anger and emotion' " (Yogi citing Kitano 1992, 135). The silent but moving scene, narrated so minimally by the naive Olivia—where the mother looks out the window at the former lover on the walk outside the house—is also intertextual with the moving scene between the lonely mother and her beloved but "rejected" lover depicted unknowingly by her naive daughter in Hisaye Yamamoto's "Yoneko's Earthquake." Cheung describes this scene as "constructed to 'make the invisible visible, to make the silent speak' " (Cheung 1993, 46), much as Kadohata constructs hers.

As in traditional Japanese literature like Lady Murasaki Shikibu's *The Tale of Genji* and Sei Shonagon's *The Pillowbook of the Red Chamber* (both ca. 1000 A.D.), correspondences and allusions to human experiences are sought for in nature as a means of expressing the internalized perspectives of Japanese American psyches. For example, the mother is not concerned with conveying through parallels with nature what is considered morality in the Christian sense to her daughter, but, rather the precise nature of female desire. Like Obasan, she teaches Olivia the facts of life when the child is at an age that would be considered inappropriate in Western Judaeo-Christian culture: "I remember how, when I was seven, we passed a plot of opened morning glories. She pointed at them. 'That's the way you'll feel inside the first time a boy you love touches you.' Later we passed the same flowers, closed into tight little twists. 'And that,' she said, 'is how you'll feel inside the first time a boy you don't love touches you' " (43). Neither Isura nor Olivia's mother distances herself sexually from the female child when assuming the role of mother as is the common practice in Western culture. Olivia's mother's observations enable the little girl to see her mother not so much as her judge and jury, but relationally, as a three-dimensional human being like herself.

Her friend Trina's mother, Ugly Sarah, also gives Olivia what might be considered an odd earful for a child to hear by traditional Western standards, but not by feminist ones:

"The night of my wedding right before we had sex," the mother, Ugly Sarah, said one night during supper, "I thought, Is this going to hurt? And then, during sex, I thought, Is this sex? When it was all over, my husband said, 'Are you alive?' She took hold of my nose and turned my face back and forth. "Honey, that was a long time ago." . . . She said her husband's last words the day he walked out, when she was twenty-eight, were "Your tits have sagged two inches in two years." At times I loved her so much I wished I could offer her my youth, though I doubt she would have wanted it. (106)

But Ugly Sarah has the last laugh. She remarries happily. Until then, the Mason family was "forbidden" to Olivia, as disreputable: "You weren't supposed to walk by alone. . . . [T]he main reason parents warned their kids away was because the mother and boyfriend were living together" (106).

ISURA, OLIVIA'S OBASAN, THE OLD HAG

As for Olivia's Obasan, she is the most unconventional of characters. Among other unusual activities for a Japanese woman is her smoking of cigars. She also informs her grandchildren that she had made love to her first husband in a public bathroom (4). At the end of her life, she is deep in an affair with a seventy-three-year-old lover who dies (14). As her (and our) world would define her, she is outrageous, and as she defines herself, "diabolical." In his essay on Wakako Yamauchi, Stan Yogi maintains that Yamauchi creates "a disgraceful mother" type in "And the Soul Shall Dance" (1966) (Yogi 1992, 147), and clearly Isura matches this description. In fact, Kadohata, like Sasaki, may be influenced by Yamauchi in other ways, as well. She may be using as the model for Olivia's experience with her grandmother's diary. Yamauchi's experience with a diary in Japanese left by her mother, which she bemoans she was unable to read (M. Chin 1990, 192). With her mother's somewhat unwilling assistance, Olivia does read, study, and attempt to translate her grandmother's diary into English.

Whereas the feminist Yamauchi "was unable to read" her mother's diary, Olivia the postfeminist perseveres in attempting to do so with her grandmother's diary, to decode it and use it for herself as a model. She shares the feelings of the narrator Maxine in *The Woman Warrior,* according to Cheung, that "[t]he emigrants confuse their offspring, who are 'always trying to get things straight, always trying to name the unspeakable'(6)" (Cheung 1992, 170). For example, Isura tells the child another revelatory piece of information, historically accurate in relation to the predicament of Japanese Isei women—that the only reason she had married was "Because they asked." Olivia takes this opportunity to make a postfeminist comment directly to the reader, that "Japanese women were nothing without husbands, and she probably had not wanted to be anything" (3). This sardonic comment, like the one her grandmother would make, shows that Olivia is aware of Isura as a remarkable woman for her time and does appreciate this aspect of her personality. She likes "finding out things about her" grandmother. She only wishes "it weren't such hard work" (8). In her childhood the "hard work" consisted of being beaten by her grandmother. In her young adulthood it consists in having to painstakingly translate her grandmother's diary, parts of which are written in Japanese.

One could also take this passage as allegorical: that each generation has to "reinvent the wheel"; has to painstakingly recuperate the diaries, the privately recorded and publicly suppressed lives of their foremothers [and forefathers, as we have seen in Myenne Ng's allegory of the suitcase]—has to translate them over and over again, with minimal assistance, and privately. As Mitsuye Yamada, a Nisei poet, tells us:

> I have heard of a few personal diaries by first generation Issei women, but they remain in the hands of their families, untranslated, and therefore inaccessible even to the diarists' own Nisei children. An exciting prospect for some future researcher in Asian Pacific American history may be to look for "letters home" which surely must exist among personal papers hidden away by families in boxes throughout Asia. We now know that such writings, especially the intensely personal accounts, are building blocks to the dreams of future generations of writers. Had the writings by early immigrant Asian women been accessible in whatever form, they might have become grist for my own creative efforts when I was growing up. For myself, I yearn to read personal accounts by those Asian women who struggled beside their men. . . . I felt a gnawing sense of regret that such primary materials by pioneering Asian women written "in their own voice in their own time" are almost nonexistent. (Yamada 1990, 128)

Of her family Olivia says that "[w]hen I wanted to know about work, I asked my father. When I wanted to know about love, I asked my mother. But when I wanted to know about sex, I asked my grandmother." The passages in the grandmother's diary that most fascinate and influence Olivia in her own relationships with men are where the grandmother changes "the signs and the language for gender" with her lovers in private. Olivia is also influenced by her grandmother's reminiscences of her "diabolical" public sexual conduct with other lovers, including her future husband, and her continual brandishing of that masculine signifier, the cigar. Consequently, since her grandmother has "already punched the clock," as Olivia puts it so irreverently, she has to get "her opinion through her diaries," some written in Japanese. Her mother's role in relation to the diaries reveals her as a second generation bridge between the generations, and as is characteristic, possessed only of a minimal knowledge of her ancestral language. By Olivia's generation, the third, it is lost. For this reason, the mother has to do "the hard parts, and some parts she refused to translate at all" (109). A comment Olivia makes—"My mother said the older she got, the harder it was to surprise her" (153)—may well mean that if her mother feels the passage reveals something about herself, she withholds it from her daughter, rather than that she censors intimate details about her mother's sexuality. Here speaks the voice of the postfeminist Japanese American young woman:

> My grandmother's diaries were a revelation to me. Besides her three husbands, she'd had seven lovers—unusual for her day. Her first great lover was not someone she'd married. Before she ever slept with him, she wrote: "I like the diabolical quality, the clarity of admitting I want, knowing he knows, and now waiting to see it happen, or not happen." The first time I read that, I was stunned, that such wanting could have a "diabolical" quality. I became enamored of the very word. That man, who could inspire diabolical wanting, was the only one of her lovers I cared to read about just then. Later she wrote more about him: "He still had all his clothes on and I was undressed when we

started to argue, yet I didn't feel vulnerable. I felt strong." That's what I wanted, to feel the same strength, more than I wanted love. (115)

In this regard, Olivia's perspective toward men, as well as that of her grandmother's in her diary is modeled on Marguerite Duras's memories of herself in *The Lover* as an adolescent girl in Vietnam, observing herself and her Chinese lover. The quote in my epigraph to this chapter, which is taken from the above passage in Isura's diary, contains a curious, destabilized Durasian double vision.

The autobiographical subject seeks to unlock the genre and thereby unlock those compulsory identities. For instance, through the shifting of voices from first to third person and through the shifting of subject positions within the scene of prostitution, Marguerite Duras in *The Lover* shuttles back and forth between the positions of object and subject of desire, gendered as feminine and masculine, respectively, with the result that "the desiring subject," and by extension, the autobiographical "I," are shown to be positional effects, not absolute origins. . . . In other words, Duras challenges the notion that the "I" secures itself in any stable and essential difference. (Smith 1993, 405)

In Olivia's grandmother, Kadohata also creates a wild, somehow uncontrollable character with sadistic tendencies which she deplores, but which we observe Olivia sometimes shares, as does Duras's persona. Again, note Kadohata's subtle, yet tender wit:

My life seemed less frantic without Obasan, yet I also felt more vulnerable: through attrition, we were a weaker family now. I dreamed I told my mother about the night of Obasan's death and she didn't feel I'd killed anyone. "My mother was a guilty woman. She told me once she felt guilty about the way she treated you, and about other things from her life. My mother was also frugal. She didn't believe anything should be wasted. She gave you her boxes, her fans, her pictures, your memories of her nice walks. The night she decided to die, she gave you her guilt. Use it." She thought that over and added, "Of course, you were very bad and deserve to be guilty." (68–69)

Olivia's response in this dream is less generous than what she imagines emanating from her mother. Despite her bravado, she is defensive because she is guilt-ridden without wishing to admit it: "Neither of my brothers liked her any more than I did, and none of us cried at the funeral" (1), she rationalizes, a justification of herself that holds up when we take into account our current definitions for an abusive (grand)parent:

[S]he used to box our ears whenever she pleased, and liked to predict ghastly futures for all of us (1). . . . She reached out and grabbed my wrist, but I tried to pull it away and run. She held fast, though. I wouldn't have thought she was so strong, but I couldn't get away. We called her Pincher Obasan behind her back. One of her methods of punishment was to smile as if she loved you with her full heart, all the while squeezing you inside the wrist. You were supposed to smile back as best you could. (25)

Another frequently made point about the problem of gender asymmetry is that because abused children see violence as "a normal way of living, they become predisposed to marrying abusers or becoming abusers themselves" (Rimonte 1989, 336). Again, this is a global issue, because violence is the habitual way of resolving problems and conflicts in most cultures, globally, and it should be remembered that most cultures are patriarchal. As the Brazilian educator Paulo Freire notes, "With the establishment of a relationship of oppression, violence has already begun. Never in history has violence been initiated by the oppressed. How could they be the initiators, if they themselves are the result of violence?" (Freire [1970] 1985, 61). The solution presented by Rimonte is "to change the mothers' and children's behaviors to one without verbal abuse or physical violence" (Rimonte 1989, 336) and by extension to change the various cultures' behaviors in the same manner.

However, Obasan's treatment of Olivia and her other grandchildren is not perceived as abusive by her. By her lights, she was doing her best to raise her offspring in accordance with what she had observed and internalized about mothering techniques from her foremothers and her culture. The guilt that Olivia attributes to her she has dreamt up as wish-fulfillment. It is not reality. Olivia's Obasan was not conscious of wrongdoing, nor was Brave Orchid, Maxine's mother in *The Woman Warrior*, nor Old and New Aunt in *The Kitchen God's Wife*. Such awareness had not yet come into their culture and consequently into their psyches at the time these foremothers were raising their children. Therefore they could not be expected to change and transform without access to and consciousness of concepts other than those that their traditions and customs had inscribed in them. If what appear to be Isura's sadisms are viewed from a historical perspective and not from Olivia's postfeminist, anachronistic, and unreliable perspective, they would reveal themselves to be motivated to a large extent by Isura's belief system in regard to methods of parental disciplining. Here another crucial issue arises in relation to Olivia's grandmother, as well as women globally, which will shed light on another cause for her sadistic behavior to her grandchildren. As I have previously pointed out in Chapter Two, women's anger is a byproduct of gender asymmetry. Kadohata creates Isura as the embodiment of anger: to "be" what she "represents"—the raging "witch" spirit as created by her culture, as well as battling it.

Both Kadohata and Yamada represent raging older women who leap out at the reader with overdetermined ferocity, both what the culture perceives and transmits as appropriate to such repulsive characters, as in the Noh dramas, and what the "repulsive characters" themselves experience in looking at the society looking at them. Kadohata's grandmother character, as well as other oppressed women, both embody and use the witch mask provided by their culture(s). She habitually smiles while performing violent acts motivated by anger—at others besides *hakujin* and her own grandchildren—as when she smiles her "widest smile" before driving off a man who is about to molest and murder Olivia. When Olivia tells her that the man was going to kill her, her grandmother jokes in her characteristically harsh way with the child: "I should have let him" (11). Even so, it is evident that Isura really does love her granddaughter in her way. When they drive away from the scene and when "she thought I wasn't looking, she glanced at her hand." On it Olivia sees "several deep indentations and a thin cut on her palm." The grandmother tells Olivia to "mind her own business." After a moment, Olivia realizes exactly "what had happened—she'd been squeezing the stick [that she had used to drive the man away] so hard it cut into her hand. I bet she would have killed that man had he tried to hurt me" (12). In such representations of Isura's and Olivia's furious responses to outrages against them, Kadohata indicates that women's anger needs to be included in the text, both of the book in question and of their lives, as well, and not suppressed as it is now.

Many ethnic and women of color writers have displayed courage, strength, and endurance equal to Isura's when under unrelenting attack for their representations of angry "woman warriors"—Maxine Hong Kingston, Amy Tan, Alice Walker and Zora Neale Hurston, to name a few. Unfortunately for most women, however, their anger has not hitherto been utilized so productively by these authors for the purpose of ending gender asymmetry. This is because, as Brenda Silver points out: "the judgmental aspect of anger . . . demands an ability to trust one's own feelings enough to criticize and judge." This is difficult for women who "have been prevented from understanding their feelings as anger." It is "psychologically" difficult for such women to make such judgments because generally women are "in dependent or subordinate positions." Nevertheless, anger "carries with it the potential for insubordination and change," for "by becoming angry, by judging, we make ourselves equal to the person we judge and see the validity of our own standards and views" (Silver 1991, 963). On the other hand, Alcoff and Gray are not as optimistic as Silver, because women's anger is successfully suppressed globally in a variety of effective ways:

"Too much" emotion is often viewed as conscious manipulation, evidence of lack of control, or as simply inappropriately personal. The emotional content of survivor discourse is policed in regard to certain rules and codes, which vary from context to context. Within a context where the figure of the female hysteric—popularly understood as imagining and thus producing her own trauma and incapable of self-control—is ever present as a background code interrogating each representation of female anger. A discursive strategy that might be viewed in another context as original and effective is here always under suspicion. The fear of being seen as "overreacting" has quelled many survivors' desires to speak out. . . . Women's anger is generally sanctioned only when it is on behalf of others—primarily children and other family members; anger on our own behalf is a success won through political and theoretical struggle. The difficulty we face in experiencing anger on our own behalf is indicative of the threat it poses for patriarchal society. (Alcoff and Gray 1993, 285, 286)

And Sarie Sachie (Munemitsu) Hylkema in an important essay on this topic, "Victim of Nice," addresses not only Japanese American women, but all Asian American women, as well. She maintains that "we need to confront our anger and release ourselves from this victimization":

Women have never had permission to be angry, let alone to show any signs of anger. We are afraid of showing anger because we would be condemned as bitchy or castrating.

We are afraid of being in touch with our anger. What would we do with it if we were? And so the quiet seething continues. . . . Why can't I be independent, straight speaking, and feminine as well? Again, this imposed standard of how a Japanese woman should be reverts to the cause [—] her anger. . . . We think that suppression of anger makes us attractive to men, but it ultimately causes the death of many relationships. . . . Do I want to live my life as a Victim of Nice? I could continue to live as a victim of patriarchal and cultural injustices; or I could put all that garbage into a box and throw it away. The first step is to admit to my anger. Having done that, I need to choose. Part of the difficulty is finding a balance, a compromise in which I do not give up who I am and still be able to work out my anger. We need to not let our anger run our lives, but use it to propel us toward our potential. (Hylkema 1990, 124–125)

When in all innocence Olivia asks her grandmother "whether she'd cried for weeks after her first and third husbands died" (6) she gets an unforgettable response in the form of a rhetorical question that exposes the woman's simmering rage. " 'Does a slave cry when the master dies?' " (6).

Before her death, the grandmother incessantly tells stories of her life to Olivia in order to bequeath to her grandchildren a sense of their past, such as "the murder story," their favorite. One of the boarders in Obasan's house is a "beautiful man." He attempts to seduce Isura, "but she didn't sleep with him," not because of "conscience," she insists, as Olivia originally assumes, but from "instinct." It takes her grandmother many years to realize "that the beautiful man was the devil and was actually trying to take her husband from her. A few months later, he succeeded, when her husband drowned in Hawaii. They'd been married almost twenty years" (34). The triangle between Ralph, Helen, and Grover in *Typical American* is handled similarly by Jen, with Grover playing the part of the diabolical tempter, except that instead of drowning, Ralph is ruined financially. Then there is the story about Isura's father who originally "worked as a fisherman when he came to the States." Because of the "many fights" that broke out between the whites and the Japanese fishermen, he had "decided to find more peaceful work" and had bought "a boardinghouse in San Francisco" (31). This is like the situation in *The Loom*, where the mother's parents had run a boardinghouse, also in San Francisco. However, according to Obasan, her parents' house was "clean," whereas Jo's grandparents' boarding house was not, because they "allowed gambling and drinking" (33).

In relation to whites, Kadohata's grandmother reacts in a few ways like the mother in *The Loom* who cleans the house thoroughly before going out for fear that the *hakujin* might see it with any imperfections: "Though Obasan always went inside early, she usually came to the door when a car approached the motel office. 'Get in. What will people think, with Japanese hanging around like hoodlums at night?' " (27), she demands. Clearly Isura, like the mother in *The Loom*, has also internalized "the master's script." On the other hand, she is more self-respecting than the mother of *The Loom* in her response to *hakujin*. She is even ahead of her time in expressing separatist contempt for whites, as when Olivia shows off her fine way of talking, so that if people couldn't see her they wouldn't know she was Japanese:

When I spoke with outsiders I was showing off, but they never understood this. I was trying to impress them, to make them like me. But at the same time I was always taunting them. See, I can talk like you, I was trying to say, it's not so hard. My grandmother didn't like that I wanted to impress them, but she liked the taunting part. "Smile at them," she would say. "Hakujin don't know when a smile is an insult." Hakujin were white people. She always said her experience showed that if you hated white people, they would just hate you back, and nothing would change in the world; and if you didn't hate them after the way they treated you, you would end up hating yourself, and nothing would change that way, either, So it was no good to hate them, and it was no good not to hate them. So nothing changed. (9)

OLIVIA, THE WILD GIRL, THE POSTFEMINIST

Kadohata can be defined as postfeminist in her perspective, unlike Hong Kingston, Tan, Myenne Ng, and Jen who write as if gender asymmetry and all its woes are relevant, are part of the present and a recent past. Sasaki and Kadohata write as if there were no such thing, as if it has never existed, or existed in the dim and distant past and is scarcely comprehensible, like a diary in a foreign language such as Olivia's grandmother writes. Where in the Chinese American texts under discussion there has always been stress associated with gender issues, we notice this seeming absence in *The Loom and Other Stories* and in *The Floating World*. The protagonist-narrator Olivia of *The Floating World* has no difficulties in this area. Moreover, there is no traditional sense of internalized guilt displayed by the narrator anywhere in the work. Kadohata's characters seem to exist without preconceived gender hierarchies or sexual taboos. All three generations of her female characters appear to have a healthy sexuality that they fully express, although the grandmother has paid the price by going insane, at least in her grandchildren's eyes. After all, "[f]emale defiance of gender roles is often interpreted as mental deviance" (Cheung 1993, 58). Olivia's mother does, however, seem to have some lingering guilt feelings in connection with Olivia's "illegitimate" birth. Nevertheless, she is not represented as therefore being considered less desirable by Charlie-O because of her first love affair.

Like Lei of *Bone*, also another man's child, Olivia is never perceived as an outsider in the new circle composed of her mother, Charlie-O, and three younger half brothers. Again, like Lei, Olivia is caring, even maternal to her younger siblings, especially her youngest half-brother. "Sometimes my mother let me give him [Peter] his bath. He had extremely sensitive ears, and if you got even a little water in them he would be in pain for hours." And once when away from him, Olivia "worried all night, even in bed, that my aunt might not be washing his ears carefully enough" (15). The feeling of mutual trust and love between all the siblings is evident in every scene in which they appear. This was also the case with Lei and her two half sisters in a parallel situation in *Bone*. It becomes an issue in *The Joy Luck Club* and *The Kitchen God's Wife*, only because the mothers never admit that their daughters' presumptive fathers were not their biological fathers until long after the latters' deaths. Nevertheless, as in these two texts and as in *Bone*, the stepdaughter and stepfather are very close and love one another deeply: "I knew that Charlie-O loved me, though once in a while I worried that he loved me because I was what had brought him together with my mother. My real father visited me several times, but he was married and had two children, and we never became close. So I was devoted to Charlie-O and had followed him everywhere when I was quite young—he even took me to his poker games—and sometimes I brought him to Parents' Day at school" (44).

Another manifestation of postfeminism can be seen when Olivia has a first boyfriend. She graduates to a sexual relationship with him without guilt, without feeling used. When her boyfriend Tan has to move away, Olivia feels terrible because she loves him, and that's that. Then when she moves to LA, she meets her next lover. Again, she enjoys sex without guilt. Moreover, her parents visit her without making scenes. "[W]hen my parents had visited Andy and me, she [Olivia's mother] kept staring at us in a funny way. Later, when I asked what made her stare, she said we'd both had the same look on our faces, as if we'd been washed over with the same water. I tried to picture her with Jack, both of them washed over with the same water" (185). In great contrast, when the mother in *The Loom* visits her daughter Jo and discovers that Jo's white lover lives in the apartment, she is upset:

She whisked her mother straight from Kennedy Airport to her cramped flat in the Village, and no sooner had they finished dinner than Jo's boyfriend, Michael, arrived. Her mother was gracious.
"Where do you live, Michael?" she asked politely.
He and Jo exchanged looks. "Here," he said.
Despite her mother's anxiety about the safety of New York streets, the two of them walked furiously in the dusk and circled Washington Square several times, mother shocked and disappointed, daughter reassuring. At the end of an hour they returned to the flat for tea, and by the end of the evening the three of them had achieved an uneasy truce.
"I knew you wouldn't be happy about it," Jo said to her, "but I wanted you to know the truth. I hate pretending."
"Things were different when we were your age," her mother said. "What's Daddy going to say?" (Sasaki 1991, 31).[1]

In *Bone*, Mah, who wants Lei to marry her long-time lover, says simply but meaningfully: "You shouldn't sleep with him so much." She says this, not from a moral position, but because "You never know. Mason's good now, but he could change" (Myenne Ng 1993, 190). Similarly, Charlie-O is jealous of Olivia's first boyfriend, but not for moral reasons. " '[D]idn't you tell me when you were in high school that eating too many vegetables would make your complexion orange? . . . You had a date with Tan, or Span, or whatever you used to call him, and you wouldn't eat any carrots all week.' Tan, I said, but he was looking at the menu" (186–187).

Like Hong Kingston, Tan, Jen, and Sasaki, Kadohata does depict other issues than gender asymmetry as crucial in affecting her characters' lives. For example, there is the issue of survival as a group in a hostile, racist environment. Kadahota uses Olivia's description of her experiences on her first job to show how the

Japanese American workers created solutions to race asymmetry through the formation of close-knit groups as units and utilizing informal grapevines to assist each other in job hunting. They go only where other Japanese already are and always cling together. Ever on guard about the *hakujin*, as we have seen in Sasaki, they take care at all times never to come to *hakujin* attention in a negative way. In this regard, Kadohata exposes the exploitative white owners of the hatcheries, the deplorable working conditions of the Japanese American chicken sexers, and their courage in enduring inhuman conditions. They work seventeen hours a day, going on Dexadrine, determination, and little more.

The hatchery was an ugly building in one of the most beautiful parts of Missouri. . . . [It] sat back from the highway, fronted by tall maples. It was concrete, windowless, and I imagine no one who passed took notice of it. Because the building had no windows, on warm days it seemed to exist in a cavern of heat and moisture. . . . The sexers worked seventeen hours, slept five, worked seventeen. . . . All the sexers had jobs at other hatcheries, and they often worked as long as thirty or forty hours in a row at their various hatcheries. They took Dexedrine to stay awake and to help them drive from one hatchery to another. . . . Sexers were hired not as individuals but as groups: the management hired and fired groups, not individuals, while the group hired and fired the individuals. . . . Unless you were with an agency, every group had a leader, who negotiated with the management in return for a commission from the rest of the workers. When one person did bad work, that put everyone's job in jeopardy. (119–120)

Without evading the necessity of depicting the constraints of their harsh lives, Kadohata nevertheless draws portraits of her characters in which light touches of humor are used to reveal their salient characteristics. Olivia loves to meet new people who intrigue and entice her by oddities and quirks of their character. Her grandmother was such a human being, as she herself is. And like her grandmother, she is contrary, "grouchy." When she goes away to college, her parents fill her with advice. Her mother does not want her to read too much because then " 'she'll hurt her eyes and get headaches and ruin her good nature.' I saw my father look sideways at her, like: What good nature?" (138). In keeping with the postfeminist perspective, Olivia herself is neither moral nor immoral in the traditional Western religiously grounded moral sense. She is more a creature of aesthetic, sensual, and emotional reactions and responses, again much like her grandmother and the narrator of Duras's *The Lover*. She is impish in personality, a little devil in the making toward her grandmother's fully-formed "diabolical" persona:

Before my grandmother died, she told me everything about herself. Sometimes, sitting next to me, she might suddenly grab my hair and pull me over to tell me one more fact about herself: how she had never seen a book until she was twelve, or how she had never cut her long, long hair. She lived with us after her third husband died. But my brothers and I were way ahead of her. Right before she moved in, we gave her a neck chain with a bell attached so we would always hear her approaching and could hide before she reached us. We bought her the bell one Christmas, and she always wore it. (2–3)

When after the funeral, Olivia's mother cuts off her grandmother's braid and gives a different strand from it to each of her children, Olivia ties a string around hers and keeps it for the rest of her life. After the family drives away from the cemetery, Olivia realizes that she has waited all along to be free of her abusive, cruel, but fascinating grandmother: "I stuck my head out the window. I was free. But I didn't feel free" (30).

Olivia is strong-willed, as are all the women in her family. They had to be in order to be so independent of cultural and religious taboos and limitations on themselves. In fact, she begins her narration by a shocking statement both about and by her grandmother whom she claims to hate. Yet after the old woman's death she not only keeps the strand of her grandmother's braid, but her diaries, as well. Further, Olivia painstakingly studies and translates them, actions that are common to the feminist project of translating and reclaiming the buried past and perspective of our foremothers. Evidently postfeminist even as a child, Olivia doesn't obey the strictures. She openly reveals her recalcitrance by sitting "with them [the Masons] on their porch for supper every day for six months," even though it wasn't until after the couple married that "my parents reluctantly allowed me to be their friend" (105–106). Olivia herself recognizes no barriers imposed by convention against the Masons in the form of their neighbors' opinions.

Again, like her grandmother, Olivia is "ornery" and "mean," but she goes beyond her grandmother's bold, but self-conscious sexual freedom into postfeminism. Here is what she says about her first boyfriend Tan: "The thing about our sex life was it made us feel close, not because it was romantic or beautiful or sweet or anything like that (although at times it was all of those), but mainly because it was a prodigious adventure we were going through together" (135). Because of her balanced attitude, she feels she knows parameters, unlike Charlie-O who is an idealist about human beings and human nature.

Olivia may not know "the best" about herself, but she does know "the worst." When she discovered her grandmother dying on the motel bathroom floor where the family were staying, her grandmother begged Olivia to bring her daughter, Olivia's mother, to her. "Diabolically," Olivia does not do so, thereby depriving Isuru and her daughter of bidding farewell to each other, of final moments with each other. Nevertheless, the novel ends with Olivia at peace about herself. She begins "to worry about my work" and in doing so "forgot about Jack" with whom she had been obsessed for years. " I tried to calculate from the night sky what time it was, but then I gave up. It didn't matter; it was high time I left" (196). Note that this is the same ending expressed in the same language as in *Bone* to convey that a young narrator is finally taking leave of the past in the form of a parent. In good postfeminist style, Olivia is getting on with her own life and leaving behind the baggage of the past.

Until then, the demands of sexual passion, and/or of love for a man take precedence over the demands of ethical conduct to another human being, regardless of gender. At the end, Olivia has an illumination about her biological father, Jack. She sees the ghost of Jack beside her as he was shortly before she was born. She now understands why and how her mother broke up with Jack. "I hadn't been born yet as he sat there. When my mother fell in love with Jack, she must have realized how young they were and that things wouldn't turn out well. But she didn't care. I liked to think of her then, not caring" (195). In previous generations, her mother's not caring would have been traumatic for the daughter. But here the character views it as a source of pride and goes forward into her own life. Nevertheless, from a feminist perspective, this is a significant issue. It is something to care about. Olivia's mother had for a time been disloyal to another woman, Jack's wife, but once she had begun to relate to her lover's wife, a humanizing identification process had also begun and continued to the point where she could give up Jack.

Under the system of gender asymmetry, women have been trained to distance and separate themselves from other women, from others as women. In this way they see each other as rivals for men and betray one another easily. But Olivia's mother does show a nascent consciousness of the necessity to be loyal to other women, to her sisters in suffering in the act of "doing the right thing" by another human being who just happens to be another woman. Couldn't the same betrayal be done to her by another woman in her turn, and so on in perpetuity? In *Typical American*, we have seen the suffering which Theresa endures as a result of her becoming "the other woman." On the other hand, Grover, the con man who sleeps with Helen, Ralph's wife, uses it as a means of "putting one over" on both Helen and Ralph simultaneously.

Olivia's emphasis here is not so much on the aspect of passion in her mother's affair with Jack. What is more important to her is that her mother ultimately was a decent enough human being to stop the affair when she perceived the reality of the other woman in the triangle. In terms of sexual passion, Olivia is proud of her mother—that the latter gratified her desires freely, as her mother before her had done, "not caring" about social sanctions against females who do this. She sees her mother as a free spirit, unconstrained by cultural prescriptions and gender asymmetrical taboos for women. Olivia admires and identifies with these qualities. Thus, Olivia does not see solutions for gender asymmetry in terms of traditional concepts of "justice" and "morality," but in "doing unto others [including women] as thou wouldst have others do unto you."

Neither Jo of *The Loom* nor Olivia in this text expresses fears or concerns about retribution from their culture because of their nonconformity to its decree of gender asymmetry. Their upsets arise from personal, familial concerns. Their sufferings are mainly due to compassion for the suffering of their parents. They can be controlled through their love for their parents because their parents' suffering causes them to suffer. As we have seen in the authors analyzed in this text, all the mothers' daughters suffer over their mothers' stunted and narrow lives. Like Lei of *Bone*, Olivia suffers over her parents' unstable, clouded relationship. She continually worries about whether or not her mother loves her stepfather. It turns out that she does, and it turns out that the couple nearly breaks up on several occasions, primarily because of the mother's infidelities. This is a common theme in other Asian American writing, as well; we have seen it in *Bone* and in *Typical American*. It is also a theme that Louis Chu in *Eat A Bowl of Tea* is credited with first using, as Ruth Hsaio (1992a) has pointed out.

CHARLIE-O

In Hisaye Yamamoto's "Las Vegas Charley" (1961), in Hong Kingston's *China Men*, in Sasaki's, and Myenne Ng's work, as well as in the work of Louis Chu, Frank Chin, and others, gambling is described as one of the major outlets of Asian American men in their efforts to "transcend their frustration and difficulties" (Kim 1982, 172). Kim and many others ascribe historical roots to this activity, primarily among the Chinese men forced by the American government's prohibitive immigration laws to "sojourn" without their women for many years in Chinatown communities. In *The Floating World*, Olivia describes her experiences when she accompanies Charlie on his recreational gambling outings. The gamblers are all Olivia's fellow hatchery workers, although Charlie-O, like Mason Louie in *Bone* is a mechanic. At these poker games, there is even a female worker who earns Olivia's admiration because she has the daring to play with the men and never lose. Nevertheless, as in other Asian American texts, we see here that gambling is still commonly used by Asian American men not only as an escape outlet, but as their preferred form of recreation. It is a way of socializing with their male peer group, even for men with wives, like Charlie-O.

As in Wakako Yamauchi's *The Soul Shall Dance* and Hisaye Yamamoto's classic "Seventeen Syllables," women are depicted as sensitive, elegant, aesthetes married to coarser types. Charlie-O, however, is more like Leon of *Bone*—only outwardly bluff and hearty. Ultimately we discover why Charlie-O stays with his wife, above and beyond his love for her. His reasons expose the nature of his strong and noble character. Once his wife had told him why she broke up with Jack, Olivia's father. Suddenly one day she had realized that he had a wife: the reality of it. She was visiting Jack when she happened to notice on the wall "this thing called a Wish List." One of the wishes was from his wife, and it was for a new couch for her birthday. A few weeks later when Jack took her to the house again, "[A] new couch was sitting in the living room. His wife wanted this thing for the house, and he got it for her, and that made your mother see for the first time the way his wife was connected to him and the way he was connected to her. She and Jack went into the bedroom then, but the whole time she just lay there feeling sad" (190).

Then when Charlie-O himself is tempted to have an affair, he confides: "I kept thinking about that when I met this other lady, and somehow that stuff your mother told me meant more to me than the other things, the things she did to me. . . . It's wrong! . . . Two people get married! They get married. Period" (190). In this response, in his loyalty to an ideal lies the crux of Charlie-O's character, again, much like Leon's in *Bone*. Olivia feels that although she is nostalgic about Charlie-O's morality "there had always been something primitive about his morality; it was as if his need for a moral order were as strong as the need for food and water. When I was growing up, I always felt sheltered by his convictions, and by his belief that all his children would grow up "good." Whenever we did something "bad" or "wrong," he wasn't so much disappointed as confused and disbelieving. I guess most people never learn the best or the worst they're capable of " (190).

The couple's marital problems are posed by Kadohata as based on Charlie-O's sufferings and torment. It is not so much the other men in his wife's life, or what they represent to Charlie-O. What is depicted as hurting Charlie-O is that his wife might not love him. The uncertainty of whether or not the wife married unwillingly and/or truly loves the second husband concerns both the narrators, Lei of *Bone* and Olivia of this text:

"What do you like to think about?" said my mother. "About you," he said (50). . . . "What do you want?" said Charlie-O, very quietly. "I don't want anything," my mother said. "You don't understand—I want you to want something." "I just don't want you to be mad," my mother said to the window. . . . I knew she'd only said that for him. What she'd said first was closer to the truth; she didn't want anything he could give her. (57)

Like all the other male characters in the same situation, Charlie-O comes through as a loyal human being, an extraordinarily hard worker who endures poverty and survives. Maxine's father in *The Woman Warrior* and *China Men*, Leon in *Bone*, and Jo's father in *The Loom and Other Stories* all pursue the same dream as Charlie-O, the American success mythology. Only Charlie-O succeeds. He ends up with his own business, with a childhood friend as his partner, sharing with him the fulfillment of the dream of their youth. Much like Leon in this respect, Charlie-O does not labor with his hands only, but with his imagination, which he puts into what his hands create. He brings to whatever he does a certain philosophical perfectionism. He creates challenging intellectual games for physical necessities. He also designs himself into a talkative, upbeat personality.

CONCLUSION

Charlie-O appears to be the opposite of his wife, who is aloof and phlegmatic, yet romantic and passionate about sex. She is also equally practical, strong, and enduring in the challenges of everyday survival and in handling social obligations. As for her mother Isura, in her lifetime she had been totally unconventional, a strong individual who did what she pleased and made her own rules to suit herself. Both women, like women globally, are amalgams of their society's cultural and religious taboos and training, which in many ways conflict with their deepest desires and needs.[2] Isura in her lifetime ruled the roost. Interestingly, she does label her own and others' actions, when they do not conform to social conventions, as "devilish" or "bad." This reveals that she does distinguish between what the world wants and what she does. Remarkably, however, she has not internalized her training when it competes with her personal wishes, needs, drives, desires, and decisions. Her children and grandchildren must obey her. As the sign of her free-wheeling power, she smokes cigars and sleeps with men to the end of her life without guilt.

Olivia's mother seems to respond to her mother as if she were a force of nature, without attempting either to change her or do battle with her. Moreover, she perpetuates her mother's strategies of selective morality. She is conventional when it is to her best interests, or what she perceives to be for the interests of her family's survival. Like her mother, she is "unconventional," but outwardly compliant when her emotions and ideals conflict with what her society decrees is safe and proper conduct. If "They" think some actions of hers and other women are "shameful," like childbirth outside of marriage, then she is "ashamed" and will be most concerned that her daughter not get caught in the same trap as she was.

Her motivation is not the innate wrongness of "improper" conduct for a woman, but avoiding social disapproval. She is embarrassed and constrained and modifies her own and her family's conduct according to whether social stigma or "shame" is attached to the action by her society, as when she does not allow Olivia to play with her best friend Trina Mason because her mother is not married to the man with whom she lives. Olivia disobeys her, anyhow. As Maxine in *The Woman Warrior* "rebels against her mother's teaching that a woman must subordinate herself to her society, must conform to its patriarchal code," so Olivia in befriending the ostracized Mason family "questions the values of her conservative community" (Cheung 1993, 174). When it comes down to it, Olivia's mother's decision is based only on concern that her daughter not be ostracized because of guilt by association. A member of "the silent generation," she doesn't really care either for herself or for others about whether "Ugly Sarah" lives or does not live with a man legally or otherwise, but she cares about the appearance of things.

Olivia both hates and admires her odd, devilish, often cruel and brutal grandmother, but she herself is depicted as much more like her grandmother than her mother. A free spirit, she does things according to her whim, most often according to how she feels about someone, not according to what the society would decree is appropriate for a female. This is how readers can tell that the system of gender asymmetry has all but broken down, or so Kadohata would make it appear. Older women act in conformity with its regulations only when they perceive it as a protective muffler against the harsh winds of community criticism, disapproval, and ostracism. The internal impetus of a self-generating belief system is missing. For Kadohata, the most postfeminist of a generation of women writers born after 1950, gender asymmetry either should be or is a thing of the past. All the authors I have analyzed in this text, whether feminist or postfeminist, agree on this point.

NOTES

1. A young social worker in Elaine Kim's *With Silk Wings* records a response similar to Jo's mother's by her Korean-born mother: "They were shocked when I told them I wanted to move to an apartment even though I wasn't married. My mother knows that I'll be going away some day. But that's her way of showing me her affection" (19).

2. In striking contrast to the Asian grandmother's personality and conduct, which are based on Asian cultural inscriptions, is the American stereotype of "a typical grandmother." Proof of Isura not being unusual is this description of her grandmother by a Korean-born lawyer interviewed by Kim: "Grandmother always carried some deadly poison dried fish eggs in her belt sash. She'd threaten to kill herself every time I didn't obey her. I had waist-length braids, and I hated to have my hair washed because she'd use scalding hot water. She said it was to kill any lice I might have. If I resisted, she'd threaten to commit suicide on the spot. One day, my friend and I tied a piece of hemp between two trees and used my grandmother's laundry board to make a swing. Some little boy cut the rope, and I fell flat on the ground, breaking the laundry board in half. My grandmother was furious. She came running after me with a whip. I ran as fast as I could toward the sea, until there was nowhere to go but into the ocean. I stood there hesitating—my grandmother was behind me, waving the whip and threatening to kill herself if I didn't stop (Kim with Otani 1983, 33).

Conclusion

"Fundamentally, I muse, all people are the same. My mother's race is as prejudiced as my father's. Only when the whole world becomes as one family will human beings be able to see clearly and hear distinctly." (Sui Sin Far, "Leaves" in *The Big AIIIEEEEE!*, 117)

It has been my aim in this text to analyze not only those writers who forward the feminist project, like Maxine Hong Kingston, Amy Tan, and R. A. Sasaki, but also "postmodern" writers like Fae Myenne Ng, Gish Jen, and Cynthia Kadohata who include and/ or advocate a postfeminist perspective. The feminist writers perceive historic time as a crucial time that they stress with intensity and passion. Still, all the writers embody both historic and present time in their representations of their mother and/or daughter characters. Unlike Hong Kingston, Myenne Ng, and Tan, some feminist and postfeminist authors do not expose gender asymmetry's causes, only its effects. Nevertheless, all these authors have profited from the feminist movement to the extent that they have in their works represented their mothers' and grandmothers' generations as suffering and struggling as individual young women coming to consciousness before the Seventies, while their daughters no longer have to do so.

All the authors without exception represent these women as in private situations choosing individual solutions. Since "it is impossible to step outside culture and thus to shed the culturally constructed self" (Friedman 1993, 243), the (fore)mother characters remain embedded within the culture of their historic period, while their daughter characters are beneficiaries of the gains of the civil rights and feminist movements of the Sixties and Seventies. These young characters are in the enviable position of accepting the good things that have come their way without any effort on their part. They all take their privileged situation for granted. They strike postfeminist attitudes and make postfeminist cracks that create a sense of distance between the generations, as well as the opportunity for sardonic humor on the part of the authors. However, neither the generation gap nor the satire should be assumed to be at the expense of the older generation.

In the case of the daughters in *The Joy Luck Club*, Pearl of *The Kitchen God's Wife*, Nina of *Bone*, Jo of *The Loom and Other Stories*, and Olivia of *The Floating World*, young women occasionally expose smug superiority and judgmental self-complacency toward their elders. Meanwhile, their creators expose how similar they are in so many crucial ways to their (fore)mothers. On the other hand, the young women's discourse and perspective in relation to their men folk uncover a self-consciously critical and disturbed attitude that would not have been possible only a few years ago without the effort and work of the Second Wave mainstream feminist movement which Friedan's work inspired. Asian American women writers of previous generations such as Sui Sin Far, Hisaye Yamamoto, Mitsuye Yamada, and especially Maxine Hong Kingston, to name only a few, have made a substantial contribution to efforts to end gender asymmetry, and contemporary Asian American women writers born after 1950 are continuing those efforts brilliantly. Yet although like their young female characters, contemporary Asian American women writers have all reaped the benefits of the feminist movement, still it has remained unacknowledged, unmentioned, and thanks to the efforts of such cultural watchdogs as Frank Chin, unmentionable, as well, in their texts.

This silence has not gone unnoticed by Asian American critics, who interpret its sources as due to a variety of factors that have kept Asian American women writers and critics at a distance from the mainstream feminist movement. First, they note resentment of and antagonism to the overrepresentation of white, middle class constituents in the mainstream feminist movement to the point of perpetuating the marginalization, even invisibility, of their Asian American sisters and other women of color. Second, Asian American critics privilege race and class issues over gender issues. For example, Evelyn Nakono Glenn commends (white) feminists for having made "considerable strides in deconstructing gender" and tactfully calls attention to their sin of omission by reminding them that "gender and race" should be deconstructed "simultaneously." Her suggestion for a first step in doing so "is to expose the structures that support the present division of labor and the constructions of race and gender around it" (Glenn 1992, 35). Sucheta Mazumder ranks ethnic and race asymmetry over gender and class asymmetry in importance and gives as the reason for doing so that in crisis situations "when an entire racial or national group has undergone severe trauma—such as during the World War II internment of Japanese Americans or the resettlement experience of Southeast Asians—ethnic identity supersedes gender and class." For these reasons concerns arising out of racial identity rather than class and/or gender are for women of color . . . "an integral aspect of their overall identity" (Mazumder 1989, 15). Such thinking as Mazumder's privileges the battle against racism over the battle against sexism, which has been the undoing of many a revolutionary female group, because the battle is simultaneous, as Glenn perceives. It is impossible to separate the intersecting strands of gender, race, ethnicity, and class asymmetry.

Esther Chow and the Asian Women United of California also critique the mainstream feminist movement and call upon them to link with Asian American women against race and class asymmetry and to be self-reflexive about their own race and class attitudes and conduct toward other women. They argue that racism and class oppression should take priority over sexism: that mainstream feminists are not consistent in their "attitudes and behavior" toward Asian American women, lack "sensitivity" toward them, and that they are responsible for educating the general public about cultural and ethnic differences" (Chow 1989, 377). Like Mazumder's, Chow's call for both white women and women of color to link on the basis of race and class oppression does not include sexism. Her language makes it seem as if feminists should band together only to add to those numbers who fight racism and class oppression. In point of fact, feminism combats all three asymmetries simultaneously—with a priority on sexism. Moreover, in calling for white feminists to be self-reflexive about "their attitudes and behavior" toward other women, she does not make the same demand on ethnic women and women of color, including herself. Furthermore, Chow interprets Asian American women's failure to participate in the feminist movement as due to their greater internalization of traditional gender roles. Accordingly, Asian American women perceive the feminist movement "as alien, radical, and irrelevant to their needs." For these reasons it becomes difficult for such feminists to liken their problems to those of other women, let alone other women on a worldwide basis (Chow 1989, 372). Chow here fails to perceive what Rey Chow does, namely that the term "*Woman* deals not only with gender but also with the power-invested processes of hierarchization and marginalization that are involved in readings of culture" (R. Chow, 1991, 52). As Ebert eloquently explains it:

[F]or all their differences in relation to each other, [patriarchies] share the same dominant organization of differences according to the gender opposition of male/female. . . . All these various patriarchal arrangements, in short, produce the same effects: the oppression and exclusion of woman as other, the division of labor according to gender—specifically, the exploitation of women's labor (whether in the public or private sphere)—and the denial of women's full access to social resources. Women thus occupy the "same" position within patriarchy differently, divided by the conjunctions of race, class, nationality, (post)colonialism, and so on. Their "identity" is not identical; they are not the "same" as each other, yet they are all subjects of the same structures of oppression. By understanding women's subjectivities as the effects of difference-in-relation, I believe, we can rearticulate a collective subject for feminism. (Ebert 1993, 22)

In Esther Chow's opinion, Asian American women writers have never failed to be concerned about class issues. White feminists, in contrast, have revealed a lack of concern for "working-class women," which has "unfortunately" set up social barriers between working-class women and middle or upper class women. She insinuates that due to their greater class privilege, "affluent" white women cannot comprehend or relate to the factors that constrain other women. Thus a "class cleavage" exists between Asian American women and the feminists who are mostly middle class women. Unlike white women, Asian American women "tend to see economic survival as a primary concern," although the more educated and affluent also are primarily concerned "with job advancement, professional licensing requirements, and career development." Gish Jen's *Typical American* would seem to dispute this point, since Theresa's experiences as a medical student and intern expand her feminist consciousness, but then Theresa is not from the working classes.

Nevertheless, because of Asian American women's immigrant class status and more precarious economic conditions, they do not "adapt easily to current demands and requirements of the American labor market." As a result, "many experience tremendous status and financial losses as the result of immigration" (Chow 1989, 372). This loss of status after immigration is borne out in the mother's comment in *The Loom* about college friends of hers who are forced to work as servants although they had better education than their employers in most cases. The reason class barriers are easier to overcome for Asian American women than for white feminists and Asian American women from working-class backgrounds, Chow contends, is that bridges are routinely constructed by Asian American women between the groups. They provide "multiculturally sensitive programs,' not only programs for the purpose of addressing gender asymmetry, but community programs such as Lei serves in *Bone* (Chow 1989, 371, 373). Chow's point is reinforced by Lei, who conceives of herself as a bridge to her family and her community, both literally and allegorically. She deals with that fact both as a celebration and as a problem in terms of her personal life, which she ultimately resolves by "leaving home" in the various mainstream meanings of that term.

Chow does see some positive elements to feminism. To the extent that they joined mainstream white feminists, specifically in their powerful consciousness-raising group sessions, Asian American women's level of consciousness was raised to the point where they were inspired to examine "their subordinate status and limited role" in their families, community, and culture (Chow 1989, 373). Such an examination constitutes the major theme of the authors analyzed in this text, as well as the necessity to practice syncresis: to combine their Asian American heritage with "what is good in the larger world" (Chow 1989, 361).

Another solution to gender asymmetry that the Asian American women attempt is of interest for two reasons. First, according to Chow, they are not so much influenced by the feminist movement, but instead are emulating African American organizations in creating Asian American organizations dedicated to ending racism and to unifying with other ethnic groups of color. In many of these organizations, as in the African American Black Power, Muslim, and Afrocentric groups, Asian American women also "occupy subservient positions and are relegated to traditional women's functions." Although aware of these drawbacks, they remain in the organizations (Chow 1989, 364). They prefer to focus on confronting racism and class oppression within radical groups "critical of the American system" rather than confronting sexism within the mainstream feminist movement because they perceive these other groups as part of "the larger society." However, after actual experience within these radical groups, Asian American women come to realize that these groups also exclude Asian Americans, other people of color, and most "working class Americans." Chow then lists the various ways in which Asian American women are faced with a variety of "barriers" that confront them personally and as a group in education, politics, and culture due to "patriarchal and structural impediments" (Chow 1989, 367). In this regard, all the authors analyzed in this text bear out her observations and conclusions. Chow specifically indicts the American society for having kept Asian American women from fully participating in the women's movement. In her opinion, these "[e]xternal barriers" are more difficult for Asian American women "than internal ones." On the other hand, since both of these barriers are "dialectical" they may thereby provide "stability as well as contradiction in the life experience of many Asian American women" (Chow 1989, 367). Whatever else they have or have not done, they have certainly provided common thematic elements for Asian American women authors of previous generations. And these elements have continued in the works of the contemporary Asian American women writers analyzed in this text.

Chow sees the main challenge for Asian American women as learning how to adapt syncretically (Chow 1989, 368). The majority of the Asian American writers and critics who appear in these pages conceive of syncretism as a major solution to these challenges. In fact, the flexibility which Chow envisions is much like that of the Black feminist historian Elsa Barkley Brown and the Black feminist sociologist Patricia Hill Collins. As Brown points out:

African-American women's history is based upon nonlinear, polyrhythmic, and what white Western traditions term "nonsymmetrical" notions of the world in which individual and community are not competing identities" . . . African-American women did seemingly contradictory things simultaneously. It is the simultaneity of their seemingly contradictory actions and beings for which we must account in our historical analyses. . . . [T]he simultaneous promotion of two seemingly contradictory sets of values (some of which may be unconscious but understood as conscious, some of which may be unconscious but understood as necessary) is essential to the survival of individual African-Americans and to the African-American community as a whole. (Brown 1989, 926, 929)

However, there is a problem in valorizing ambivalent responses to external circumstances rather than a revisionary movement toward change, as we have seen in Hong Kingston, Tan, Myenne Ng, and Jen. Like Sasaki's, Barkley Brown's is a view of women as pliable, flexible, contingent subjects who adapt with the flow. Both Winnie's New and Old Aunts in *The Kitchen God's Wife* are examples of such a perspective, which Tan views as limited, as are those of the characters of the mother and Jo in Sasaki's *The Loom and Other Stories*. Like many feminists, Chow perceives the source of the problem as emanating from cultural patriarchal constructions such as school, family, and workplace which devalue and subjugate women. As do Hong Kingston, Tan, and Sasaki, she singles out patriarchal educational institutions for depriving women of a "knowledge of their legal rights" (Chow 1989, 369). She links women's political activity with traits of independence, spontaneity, and aggressiveness, which she believes will come, not from the assimilationist goal of fitting in, but from internalizing the "American values of independence, individualism, mastery of one's environment through change" (Chow 1989, 368). Education in certain "American values" will somehow imbue Asian American women with activist political tendencies. As I pointed out in my discussion of Jen's *Typical American,* when Franklin, Emerson, and Thoreau, for example, created the basic list of American values, their language and discourse specifically exempted women who were conceptualized as "The Other" from emulating these values. Emerson and Thoreau went so far as to view females as ties that bind, as preventing "rugged individualists" from marching to a different drummer. Whenever women read traditional American texts, they are therefore forced by the discursive intent to make two moves in order to apply to themselves the American values that Chow would have them appropriate. First, female readers have to consciously note that American discourse (as well as the narrative) excludes them altogether; performs "gender erasure" on them, in Ann Folwell Stanford's apt term (1993, 17). Secondly, women have to force themselves to press through these literal and conceptual discursive barriers in order to include themselves into an epistemology that does not take them into account.

Under these circumstances few women read themselves into mainstream American texts as active participants in mainstream American cultural value systems. In requesting that Asian American women do so, and then in envisioning that once they do, they will then become political activists, is for Chow to imagine that one action automatically follows the other. Additionally, there is no proof that greater self-relational readings of the American cultural values and discourse on the part of Asian American women will necessarily lead to the kind of transformative work necessary for active opposition to it. Although she perceives a major barrier between white, primarily middle and upper class mainstream feminists and Asian American women as caused by the latter's identification with "working class" women, there is also class élitism in Chow's assumption that only educated Asian American women will be politically active—that oppressed women of the lower classes are incapable of seeing their oppression as astutely and as clearly as educated women of the feminist movement (Chow 1989, 372).

Nevertheless, Chow still believes that it is vital for Asian American women of all ages and classes to be integrated into their own communities as well as with the feminist movement for political reasons (Chow 1989, 369). Unfortunately, like some other ethnic critics, she then calls for Asian American women to observe white women's flaws as those of an "Other," separate entity, rather than concluding that under patriarchy their flaws are shared by all women, since class for most women is a by-product of their relationship to men. The power to structure levels of women's subordination and oppression globally must be destabilized and disarmed. Striking at those women higher than other women in the hierarchy does not get rid of the offending power, but of its adjuncts, supporters, servers, seconds in command, hangers-on, complicitous victims, Aunt Toms, and flatterers. It is like tearing off buds on the leaves of a weed, rather than digging it up by its roots.

Chow's alienation from white women is shared by other ethnic and women of color feminists. For example, Patricia Hill Collins, in making up her list of exemplars of "an alternative epistemology," which calls for a separate way of women's being and knowing, theorizes that it may not only be sourced from Afrocentric tradition but from a women's tradition, as well. She then describes Black feminist thought as "Afrocentric" without defining how she means the term "Afrocentric." This is problematic because of the overdetermined nature of the term. Further, her list of practitioners of such an alternative epistemology includes Joyce Ladner, Elsa Barkley Brown, June Jordan, Deborah K. King, Bonnie Thornton Dill, and the Canadian sociologist, Dorothy Smith (Collins 1991, 762)—to my knowledge all Black women. How then does Collins's perspective differ from the ethnocentrism and racism of which white mainstream feminists are accused when, like them, she uses the inclusive term "women" and then composes an exclusive rather than an inclusive list?

On the other hand, Collins is positive about "poststructuralism" because she sees it as "a real corrective to . . . a fundamental problem of structuralism and positivism." What she finds troublesome about poststructuralism is its "lack of attention to the role of power and domination in the construction of difference." For this reason, poststructuralist scholars have difficulty in perceiving "communities of common experience or common discourse" (Collins 1991, 24). Here Collins reveals that she is one of the few "centric" scholars to conceive of any grounds for commonality between "Others" and their own group's unique "experience" of oppression. Certainly she is one of the very few who is willing to acknowledge that "shared material conditions" might "transcend divisions among women created by race, social class, religion, sexual orientation, and ethnicity" (Collins 1991, 26).

It has been my aim in this work to provide an expanded perspective that will reflect the commonalties of experiences and discourse of Asian American women, other ethnic women and women of color, and white American women, as well. Only then can we create a broad enough theory to encompass these diverse groups and at the same time not fall prey to the tendency to preoccupy ourselves with being "the antithesis of MAN," much as race and ethnic "centrics" see themselves as the antithesis of Eurocentrics. In doing so, they replicate their oppressors by becoming their mirror image, thus falling prey to the very racism they are confronting. What Patricia Lin (-Blinde) cautions feminist and ethnic women writers and critics against should apply to "centrics" of all kinds as well: "[P]articular care needs to be taken lest they themselves replicate the exercises that amount to acts of intellectual imperialism" (Lin 1992, 116–117).

At this point we might remind ourselves of one of mainstream feminism's strengths: their "stress on cross-cultural differences among women." Although "often not highlighted enough in feminist theory," this stress does lead feminists "to emphasize the importance of building an international feminist community" (Jones 1990, 788). But how to do so? Especially in view of another argument used to prevent diverse women's groups from forming affiliations to which Collins objects, namely, that there is no way of "negotiating the competing knowledge-claims of multiple groups." Such an argument tends to ignore what she terms "communities of common experience or common discourse," whereas "diversity" degenerates into "merely identifying and describing differences, rather than weighing the meaning of those differences for some larger, comprehensive reason" (Collins 1991, 24).

What is especially dangerous in her view is that "members of different and historically marginalized groups run the risk of not being listened to because there are too many perspectives, too many 'others' to be accommodated. The result can be a scattered discourse lacking a center" (Collins 1991, 25). Rather than fearing this lack of a center or perspectival multiplicity, I suggest that we view it as one of the characteristics of the multiple experiences and consciousnesses of Asian American women and women of color. "Centrics" see such variety as cacophony, or chaos, making it inherently obscure or difficult, if not impossible, to cross from one culture's "essential experience" to another, or even to cross several cultures. To erect barriers against doing so is to practice mystification. Instead, we might inquire as to whether those who do so might perceive benefits from preventing women locally and globally from unifying. How "scattered" and "diverse" can oppositional "discourse" be to patriarchal prescriptions that always, century after century, all over the globe end up in the same asymmetries of gender, race, and class?

My lengthy research across the ethnic field over a period of twenty years has enabled me to observe commonalties, patterns of oppression experienced by women of all the groups. Mystification extends out to the global level. There is an overemphasis on differences and consequently difficulty in unifying, which is more of a reflection of a divide and conquer mentality than reality. As Ebert puts it, it "is especially strong among women of color although they have not usually articulated it in consciously post-modern terms" as Collins does (Ebert 1993, 25). Collins's objections to "post-structuralist discussions of diversity" read suspiciously like her own and other ethnic "centric" Asian American and women of color feminists' objections to mainstream feminism.

The leading postmodernists (Foucault, Lyotard, Derrida) deny the objective existence of totalities, arguing that social relations are heterogeneous and traversed by a multitude of differences, and that power and domination are diffuse, local and nonsystematic. Moreover, they contend that theories (such as feminism) that articulate totalities—even in order to overthrow them—are themselves "totalizing." "Any assertion of unities or systematicity are [sic] seen as exclusionary, homogenizing and dominating." Nevertheless, the postmodern "war on totality" is in some ways appealing to feminists because it "provides an effective critique of many of the oppressive and reductive aspects of dominant (patriarchal) theories." Unfortunately, it also "conflates social totalities (such as class, women and even society itself) with the theories, or metanarratives, used to make sense of them." For feminists, "the [postmodernist] war on theory has meant especially a war" on those feminist theorists like myself "who have attempted to articulate the systematicity of patriarchal oppression." It must be stressed that the postmodern critique "of radical feminism as reductive and totalizing . . . raises serious political problems for feminism because it suppresses any theories that go beyond the local to engage systematic, global relations of oppression" (Ebert 1993, 24). Concentration on the exterior trappings of outwardly diverse cultural institutions globally primarily serves as mystification, as diversionary tactics.

Throughout this text I have continually striven to emphasize the global implications of gender asymmetry in order to augment "theories of the 'local' " . . . which generate "critiques of the specific historical, race, class, sexual positions of particular women—the differences 'within' women" (Ebert 1993, 25) because such (over) emphasis on our cultural differences serves to conceal underlying global patterns of oppression. Too much is made of our differences; how complex, how confusing they are. Under such circumstances, only members of individual groups are qualified to study and interpret those groups. But when groups are studied across as well as interculturally, as I have done for so long, they reveal their differences to be not so much contextual as content. For example, soldiers are employed in warfare across all cultures. They are members of the military institution, which is a global institution in context. They all wear helmets (content). Some are round. Some are covered with camouflage. Some are made of steel. Some are cushioned differently. Some are decorated. Some have visors. They have different kinds of straps, different insignias. Aren't they all helmets, nevertheless?

Aida Hurtado in yet another "centric" attempt to separate women, divides them into "feminists of color" and "white feminists." She defines the former as working class and the latter as middle class on the grounds that she wants "to provide a framework for discussion by defining the different positions of these groups of women to white men . . . [to] help us to understand the difference between women of Color and white women in general, and feminists in particular." She wishes to point out "important differences between . . . feminists of Color and white feminists" in order to " elucidate the race/class nexus so lacking in white feminist theory" (Hurtado 1989, 838). Ironically, her theory is "lacking" in any awareness of "race/class nexus" for any other group of feminists than her own—for instance, Asian American women in relation to stereotypical "white feminists."

Where Hurtado perceives "white feminists" as the enemy and the Other, on the basis of intrinsic "difference" Esther Chow more productively looks to extrinsic factors as having created artificial barriers, distinctions, and distances between Asian American women and the feminist movement. She attributes Asian American women's distrust to the influence of other Asian American women and especially of Asian American men. They do not wish to threaten the "male ego" and damage "working relationships" with their men. For these reasons, they feel that if they join white feminists they will "dilute . . . the Asian American cause" (Chow 1989, 370). This argument, also advanced by Frank Chin in Asian American circles, is that faced by ethnic women of color involved in the radical and Black power movements. So far, it has served as a common and powerfully effective deterrent to women from all these different groups coming together. In keeping with these arguments, Chow maintains on the one hand that because "[w]hite supremacy and male dominance" constrain Asian American women politically, therefore "white women are seen as partly responsible for perpetuating racial prejudice and discriminatory practices" (Chow 1989, 371). On the other hand, she sees Asian American women as not responsible in any way for their men's and their cultures' discriminatory practices against them. According to her, because they are manipulated and controlled by their men and their culture, they have become hostages to the gender asymmetry of their situation. Yet Chow denies parity to the white feminists by failing or refusing to provide the same rationale for white women relative to their men and their culture as she does for Asian American women and their men and culture. She therefore assumes a power for white women in relation to their men and the white patriarchal social structures that in fact does not exist. In fact, white women's experiences within their situation are parallel to Asian American women's.

It is only as long as white (and all other) women are in relationship to their men on the men's terms that they enjoy whatever privileges they are granted by those in power over them. When cast aside and/or down and out by their men, women are in the same position all over the globe. In Gloria Steinem's words: "Most women are one man away from welfare." To stress the privileges of white women, to distance and separate from them on this basis alone does not solve the underlying causes of gender asymmetry. Instead. the root of the problem— worldwide oppression and injustice—is shared by all women, and linkages should be forged on this basis. For, although it is necessary to relate sexual differences to the practices that construct them, it is also important to realize that "overdetermination among disparate subject positions produces a system of sexual division that, no matter how heterogeneous the various structures of sexual differences may be, situates the female in the inferior position" (Przybylowicz 1990, 283).

In yet another example of ethnic Balkanization or "centricity," the Native American Vicki Sears in discussing her group's solutions to gender asymmetry in terms of "batterers" blasts the celebrated writer and activist Alice Walker. An African American "womanist" with some Native American ancestry, Walker has devoted herself to Native American causes for years. Sears orders Walker to mind her own business, to cease and desist on the grounds that as an American Walker has no business traversing the globe to battle the customs of clitoridectomy and infibrillation practiced by millions of Muslims, African Muslims, and Africans. "Every time a non-Indian feminist tells us, without understanding Indian family values or how our system can be used, to break away from batterers, they are saying our values and our culture are unimportant. My sister feminists still need to understand the importance of paying attention to cultural differences" (Sears 1993, 8). A given group's "values and . . . culture" are important, but there are values that are more important. Greater "attention" has to be paid to "man's inhumanity" "to man" and to "woman" than to "cultural differences." Cruelty, sadism, torture, murder, death, injustice, and oppression to anyone cross all religious, ethnic, racial, and cultural boundaries and are of global concern. They cannot and should not be respected or compromised with, or paid "attention to" on the basis of "cultural relativism" or "cultural sovereignty" within any cultural borders and boundaries.

In this context, Lee Schweninger's statement about M. Scott Momaday's character Tayo in *House Made of Dawn*—that "[h]is racial memory is an essential part of his understanding" (53)—reminds me of the remarks of three individuals on television recently. An African American stated that African Americans do African dances "instinctively and naturally." The son of a Grand Ole Opry star maintained that his son "picked" naturally; that it was "in his genes." If either were true, then in reality an African American child would not have to be painstakingly taught to speak African languages and learn to do African dances and Asian American children would not have to spend years in school learning their ancestral languages. Conversely, a third individual maintained that Asian and Asian American musicians could never really excel in interpreting and playing European classical music such as Beethoven's. Both "centric" positions are the same, only different sides of one coin.

Like all other descendants of immigrants (and like the Africans who for the most part were brought here involuntarily, and the Native Americans who are indigenous), the work of the Asian American writers discussed in this text decisively refutes ethnic Balkanization. Their characters' responses to the loss of ancestral languages and arts are multiple and diverse. Some describe their ancestral languages as difficult and strange-sounding to them. Some, like Olivia in *The Floating World*, strive to learn them, even so. Some know them well from having been trained in them from birth. Some, like Lei of *Bone*, cannot speak any other language except English, although they understand their ancestral languages. Clearly they fall in the three categories that Boelhower has identified as the three stages of ethnicity: "Construction, Deconstruction, and Reconstruction."

In terms of literary criticism, the "centric" emphasis on "unique" content differentiation across cultures has recently constrained, if not actually hindered, scholarship across literatures involving the exploration of contextual global patterns of suffering such as gender asymmetry. Perhaps those "centric" ethnic and women of color feminists who most vociferously argue for separatism discern benefits for themselves and their own groups from splitting off from all other groups when they argue that the only authorized and truly authentic kinds of scholarship can come from their pens alone by virtue of their unique experiences as members of their given groups. Therefore their writing, their voices alone should have a "womanopoly" by blood right over any scholarship about their group. Members of other groups are ignorant about, have not shared their unique experience. Further, only members of a given "minority" or "Third World" group can be authorized to speak or write about their group because they alone can be assured of authenticity about matters pertaining to their group.

Scholars should not dare to presume to study any group other than their own group. The untenability of these arguments has been exposed by Henry Louis Gates, Jr. by carrying them to the extreme of their logic, as Swift did in "A Modest Proposal." Gates used as his example Stanley Fish, a colleague of his, a prominent American scholar whose specialization is seventeenth century English history. If the "centric" arguments prevail, Gates pointed out, Fish would be disqualified on the grounds that he is neither English nor living in the seventeenth century.

Nothing comes magically or by blood to any member of any group. It is all painstakingly taught and learned. As John Locke maintained, we are each born *tabula rasa* (blank tablets) and as the great pan-Africanist Aimé Cesaire concluded late in life: "Identity in suffering, not in genetic material, determined the bond among black people of different origins" (Cesaire 1983, 6). This truism is reflected in the observations of the selected contemporary Asian American women writers whose works have been analyzed in this text. As humanity is characterized by cosmopolitan mingling that actually strengthens its survival capabilites, so is passionate intellectual curiosity, interest, and inquiry, which like bodily love continually crosses boundaries, or, rather, knows no boundaries. In the twenty-first century, Asian American and other ethnic women and women of color will continue to live with multiple and diverse identities. As such, they will serve as models for mainstream feminists and for woman globally, as well as for the rest of humanity. To survive in a global environment, human beings will of necessity contain and include "multiple identities" regardless of gender, race, class, religion, and ethnicity. Individuals with single identities, such as Eurocentrics or any other kind of "centrics" committed to one "essential" identity will become dinosaurs, throwbacks. Under much pressure, Gates dares to stand firm against current "centric" Balkanized groups' insistence that "multiple identities" are to be deplored and cannot be held simultaneously. He sees his critical project as guaranteeing that "black and so-called Third-World literature is taught to black and Third World (and white) students by black and Third World (and white) professors in heretofore white mainstream departments of literature" (Gates 1987, 34).

Donna Przybylowicz points out that Bakhtin's "notions of dominant/muted discourses and hegemonic/nonhegemonic formations" differ from Julia Kristeva's in that the latter "recognizes a heterogeneous preverbal, pre-oedipal, and unconscious level of signification in language that represents what the ruling society has repressed" (1990, 282). This concept forms the basis of Kristeva's "essentialist feminism," which Przybylowicz rejects. Gender asymmetry is a transnational, global reality that proves the universality of patriarchal systems of domination. What the traditional discourse puts out as "truth" about various categories of life (such as "female gender") becomes shaping reality, which, in turn, keeps the hegemonic system in place. She wonders how we can then destabilize negative discursive practices replicated in its categorization of subjects and its institutions like a giant web woven by a huge spider in which everything gets trapped up and down the line and through the interstices. Here Przybylowicz and I part company. She maintains with Bakhtin that "[h]egemony is plural, not monolithic, and power is no longer attributed to a central nodal point but to multiple determinants. . . . [A] hegemonic formation . . . absorbs . . . oppositional forces within its parameters as long as the counterhegemonic groups accept the basic articulations of that structure as the site of criticism and negation" (Przybylowicz 1990, 283). The global patriarchy may have external plural trappings locally (content). In some cultures the rulers wear suits, in others long gowns and turbans, in yet others, dashikis. The content may differ, but the context is always the same. In whatever assorted culture and colors they come, they are phallocentric globally. Nevertheless, Przybylowicz still hopes for the formation by women of "a counterhegemonic force" even though they come "from different and overdetermined, articulatory positions."

Again, I maintain that despite the diverse, contradictory, "conflictual and antagonistic" forces, despite a cacophony of intersecting calls on the subject ideologically, despite the fact that all subjects contain layers of disconnected voices, the historic fact is that the system of patriarchy that rules the globe does so because it acts universally in all cultures according to the dictates of its own self-interests to perpetuate its power and dominance. It is in place and remains in place on this basis. It is delusory to point to "this moment of affirmation and revolution [which] is deconstructive and based on a form of politics characterized by contingency, ambiguity, multiplicity, and a rejection of essentialist notions—out of antagonism and division evolve the possibilities for a radical democracy" (Przybylowicz 1990, 284). Such "possibilities" have never thus far come to fruition by any means in any culture. Chers and Madonnas can strut and "meta-perform" to satirize male fantasy; African Americans can "signify" behind masks, or come out for "human rights" as opposed to "civil rights," radical feminists can plot "destabilizations," Marxist feminists can apply theories of production endlessly and battle with essentialist feminists who opt for a separate realm founded on male definitions of female gender, and so on. Despite all this, patriarchy on a global scale still remains in place.

The postmodernists tell their readers not to despair; that various "heterogeneous impulses from antithetical modes of cultural production" are present" (Przybylowicz 1990, 285), when in actuality there is an "antagonistic coexistence of various synchronic systems or modes of production" in which "certain social formations try to overcome opposing forces yet inevitably move within their own dynamics" (Przybylowicz 1990, 295). True, there may be many "antagonistic modes" coexisting within patriarchy. Yet patriarchy remains consistent in holding to certain basic fixed positions and ideologies that are not negotiable or contingent and from which it will not be swayed. It will bend a bit here, seem to yield a bit there. Still, its basic adherence remains to one premise throughout various external situations—to self-interest and retention of power and dominance. Patriarchy is pliable and flexible only to the extent that in whatever maneuvers it makes it always retains the reins of dominance.

What keeps women in line around the globe is complex. One of the ways is deprivation by/of their men. Where women cannot support themselves, the

Sword of Damocles over their heads is economic or sexual. When heterosexual and even lesbian women are economically self-sufficient, they still "need" men, or are "burdened" with children, because men are in positions of power above them in some crucial economic, political, and religious ways. Asian American women use this argument as yet another reason for their resistance to the feminist movement: their dependence on their sexual needs, their "either staying with or returning to an abusive partner" (Rimonte 1989, 331).

In Gish Jen's *Typical American,* where such dependency seems to be the case with Helen in relation to both Grover and Ralph, there is no question that the husbands are abusing their wives and mistresses, and engaging in family violence in general. Abuse and violence are part of many Asian American women's experiences and cultural expectations (as well as all other women's experiences globally). Winnie's first husband Wen Fu in *The Kitchen God's Wife* and Ralph in *Typical American* physically beat and verbally abuse their wives, and Leon and Mah in *Bone* verbally abuse one another. Many women are represented as being verbally and physically abused as a matter of course. In fact, women frequently are attracted to emotionally difficult men who make constant demands on them without offering reciprocal support or nurturance. We can see this in the beginning of Winnie's relationship with Wen Fu in *The Kitchen God's Wife* when she is besotted with his oily charm and in *Typical American*, in both Helen's and Ralph's infatuation with Grover, a similar character to Wen Fu in some ways. Due to cultural training, easygoing, gentle, "maternal" men who are primarily friends and supporters of women; men who are flexible and negotiate, men who are gentle lovers do not as a rule get the attention from women that many disturbed men do. In the texts I have analyzed in this work, the women characters eventually learn better—to judge men by their conduct. After too many beatings by her husband, accompanied by verbal abuse and perversions, Winnie of *The Kitchen God's Wife* falls in love with Jimmy Louie, because of his kindness, goodness, and nobility. Mason Louie of *Bone*, husband of the narrator Lei is a fine human being, as is Old Chao of *Typical American*, and Charlie-O of *The Floating World*. At this point I hear Karen Lehrman in my imagination demanding of *(Un)Doing the Missionary Position* what she demanded of Marilyn French's *The War Against Women*: "So, now what?" Even if "men dominate or would love to dominate all women all of the time because of the way they're raised . . . [and even] [i]f women across the globe are beginning to fight back," how can "they ever succeed if this war is so pervasive, and women have always been so ineffective"? Why bother changing laws

if women are so helpless, such victims . . . which ignores the responsibility women bear for at least some of the situations they end up in? . . . [A]ttacks on men as a uniformly vicious class are not going to foster the types of behavioral, let alone attitudinal, changes that are needed. . . . [I]f "feminism" is presented to them as anti-male, anti-capitalist and anti-sex, why would they buy into it at all? . . . What's needed is a sober, rational analysis of the problems that remain and workable proposals for change. . . . After coming this far, that should not be the hard part. (Lehrman 1992, 18)

In most revolutions, the would-be revolutionaries spend much time address-ing their oppressors and using strenuous reasons and arguments to win redress for their wrongs, all to no avail, else the confrontations would not have ended up in revolutions. According to Linda Alcoff:

> We must seek a means of articulating a feminism that does not continue construing us in any set way. . . . [W]e must avoid buying into the neuter, universal "generic human" thesis that covers the West's racism and androcentrism with a blindfold. We cannot re-solve this predicament by ignoring one half of it or by attempting to embrace it. The solution lies, rather, in formulating a new theory within the process of reinterpreting our position, and reconstructing our political identity, as women and feminists in relation to the world and one another. (Alcoff 1988, 288).

Similarly, Przybylowicz suggests that we use Foucault and the other post-modernists to subvert "a paradigm of power that assumes . . . antagonism be-tween the sexes," but not in a way to involve "transcendence of binary oppositions." Rather, as I have suggested above, in countering Patricia Hill Collins's preference for "identity politics," we could work with a "proliferation of differences" . . . "that would diffuse the struggle for dominance. In other words, the point is not to transcend but to multiply the many manifestations of power so that the model of master/servant, oppressor/oppressed is no longer the central one. In this respect, the subjugated can develop oppositional practices that challenge hegemonic structures, and the dominant groups, in turn, discover that they themselves assume characteristics of the oppressed (Przybylowicz 1990, 287). Even so, a wolf in sheep's clothing does not make a sheep; a man talking softly still carries "a big stick"; a benevolent despot is still the one in power; an enlightened ruler is still a ruler. "Hegemonic structures," even when appropriating the trappings and discourse of the oppressed are still perpetuators of gender asymmetry. As Przybylowicz herself suggests, "gender must be ana-lyzed in varying contexts—class, race, family, reproduction, technology, institu-tions, etc.—in order to show how social hierarchies are formed and perpetuated" (Przybylowicz 1990, 298).

At the same time, she urges us to eschew separatism from "the phallocentric master discourses" on the grounds that "such a stance can only result in a strengthening of patriarchal power. . . . [I]deally one should maintain a dialogue with the hegemonic order, yet still advocate emancipatory and/or subversive strategies" (Przybylowicz 1990, 292). However, as I have pointed out, "the he-gemonic order" still remains firmly in place; it is just that she asks us to continue nagging inside the Father's house. Systems and institutions may change. Colors may go rainbow. Women of all ethnicities, colors and cultures may be spotted occasionally in high seats and lofty halls, or may even be televised in great num-bers at international conferences on women, such as the recent one in Beijing. Ultimately, no matter how various and diverse the personnel, all work "within its parameters." All must "accept the basic articulations of that structure" (Przybylowicz 1990, 284), that is, gender asymmetry in patriarchy. And those "basic articulations" have remained in place throughout recorded history. In whatever guise, in whatever color, in whatever culture, a patriarchal system controls wealth and power globally and has determined all the systems and institutions by which humanity has been run with an uncontrolled dominion over the environment and all else within its reach. As its system works "privately" in all areas of "family" life, so it has worked in the public domain, the "political." So it works in relation to the earth, to the sea, to the sky, to the environment—pursuit of wealth, power, and dominance over every other life form.

"The missionary position," patriarchy, is a global system, based on replicating and aggrandizing the male self seen in the mirror (and, by extension, the male selves of those who look like the male self when he looks in the mirror), or his essential extension of self when he urinates, has an erection, or ejaculates. As Ebert puts it: "the 'phallus' is a social entity and, as such, its meaning does not reside in any secure ground such as the physicality of the penis. The meaning of the phallus, in short, is not secured in the penis, but is basically a matter of power" (Ebert 1993, 28). Patriarchy crosses and transcends race, ethnicity, age, cultural and national boundaries. It is a universal, global system of rule. The prevailing system of domination flows through, around, within, and in all aspects of human existence. There is no area where the same criteria do not apply: from birth to death, from the smallest detail to the largest war—self-interest and self-aggrandizement, power and domination over all things in all areas and forms of existence—even or especially, in language discourse, literature, the media, the arts. It does not appear that the majority of men as individuals or that the majority of institutions that now continue with business as usual would have sufficient incentives and/or motivation to change because of feminist arguments. It is up to those men and women who would change the situation to do so.

Punning on the title of their text, *Making Waves*, the Asian American Women United argue that although Asian American women could use the "support of their communities and other activist movements," the fact is that "no one else can speak for them. They, like all of us, must speak for themselves. We can expect no one else to fight our battles; we must fight them ourselves. We must make our own waves" (Asian Women United of California 1993, 348). The problem with this strong and independent stance is that it has not addressed the unproductive fractionalizations between white, Asian American, African American, Native American, Latina, and Chicana feminists which my citations in this chapter have exposed. Each group sees itself as a separate entity, too often in the sense of being oppositional, different. What I suggest is the reverse of what the Asian American Women United suggest. We might instead form various elements of a united entity which together fights all "our battles"—like various parts of one body that function all together to walk, to run, to dance, even to fly in the sense of "getting off the ground." If oppressed groups traced the source of their oppression genealogically, as do many of the contemporary Asian American women writers, they would find a common Father and that we all live in our Father's House. They would find that their groups and themselves as individuals represent diversely categorized and hierarchicalized, unequally oppressed groups. But all women are oppressed, nonetheless.

Like Przybylowicz, I call for an "[a]ffinity not identity, unity not totality" for women, which "should be the basis for a new political coalition based on difference, or otherness, on opposition" (Przybylowicz 1990, 301). Postmodern feminist theory need not be "universalist but cross-cultural, comparativist, and historical"; it might "perceive social identity as plural and as rooted in complex differentiations based on class, race, gender, sexual preference, ethnic background, and age." Political alliances need not be narrow. They could be based "on alliances between diverse groups with diverse experiences and needs rather than on the notion of a homogeneous collective with similar desires, identities, and interests" (Przybylowicz 1990, 300).

Groups based on identity politics that oppose gender asymmetry emphasize their difference from other groups, as well as from the mainstream. Moreover, they are unfamiliar with or ignore writers from other groups. Fully as much as the white mainstream feminists whom they excoriate justly for their ethnocentrism and racism, their own critiques are just as uninformed about or unwilling to take into account in their discourse and theory other ethnic and women of color groups than those to which they belong. Sadly, many Asian American women, as well as other ethnic and women of color groups are alienated from the feminist movement for the various reasons that I have analyzed in this chapter. They are therefore unreceptive to what they perceive as intrusion from other women from other groups with other "agendas." It is true that "the trees planted in the Father's forests are of different varieties, but they all stand in a fathomless, uncharted forest where vast lumbering interests are chopping down their population without regard to the botanical differences of the indigenous trees. All the while the leaders of the trees are shouting: 'Maples follow me,' or 'Pines follow me.' " Instead of looking for "identity," for a politics of identity within a group, perhaps we should start, in "resistance to identity"—in other words, from difference—looking for difference understood as a continual resistance to the conservative forces of "identity" (Leslie-Spinks 1990, 15). Sadly, all of us—Asian American, other ethnic women of color, ethnic feminists, mainstream feminists—women all over the world—have hitherto been losing the forest for the trees.

Bibliography

Alcoff, Linda. 1988. "Cultural Feminism Versus Post-Structuralism: The Identity Crisis in Feminist Theory." In *Reconstructing the Academy: Women's Education and Women's Studies*, ed. Elizabeth Minnich, Jean O'Barr, and Rachel Rosenfeld, 257–288. Chicago: University of Chicago Press.

Alcoff, Linda, and Laura Gray. 1993. "Survivor Discourse: Transgression or Recuperation?" *Signs* 18 (2): 260–290.

Alcott, Louisa May. 1989. *Little Women*, ed. Elaine Showalter. New York: Penguin.

———. 1988. *Alternative Alcott*, ed. and intro. Elaine Showalter. New Brunswick, NJ: Rutgers University Press.

Bakhtin, Mikhail. 1986. "The Problem of Speech Genres." In *Speech Genres and Other Late Essays*, ed. Caryl Emerson and Michael Holquist, trans. Vern W. McGee, 60–102. Austin: University of Texas Press.

Beauvoir, Simone de. (1949) 1974. *The Second Sex*, ed. and trans. H. M. Parshley. New York: Vintage.

Bennett, Paula. 1993. "Critical Clitoridectomy: Female Sexual Imagery and Feminist Psychoanalytic Theory." *Signs* 18 (2): 235–259

Betelheim, Bruno. 1976. *The Uses of Enchantment: The Meaning and Importance of Folk Tales*. New York: Knopf.

Boelhower, Q. William. 1987. *Through the Glass Darkly. Ethnic Semiosis in American Literature*. New York: Oxford University Press.

———. 1982. *Immigrant Autobiography in the United States*. Verona: Essedue Edizioni.

Brown Barkley, Elsa. 1989. "African-American Women's Quilting: A Framework for Conceptualizing and Teaching African-American Women's History." *Signs* 14 (4): 925–929.

Butler, Judith. 1990. *Gender Trouble and the Subversion of Identity*. New York: Routledge.

Carnegie, Dale. (1936) 1981. *How to Win Friends and Influence People*. New York: Simon and Schuster.

Cesaire, Aimé. 1983. *The Collected Poetry of Aimé Cesaire*, trans. Clayton Eshleman and Annette Smith. Berkeley and Los Angeles: University of California Press.

Chamallas, Martha. 1993. "Book Review." *Signs* 18 (3): 678–683.

Chambers, Ross. 1990. "Irony and the Canon." In *Profession 90*, ed. Phyllis Franklin. New York: The Modern Language Association of America: 18–24.

Chang, Diana. 1956. *The Frontiers of Love*. New York: Random House.

Cheung, King-Kok. 1993. *Articulate Silences: Hisaye Yamamoto, Maxine Hong Kingston, Joy Kogawa*. Ithaca , NY and London: Cornell University Press.

———. 1992a. " 'Don't Tell': Imposed Silences in *The Color Purple* and *The Woman Warrior*." In *Reading the Literatures of Asian America*, ed. Shirley Geok-lin Lin Lim and Amy Ling, 163–189. Philadelphia: Temple University Press.

———. 1992b. "Thrice Muted Tale: Interplay of Art and Politics in Hisaye Yamamoto's 'The Legend of Miss Sasagawara.' " *MELUS* 17 (3): 110–125.

Chin, Frank. 1991. "Come All Ye Asian American Writers of the Real and the Fake." In *The Big AIIIEEEEE!: An Anthology of Chinese American and Japanese American Literature*, ed. Jeffery Paul Chan, Frank Chin, Lawson Fusao Inada, and Shawn Wong, 1–92. New York: Penguin.

Chin, Frank, et al. 1991. "Introduction." In *The Big AIIIEEEEE!: An Anthology of Chinese American and Japanese American Literature*, ed. Jefferey Paul Chan, Frank Chin, Lawson Fusao Inada, and Shawn Wong, xi–xvi. New York: Penguin.

Chin, Marilyn. 1991. "The End of a Beginning." In *Chinese American Poetry: An Anthology*, ed. L. Ling-Chi Wang and Henry Yiheng Zhao, 34. Santa Barbara: Asian American Voices.

———. 1990. "A *MELUS* Interview: Maxine Hong Kingston." *MELUS* 16 (4): 57–74.

Chodorow, Nancy J. 1989. *Feminism and Psychoanalytic Theory*. New Haven, CT: Yale University Press.

———. 1978. *The Reproduction of Mothering: Psychoanalysis and the Sociology of Gender*. Berkeley: University of California Press.

Chow, Esther Ngan-Ling. 1989. "The Feminist Movement: Where Are All the Asian American Women?" In *Making Waves: An Anthology of Writings By and About Asian American Women*, ed. Asian Women United of California, 362–376. Boston: Beacon Press.

Chow, Rey. 1991. *Woman and Chinese Modernity: The Politics of Reading Between West and East*. Minneapolis: University of Minnesota Press.

Christian, Barbara T. 1988. "Response to 'Black Women's Texts.' " *NWSA Journal* 1 (1): 32–36.

———. 1987. "The Race for Theory." *Cultural Critique* 6: 51–64.

Chu, Louis. (1961) 1979. *Eat a Bowl of Tea*, intro. Jeffery Chan. Seattle: University of Washington Press.

Cisneros, Sandra. 1991. *Woman Hollering Creek and Other Stories*. New York: Vintage.

Cixous, Hélène. 1980. "The Laugh of the Medusa." In *New French Feminism*, ed. Elaine Marks and I. de Courtivron. Brighton, England: Harvester Press.

Cixous, Hélène, and Catherine Clement. 1986. *The Newly Born Woman*, trans. Betty Wing. Minneapolis: University of Minnesota Press.

Cofer, Judith Ortiz. 1990. *Silent Dancing: A Partial Remembrance of a Puerto Rican Childhood*. Houston: Arte Publico Press.

Collins, Patricia Hill. 1991. "The State of the Arts." *The Women's Review of Books* 8 (5): 23–26.

Cordova, Dorothy. 1989. "Voices from the Past: Why They Came." In *Making Waves: An Anthology of Writings By and About Asian American Women*, ed. Asian Women United of California, 42–49. Boston: Beacon.

Derrida, Jacques. 1976. *Of Grammatology*. Baltimore, MD: Johns Hopkins University Press.

Dickens, Charles. (1843–44), 1994. *Martin Chuzzlewit: With Forty Illustrations by 'Phiz'*, intro. William Boyd. London: David Campbell.

DuPlessis, Rachel Blau. 1985. "For the Etruscans." In *The New Feminist Criticism: Essays on Women, Literature, and Theory*, ed. Elaine Showalter, 271–291. New York: Pantheon Press.

Duras, Marguerite. 1985. *The Lover*, trans. Barbara Bray. New York: Pantheon Books.

Eagleton, Terry. 1993. *The Crisis of Contemporary Culture*. New York: Oxford University Press.

Ebert, Theresa, L. 1993. "Ludic Feminism, the Body, Performance, and Labor: Bringing Materialism Back into Feminist Cultural Studies." *Cultural Critique* 23: 5–50.

———. 1991a. "The 'Difference' of Postmodern Feminism." *College English* 53 (8): 886–904.

———. 1991b. "Review." *The Women's Review of Books*. VIII (4): 24–25.

Edmondson, Belinda. 1992. "Black Aesthetics, Feminist Aesthetics, and the Problems of Oppositional Discourse." *Cultural Critique* 22: 75–98.

Emerson, Ralph Waldo. (1841) 1990. "Self Reliance." In *The Heath Anthology of American Literature*. Vol. 1, ed. Paul Lauter et al., 1511–1528. Lexington, MA and Toronto: D. C. Heath.

Far, Sui Sin. (Edith Eaton). (1912) 1995. *Mrs. Spring Fragrance and Other Writings*, ed. Amy Ling and Annette White-Parks. Urbana: University of Illinois Press.

———. (1912) 1991. "Leaves." In *The Big AIIIEEEEE! An Anthology of Chinese American and Japanese American Literature*, ed. Jeffery Paul Chan, Frank Chin, Lawson Fusao Inada, and Shawn Wong, 117. New York: Penguin.

Fielding, Henry. (1749) 1994. *The History of Tom Jones, a Foundling*, ed. Fredson Bowers. New York: Modern Library.

Fitzgerald, F. Scott. (1925) 1990. *The Great Gatsby*, intro. Matthew J. Bruccoli. New York: Garland.

Foucault, Michel. 1980. "Truth and Power." In his *Power and Knowledge*, ed. and trans. Colin Gordon et al., 109–133. New York: Pantheon Books.

Franklin, Benjamin. (1791) 1990. "The Autobiography of Benjamin Franklin." In *The Heath Anthology of American Literature*. Vol. 1. ed. Paul Lauter et al., 823–881. Lexington, MA and Toronto: D. C. Heath.

Freire, Paolo. (1970) 1985. *Pedagogy of the Oppressed*, trans. Myra Bergman Ramos. New York: Continuum Press.

French, Marilyn. 1992. *The War Against Women*. New York: Summit Books.

Freud, Sigmund. 1994. *Psychological Writings and Letters*, ed. Sander L. Gilman. New York: Continuum.

———. 1990. *Freud on Women: A Reader*, ed. and intro. Elisabeth Young-Bruehl. New York: Norton.

Friedan, Betty. 1963. *The Feminine Mystique*. New York: Norton.

Friedman, Susan Stanford. 1993. "Where Are the Missing Contents? (Post) Modernism, Gender, and the Canon." *PMLA* 108 (2): 240–252.

Gamble, Vanessa Northington. 1993. "The Political Is the Personal." *The Women's Review of Books* 11 (1): 12–13.

Gates, Henry Louis, Jr. 1987. "Authority, (White) Power and the (Black) Critic: Or, Its [*sic*] All Greek to Me." *Cultural Critique* 7: 19–46.

Gilligan, Carol. 1982. *In a Different Voice: Psychological Theory and Women's Development*. Cambridge, MA: Harvard University Press.

Gilman, Charlotte E. Perkins. 1993. *The Yellow Wallpaper*, ed. and intro. Thomas L. Erskine and Connie L. Richards. New Brunswick, NJ: Rutgers University Press.

Giroux, Henry A. 1992. "Multiculturalism as Anti-Racist Pedagogy." *Cultural Critique* 21: 5–40.

Glenn, Evelyn Nakono. 1992. "From Servitude to Service Work: Continuities in the Racial Division of Paid Reproductive Labor." *Signs* 18 (1): 1–43.

Goellnicht, Donald C. 1992. "Tang Ao in America: Male Subject Positions in *China Men*." In *Reading the Literatures of Asian America*, ed. Shirley Geok-lin Lim and Amy Ling, 191–214. Philadelphia: Temple University Press.

Goethe, Johann Wolfgang Von. (1827) 1949–1959. *Faust*, trans. Philip Wayne. 2 vols. New York: Penguin.

Gordon, Rebecca. 1993. "La Mujer Esta Presente." *The Women's Review of Books* 10 (8): 11–12.

Haaken, Janice. 1993. "From Al-Anon to ACOA: Codependence and the Reconstruction of Caregiving." *Signs* : 18 (2): 321–345.

Haddad, Lahcen. 1992. "Bakhtin's Imaginary Utopia." *Cultural Critique* 22: 143–164.

Hagedorn, Jessica (Tarahata). 1982. "Christina." In, *Asian American Literature: An Introduction to the Writings and Their Social Context*, ed. Elaine H. Kim, 255. Philadelphia: Temple University Press.

Hartsock, Nancy. 1990. "Postmodernism and Political Change: Issues for Feminist Theory." *Cultural Critique: The Construction of Gender and Modes of Social Division II.*, ed. Donna Przybylowicz, Nancy Hartsock, and Pamela McCallum 14: 15–34.

Hauser, Gayelord. 1950. *Look Younger, Live Longer*. New York: Farrar Straus.

Hawes, Clement. 1991. "Three Times Around the Globe: Gulliver and Colonial Discourse." *Cultural Critique* 18: 187–214.

Hawthorne, Nathaniel. (1835) 1990. "Young Goodman Brown." In *The Heath Anthology of American Literature*. Vol. 1, ed. Paul Lauter et al. Lexington, MA: D. C. Heath.

Hayslip, Le Ly. 1989. *When Heaven and Earth Changed Places*. New York: Penguin.

Henderson, Mae. 1990. "Speaking in Tongues: Dialogics, Dialectics, and the Black Woman Writer's Literary Tradition." In *Reading Black, Reading Feminist*, ed. Henry Louis Gates, Jr., 116–142. New York: Penguin.

Hernton, Calvin. 1987. *The Sexual Mountain and Afro-American Women Writers*. New York: Anchor Books.

Hirsch, Marianne. 1989. *The Mother/Daughter Plot: Narrative, Psychoanalysis, Feminism*. Bloomington: Indiana University Press.

Hite, Molly. 1989. *The Other Side of the Story: Structures and Strategies of Contemporary Feminist Narrative*. Ithaca, NY: Cornell University Press.

Houston, Jeanne Wakatsuki. 1985. *Beyond Manzanar: Views of Asian-American Womanhood*. Santa Barbara, CA: Capra Press.

Houston, Jeanne Wakatsuki, and James D. Houston. 1974. *Farewell to Manzanar: A True Story of Japanese American Experience During and After the World War II Internment*. New York: Bantam.

Howells, William Dean. (1884) 1982. *The Rise of Silas Lapham*, ed. Don L. Cook. New York: Norton.

Hsaio, Ruth Yu. 1992a. "Facing the Incurable: Patriarchy in *Eat a Bowl of Tea*." In *Reading the Literatures of Asian America*, ed. Shirley Geok-lin Lim and Amy Ling, 151–162. Philadelphia: Temple University Press.

———. 1992b. "Review of *Between Worlds*." *MELUS* 17 (3): 131–134.

Hsia, C. T. 1968. *The Classic Chinese Novel: A Critical Introduction*. New York: Columbia University Press.

Hsu, Francis .L. K. 1981. *Americans and Chinese: Passages to Differences*. 3rd Ed. Honolulu: University of Hawaii Press.

Hurston, Zora Neale. (1937) 1991. *Their Eyes Were Watching God*, intro. Sherley Anne Williams. Urbana: University of Illinois Press.

Hurtado, Aida. 1989. "Relating to Privilege: Seduction and Rejection in the Subordination of White Women and Women of Color." *Signs* 14 (4): 833–855.

Hylkema, Sarie Sachie. 1990. "Victim of Nice." In *Sowing Ti Leaves: Writings by Multicultural Women*, ed. Mitsuye Yamada and Sarie Sachie Hylkema, 122–126. Irvine, CA: MCWW Press.

James, Henry. (1877) 1982. *The American*, ed. Don L. Cook. New York: Norton.

Jameson, Fredric. 1991. *Postmodernism, or, The Cultural Logic of Late Capitalism*. Durham: Duke University Press.

Jameson, Fredric, Terry Eagleton, and Edward W. Said. 1990. *Nationalism, Colonialism, and Literature*, intro. Seamus Deane. Minneapolis: University of Minnesota Press.

JanMohamed, Abdul R. and David Lloyd, ed. 1990. *The Nature and Context of Minority Discourse*. New York: Oxford University Press.

JanMohamed, Abdul R. 1983. *Manichean Aesthetics: The Politics of Literature in Colonial Africa*. Amherst: University of Massachusetts Press.

Jen, Gish (Lillian). 1992. *Typical American*. New York: Plume.

Jones, Kathleen B. 1990. "Citizenship in a Woman-Friendly Polity." *Signs* 15 (4): 781–812.

Jordan, June. 1993. "Seeking an Attitude." *The Women's Review of Books* 10 (8): 9–10.

Kadohata, Cynthia. 1989. *The Floating World*. New York: Viking Penguin.

Kang, Younghill. (1931) 1975. *The Grass Roof*. New York: Norton.

Kant, Emanuel. (1791) 1992. *Critique of Pure Reason*, trans. Humphrey Palmer. Lewiston, ME.: Mellen Press.

Kim, Elaine H. 1992. "Foreword." *Reading the Literatures of Asian America*. ed. Shirley Geok-lin Lim and Amy Ling, xi–xvii. Philadelphia: Temple University Press.

———. 1987. "Defining Asian American Realities Through Literature." *Cultural Critique* 6: 87–112.

Kim, Elaine H., with Janice Otani. 1983. *With Silk Wings: Asian American Women At Work*. Oakland, CA: Asian Women United of California.

———. 1982. *Asian American Literature: An Introduction to the Writings and Their Social Context*. Philadelphia: Temple University Press.

Kingsolver, Barbara. 1994. "A Metaphysics of Resistance." *The Women's Review of Books* 11(5): 25–26.

Kingston, Maxine Hong. 1990. *Tripmaster Monkey: His Fake Book*. New York: Vintage

———. 1980. *China Men*. New York: Knopf.

———. 1977. *The Woman Warrior: Memoirs of a Girlhood Among Ghosts*. New York: Vintage

Kogawa, Joy. 1981. *Obasan*. Boston: David Godine.

Kohlberg, Lawrence. 1984. *The Psychology of Moral Development: The Nature and Validity of Moral Stages*. Vol. 2. San Francisco: Harper and Row.

———. 1981. *The Philosophy of Moral Development: Moral Stages and the Idea of Justice.* Vol. 1. San Francisco: Harper and Row.

Kristeva, Julia. 1986. *The Kristeva Reader/Julia Kristeva,* ed. Toril Moi. New York: Columbia University Press.

———. 1981. *Desire in Language: A Semiotic Approach to Literature and Art.* Oxford: Basil Blackwell.

Lacan, Jacques. 1993. *The Psychoses,* ed. Jacques-Alain Miller and trans. Russell Griggs. London: Routledge.

Lapidus, Jacqueline. 1993. "From the Word to the World." *The Women's Review of Books* 10 (7): 25–26.

Lee, Evelyn, and Gloria Oberst. 1989. "My Mother's Purple Dress." In *Making Waves: An Anthology of Writings By and About Asian American Women,* ed. Asian Women United of California, 99–114. Boston: Beacon.

Lehrman, Karen. 1992. "Technical Errors." *The Women's Review of Books* 10 (2): 17–18.

Leslie-Spinks, Amanda. 1990. "Different Differences." *The Women's Review of Books* 7 (8): 15–16.

Levi-Strauss, Claude. 1966. *The Savage Mind.* Chicago: University of Chicago Press.

Liebman, Joshua Loth. 1946. *Peace of Mind.* New York: Simon and Schuster.

Lim, Shirley Geok-lin. 1992. "The Ambivalent American: Asian American Literature on the Cusp." In *Reading the Literatures of Asian America,* ed. Shirley Geok-lin Lim and Amy Ling, 13–32. Philadelphia: Temple University Press.

———. 1991a. "Dedicated to Confucius Plaza." In *Chinese American Poetry: An Anthology,* ed. Ling-Chi L. Wang and Henry Yiheng Zhao, 134. Santa Barbara, CA: Asian American Voices.

———. 1991b. "Modern Secrets." In *Chinese American Poetry: An Anthology,* ed. Ling-Chi L. Wang and Henry Yiheng Zhao, 132. Santa Barbara, CA: Asian American Voices.

Lim, Shirley Geok-lin, Mayumi Tsutakawa, and Margarita Donnelly, ed. 1993. *The Forbidden Stitch: An Asian American Women's Anthology.* Corvallis, OR: Calyx Books.

Lin (-Blinde), Patricia. 1992. "Clashing Constructs of Reality: Reading Maxine Hong Kingston's *Tripmaster Monkey: His Fake Book* as Indigenous Ethnography." In *Reading the Literatures of Asian America,* ed. Shirley Geok-lin Lim and Amy Ling, 333–348. Philadelphia: Temple University Press.

Ling, Amy. 1990. *Between Worlds: Women Writers of Chinese Ancestry.* New York: Pergamon Press.

London, Bette. 1993. "Mary Shelley, Frankenstein, and the Spectacle of Masculinity." *PMLA* 108 (2): 253–267.

Lott, Juanita Tamayo. 1989. "Growing Up, 1968–1985." In *Making Waves: An Anthology of Writings By and About Asian American Women,* ed. Asian Women United of California, 353–362. Boston: Beacon.

Lowe, Lisa. 1990. "Oriental Inventions and Inventions of the Orient in Montesquieu's Lettres Persanes." *Cultural Critique* 15: 115–144.

Luttrell, Wendy. 1990. "Book Review." *Signs* 16: 635–640.

Lyotard, Jean-François. 1993. *Toward the Postmodern,* ed. Robert Harvey and Mark S. Roberts. Atlantic Highlands, NJ: Humanities Press.

———. 1981. *The Dialogic Imagination: Four Essays,* ed. Michael Holquist, trans. Caryl Emerson and Michael Holquist. Austin: University of Texas Press.

MacLeod, Arlene Elowe. 1992. "The New Veiling in Cairo: Hegemonic Relations and Gender Resistance as Accommodating Protests." *Signs* 17 (3): 533–557.

Marshall, Paule. 1991. *Daughters*. New York. Atheneum.

Maso, Carole. 1993: "The Inside Story." *The Women's Review of Books* 10 (12): 7–8.

Matsumoto, Valerie. 1989. "Two Deserts." In *Making Waves: An Anthology of Writings By and About Asian American Women*, ed. Asian Women United of California, 299–308. Boston: Beacon.

Maturana, Humberto R., and Francisco J. Varela. 1992. *The Tree of Knowledge: The Biological Roots of Human Understanding*, trans. Robert Paolucci. Boston: Shambhala.

Mazumder, Sucheta. 1989. "General Introduction. A Woman-Centered Perspective on Asian American History." In *Making Waves: An Anthology of Writings By and About Asian American Women*, ed. Asian Women United of California. 1–24. Boston: Beacon.

McCormick, Richard W. 1993. "From Caligari to Dietrich: Sexual, Social, and Cinematic Discourses in Weimar Film." *Signs* 18 (3): 640–668.

Mei, Huang. 1994. *Transforming the Cinderella Dream: From Frances Burney to Charlotte Bronte*. New Brunswick, NJ: Rutgers University Press.

Melville, Herman. (1857) 1971. *The Confidence Man: His Masquerade*, ed. Hershel Parker. New York: Norton.

Milton, John (1659) 1993. *Paradise Lost*, ed. Roy Flannagan. New York: Macmillan.

Minh-ha, Trinh T. 1989. *Woman, Native, Other: Writing, Postcoloniality and Feminism*. Bloomington: Indiana University Press.

Mohanty, Chandra Talpade. 1991. *Third World Women and the Politics of Feminism*. Bloomington: Indiana University Press.

———. 1990. "On Race and Voice: Challenges for Liberal Education in the 1990s." *Cultural Critique* 14: 179–208.

Momaday, M. Scott. 1968. *House Made of Dawn*. New York: Harper and Row.

Moraga, Cherríe. 1983. *Loving in the War Years*. New York: South End Press.

Morrison, Toni (1970) 1993. *The Bluest Eye*. New York: Knopf.

Mudimbe, V. Y. 1991. "A Conversation with V. Y. Mudimbe." *Callaloo* 14 (4): 961–986.

Mukherjee, Bharati. 1991. *Jasmine*. New York: Fawcett Crest.

Mutman, Mahmut. 1993. "Under the Sign of Orientalism: The West vs. Islam." *Cultural Critique* 23: 165–197.

Newman, Katharine. 1990. "*MELUS* Invented: The Rest Is History." *MELUS* 16 (4): 99–113.

Newton, Judith, and Judith Stacey. 1993. "Learning Not to Curse, or, Feminist Predicaments in Cultural Criticism by Men: Our Movie Date with James Clifford and Stephen Greenblatt." *Cultural Critique* 23: 51–82.

Ng, Fae Myenne. 1993. *Bone*. New York: Hyperion.

Noda, Kesaya E. 1989. "Growing Up Asian in America." In *Making Waves: An Anthology By and About Asian-American Women*, ed. Asian Women United of California, 243–250. Boston: Beacon.

Oh, Seiwoong. 1993. "Cross-Cultural Reading Versus Textual Accessibility in Multicultural Literature." *MELUS* 18 (2): 3–16.

Overstreet, Harry. 1949. *The Mature Mind*. New York: Norton.

Peale, Norman Vincent. 1952. *The Power of Positive Thinking*. New York: Prentice Hall.

Peale, Norman Vincent, and Smiley Blanton. 1950. *The Art of Real Happiness*. New York: Prentice Hall.

Pfaff, Timothy. 1980. "Talking with Mrs. Kingston." *The New York Times Book Review.* June 18, 1980: 25–27.

Poe, Edgar Allan. 1839 (1990)."The Fall of the House of Usher." In *The Heath Anthology of American Literature.* Vol. 1, ed. Paul Lauter et al., 1344–1356. Lexington, MA: D. C. Heath.

Pratt, Mary Louise. 1991. "Arts of the Contact Zone." In *Profession 91,* ed. Phyllis Franklin. New York: The Modern Language Association of America: 33–40.

Przybylowicz, Donna. 1990. "Toward a Feminist Cultural Criticism: Hegemony and Modes of Social Division." *Cultural Critique* 14: 259–301.

Radhakrishnan, R. 1987a. "Culture as Common Ground: Ethnicity and Beyond." *MELUS* 14 (2): 5–18.

———. 1987b. "Ethnic Identity and Post-Structuralist Difference." *Cultural Critique* 6: 199–220.

Rimonte, Nilda. 1989. "Domestic Violence Among Pacific Asians." In *Making Waves: An Anthology of Writings By and About Asian American Women,* ed. Asian Women United of California, 327–337. Boston: Beacon Press.

Roberts, Moss, ed. and trans. 1979. *Chinese Fairy Tales and Fantasies.* New York: Random House.

Robinson, Sally. 1991. *Engendering the Subject: Gender and Self-Representation in Contemporary Women's Fiction.* SUNY Series in Feminist Criticism and Theory. Albany: State University of New York Press.

Rodriguez, Richard. 1982. *Hunger of Memory.* Boston: D. R. Godine.

Rosenfelt, Deborah. 1993. "Feminism, 'Post-feminism,' and Contemporary Women's Fiction." In *Tradition and the Talents of Women,* ed. Florence Howe, 268–291. Urbana: University of Illinois Press.

Rousseau, Jean Jacques. (1762) 1971. *Emile: or, On Education,* intro. and trans. Allan Bloom. New York: Basic Books.

Said, Edward. 1978. *Orientalism.* New York: Penguin.

San Juan, Jr. E. 1991. "The Cult of Ethnicity and the Fetish of Pluralism: A Counterhegomonic Critique." *Cultural Critique* 18: 215–229.

Sasaki, R[uth]. A. 1991. *The Loom and Other Stories.* St. Paul, MN: Graywolf Press.

Sato, Gayle K. Fujita. 1992. "Momotaro's Exile: John Okada's *No-No Boy.*" *Reading the Literatures of Asian America.* ed. Shirley Geok-lin Lim and Amy Ling, 239–258. Philadelphia: Temple University Press.

Schulte-Sasse, Linda. "Leni Riefenstahl's Feature Films and the Question of the Fascist Aesthetic." *Cultural Critique* 18 (Spring 1991): 123–148.

Schweninger, Lee. 1993. "Writing Nature: Silko and Native Americans as Nature Writers." *MELUS* 18 (2): 47–59.

Sears, Vicki. 1993. "Review." *The Women's Review of Books* 10 (8): 8.

Sheen, Fulton J. 1949. *Life Is Worth Living.* New York: Whittlesey House.

———. 1953. *Peace of Soul.* New York: McGraw-Hill.

Shikibu, Lady Murasaki. 1990. *The Tale of Genji,* trans. and intro. Edward G. Seidensticker. New York: Vintage.

Shonagon, Sei. 1984. *The Pillowbook of Sei Shonagon,* ed. and trans. Ivan Morris. New York: Penguin.

Silver, Brenda R. 1991. "The Authority of Anger: *Three Guineas* as Case Study." *Signs* 16 (2): 961–986.

Sledge, Linda Ching. 1980. "Maxine Kingston's *China Men*: The Family Historian as Epic Poet." *MELUS* 7 (4): 3–22.

Smith, Sidonie. 1993. "Who's Talking/Who's Talking Back? The Subject of Personal Narrative." *Signs* 18 (2): 392–407.

Sollors, Werner. 1986. *Beyond Ethnicity: Consent and Descent in American Culture*. New York: Oxford University Press.

Sone, Monica (Itoi). (1953) 1979. *Nisei Daughter*, intro. S. Frank Miyamoto. Seattle: University of Washington Press.

Spivak, Gayatri Chakravorty. 1988. *In Other Worlds: Essays in Cultural Politics*. New York: Methuen.

Spivak, Gayatri Chakravorty, and Ranajit Guha, ed. 1988. *Selected Subaltern Studies*. New York: Oxford University Press.

Sprengwether, Madelon. 1993. "Review." *The Women's Review of Books* 10 (5): 14–15.

Stanford, Ann Folwell. 1993. "He Speaks for Whom? Inscription of Women in *Invisible Man* and *The Salt Eaters*." *MELUS* 18 (2): 17–31.

Stanley, Liz. 1992. *The Auto/biographical I: The Theory and Practice of Feminist Auto-biography*. Manchester, UK: Manchester University Press.

Stivers, Camilla. 1993. "Reflections on the Role of Personal Narrative in Social Science." *Signs* 18 (2): 408–425.

Suzuki, Peter T. 1991. "The University of California Japanese Evacuation and Resettlement Study: A Prolegomenon." *The Big AIIIEEEEE!: An Anthology of Chinese American and Japanese American Literature*. ed. Jeffery Paul Chan, Frank Chin, Lawswon Fusao Inada, and Shawn Wong, 370–413. New York: Penguin Books.

Tan, Amy. 1991. *The Kitchen God's Wife*. New York: Putnam.

———.1989. *The Joy Luck Club*. New York: Ballantine.

———. (1987) 1992. "Watching China." In *Patterns of Reflection: A Reader*, ed. Dorothy Seyler, 269–271. New York: Macmillan.

Thoreau, Henry David. (1854) 1992. *Walden*, ed. William Rossi. New York: Norton.

Tran, Qui-Phiet. 1992. "From Isolation to Integration: Vietnamese Americans in Tran Diieu Hang's Fiction." In *Reading the Literatures of Asian America*, ed. Shirley Geok-lin Lim and Amy Ling, 271–284. Philadelphia.: Temple University Press.

Twain, Mark (Samuel Langhorne Clemens). (1889) 1982. *A Connecticut Yankee in King Arthur's Court*, ed. Allison R. Enson. New York: Norton.

Uba, George. 1992. "Versions of Identity in Post-Activist Asian American Poetry." In *Reading the Literatures of Asian America*, ed. Shirley Geok-lin Lim and Amy Ling, 33–48. Philadelphia: Temple University Press.

Veblen, Thorstein. (1899) 1992. *The Theory of the Leisure Class*. New Brunswick, NJ: Transaction Publishers.

Walker, Alice. 1983. *In Search of Our Mothers' Gardens: Womanist Prose*. San Diego, CA: Harcourt Brace Jovanovich.

———. 1982. *The Color Purple*. New York: Harcourt Brace Jovanovich.

———. 1970. *The Third Life of Grange Copeland*. New York: Harcourt Brace Jova-novich.

Wang, L. Ling-Chi and Henry Yiheng Zhao, ed. 1991. *Chinese American Poetry: An Anthology*. Santa Barbara, CA: Asian American Voices.

Weglyn, Michi. 1991. "Years of Infamy: The Untold Story of America's Concentration Camps." In *The Big AIIIEEEEE!: An Anthology of Chinese American And Japanese American Literature*. ed. Jeffery Paul Chan, Frank Chin, Lawson Fusao Inada, and Shawn Wong, 414–449. New York: Penguin Books.

West, Cornel. 1989. *The American Evasion of Philosophy: A Genealogy of Pragmatism*. Madison: University of Wisconsin Press.

Wharton, Edith. (1911) 1995. *Ethan Frome*, ed. Kristin O. Jauer and Cynthia Griffin Wolf. New York: Norton.

Whitman, Walt. (1855) 1990. "Preface" to *Leaves of Grass*. In *The Heath Anthology of American Literature*, ed. Paul Lauter, et al., 2713–2726. Lexington, MA: D. C. Heath.

Wise, Christopher. 1992. "Review." *MELUS* 17 (1): 121–122.

Wolfe, Cary. 1995. "In Search of Post-Humanist Theory: The Second-Order Cybernetics of Maturana and Varela." *Cultural Critique* 30: 33–70.

Wong, Diane Yen-Mei. 1989. *Making Waves: An Anthology of Writings By and About Asian American Women*, ed. Asian Women United of California, 348. Boston: Beacon Press.

Wong, Jade Snow. (1945) 1993. *Fifth Chinese Daughter*. Seattle: University of Washington Press.

Wong, Nellie. 1989. "Reverberations." In *The Forbidden Stitch: An Asian American Women's Anthology*, ed. Shirley Geok-lin Lim, Mayumi Tsutakawa, Margarita Donnelly, 207. Corvallis OR: Calyx Books.

Wong, Sau-ling Cynthia. 1993. *Reading Asian American Literature: From Necessity to Extravagance*. Princeton, NJ: Princeton University Press.

———. 1988. "Necessity and Extravagance in Maxine Hong Kingston's *The Woman Warrior*: Art and the Ethnic Experience." *MELUS* 15 (1): 3–26.

Woo, Merle, and Audre Lorde. 1986. *Apartheid U.S.A.: Our Common Enemy, Our Common Cause: Freedom Organizing in the Eighties*. New York: Kitchen Table Women of Color Press.

Wu, Qing-Yun. 1992. "A Chinese Reader's Response to Maxine Hong Kingston's *China Men*." *MELUS* 17 (3): 85–94.

Yamada, Mitsuye. 1990. "The Cult of the 'Perfect' Language; Censorship by Class Gender and Race." In *Sowing Ti Leaves: Writings by Multicultural Women*, ed. Mitsuye Yamada and Sarie Sachie Hylkema, 127–146. Irvine, CA: MCWW Press.

Yamamoto, Hisaye. 1994. *Seventeen Syllables and Other Stories*, ed. and intro. King-Kok Cheung. New Brunswick, NJ: Rutgers University Press.

Yamauchi, Wakako. 1994. *Songs My Mother Taught Me: Stories, Plays, and Memoir*. New York: The Feminist Press.

Yanagisako, Junko. 1985. *Transforming the Past: Tradition and Kinship Among Japanese Americans*. Stanford, CA: Stanford University Press.

Yasui, Minoru. 1991. "Good Law vs. Good Publicity." In *The Big AIIIEEEEE!: An Anthology of Chinese American and Japanese American Literature*, ed. Jeffery Paul Chan, Frank Chin, Lawson Fusao Inada, and Shawn Wong, 450–461. New York: Penguin Books.

Yogi, Stan. 1992. "Rebels and Heroines: Subversive Narratives in the Stories of Wakako Yamauchi and Hisaye Yamamoto." In *Reading the Literatures of Asian America*, ed. Shirley Geok-lin Lim and Amy Ling, 131–150. Philadelphia: Temple University Press.

Young, Iris Marion. 1990. *Justice and the Politics of Difference*. Princeton, NJ: Princeton University Press.

Zavarzadeh, Mas'ud. 1992. "Pun(k)deconstruction." *Cultural Critique* 22: 5–46.

Zizek, Slavoj. 1989. *The Sublime Object of Ideology*. London: Verso.

Zonana, Joyce. 1993. "The Sultan and the Slave: Feminist Orientalism and the Structure of Jane Eyre." *Signs* 18 (3): 592–617.

Index

About the Author

PHILLIPA KAFKA is Professor of English Literature and Director of Women's Studies at Kean College of New Jersey. A pioneer in Ethnic American Studies since 1976, she is author of *The Great White Way: African American Women Writers and American Success Mythology.*

ISBN 0-313-30161-1

9 780313 301612   90000>

HARDCOVER BAR CODE